Shots Fired
in Terminal 2

Shots Fired
in Terminal 2

A Witness to the Fort Lauderdale Airport Shooting
Reflects on America's Mass Shooting Epidemic

William Hazelgrove

 Prometheus Books

59 John Glenn Drive
Amherst, New York 14228

Published 2018 by Prometheus Books

Cover design by Jacqueline Nasso Cooke
Cover image © istock.com / shansekala
Cover design © Prometheus Books

Trademarked names appear throughout this book. Prometheus Books recognizes all registered trademarks, trademarks, and service marks mentioned in the text.

The Internet addresses listed in the text were accurate at the time of publication. The inclusion of a website does not indicate an endorsement by the author(s) or by Prometheus Books, and Prometheus Books does not guarantee the accuracy of the information presented at these sites.

Inquiries should be addressed to
Prometheus Books
59 John Glenn Drive
Amherst, New York 14228
VOICE: 716–691–0133 • FAX: 716–691–0137
WWW.PROMETHEUSBOOKS.COM

22 21 20 19 18   5 4 3 2 1

Library of Congress Cataloging-in-Publication Data

Names: Hazelgrove, William Elliott, 1959- author.
Title: Shots fired in terminal 2 : a witness to the Fort Lauderdale shooting reflects on America's mass shooting epidemic / by William Hazelgrove.
Description: Amherst, New York : Prometheus Books, [2018]
Identifiers: LCCN 2018011847 (print) | LCCN 2018013391 (ebook) | ISBN 9781633883840 (ebook) | ISBN 9781633883833 (pbk.)
Subjects: LCSH: Santiago Ruiz, Esteban. | Fort Lauderdale-Hollywood International Airport (Fla.) | Mass shootings—Florida—Fort Lauderdale—Case studies. | Veterans—Mental health—Florida—Fort Lauderdale—Case studies. | Victims of violent crimes—Florida—Fort Lauderdale—Case studies. | Gun control—United States—Case studies. | Violence—United States—Case studies.
Classification: LCC HV6534.F6187 (ebook) | LCC HV6534.F6187 H39 2018 (print) | DDC 364.152/340975935—dc23
LC record available at https://lccn.loc.gov/2018011847

Printed in the United States of America

For the Victims

We each devise our means of escape from the intolerable.
—William Styron

CONTENTS

Note to the Reader   11

Prologue   13

Chapter 1. Reentry (January 6, 2017, 5:00 a.m.)   15

Chapter 2. The American Payoff   21

Chapter 3. Fort Lauderdale–Hollywood International Airport   25

Chapter 4. Weaponized Humans   29

Chapter 5. Baggage Claim Terminal 2 (12:50 p.m.)   33

Chapter 6. Terminal 1 (1:06 p.m.)   37

Chapter 7. The Right to Bear Arms: A Liberal Idea   45

Chapter 8. Grace Under Pressure (1:20 p.m.)   51

Chapter 9. One in Three Hundred and Fifteen (1:45 p.m.)   59

Chapter 10. The First Mass Murder (1949)   65

Chapter 11. The Feeding Frenzy (2:00 p.m.)   69

Chapter 12. Fifteen Minutes of Fame (2:30 p.m.)   77

Chapter 13. The Texas Tower Sniper (1966)   79

Chapter 14. Outside Terminal 2 (3:00 p.m.)   87

Chapter 15. Chicken Nuggets: The McDonald's Shooting (1984)   91

Chapter 16. Shell Shock (3:30 p.m.)   97

Chapter 17. A Short History of the Gun   105

Chapter 18. Return to Terminal 1 (4:00 p.m.)   115

Chapter 19. Cowboys and Indians   123

Chapter 20. No Escape (5:00 p.m.)   131

Chapter 21. A Short History of the NRA   139

Chapter 22. Casablanca (7:00 p.m.)   145

Chapter 23. Columbine (1999)   153

Chapter 24. Escape from FLL (9:00 p.m.)   163

Chapter 25. Taxi Driver (1981)   169

Chapter 26. The Warriors (10:00 p.m.)   173

Chapter 27. The Worst: Sandy Hook (2012)   179

Chapter 28. Port Everglades (11:00 p.m.)   185

Chapter 29. Quality Inn (11:30 p.m.)   191

Chapter 30. Virginia Tech (2007)   195

Chapter 31. Swimming Up from the Deep (Midnight)   199

Chapter 32. The Dark Knight (2012)   203

Chapter 33. Victims (January 7, 2017, 9:00 a.m.)   207

Chapter 34. The Survivor (2011)   213

Chapter 35. The Horror (January 8, 2017, 2:00 p.m.)   217

Chapter 36. The Bump Stock Killer: Las Vegas (2017)   221

Chapter 37. Home (January 9, 2017)   225

Chapter 38. A Professional School Shooter:
            Marjory Stoneman Douglas High School (2018)   229

Chapter 39. Males Who Fail   235

Chapter 40. Twelve Hours of Chaos   239

Acknowledgments   245

Notes   247

NOTE TO THE READER

I did not have access to the victims of the Fort Lauderdale–Hollywood International Airport shooting. The FBI investigation was ongoing at the time, and the survivors and the wounded were all in various states of recovering. So I have built this book from my personal experience, news reports, history, and the odd bits of information that float around after every shooting. So by the time of publication some of the facts might have changed as the investigation progresses. But the center of the book is unchanged. The experience of going through a shooting is like any rite of passage; you have knowledge you may not want, but it's there nonetheless.

During the course of writing this book there have been many shootings. The most recent was the Santa Fe High School shooting, where ten were killed. Before that was Marjory Stoneman Douglas High School, with seventeen dead. The most horrific, of course, was the Las Vegas Harvest Music Festival with 58 dead and 851 wounded. A congressional Republican baseball game was attacked by a man with a rifle, and a bomb blew up at an Ariana Grande concert killing twenty-two people. And, of course, there will be more before publication. But I know how the survivors feel. Shootings and bombings have the same footprint of carnage, death, shock, stampeding people, and then a lingering feeling of being changed forever. It is a club you never want to be in, but once you are in it you never view the world in the same way.

I did use secondary sources to buttress this book, but the issues of guns and gun control are changing so constantly that books are out of date soon after they are published. Sadly, I have had to add four recent shootings before this book went to press. And statistics do not tell the tale of the dead, the wounded, and the scarred that shootings leave behind. Only people can tell that tale. Which leaves personal experience, intuition, and a smidge of history.

The best I can say is that I was there, and this is what I saw and felt on January 6, 2017.

PROLOGUE

On January 6, 2017, my family was returning from a cruise in the Bahamas. My book *Madame President: The Secret Presidency of Edith Wilson* had been out for a few months, and this was a celebratory vacation for my family and me. We had a layover in Fort Lauderdale–Hollywood International Airport and we weren't due to catch a flight until 7:45 p.m. We settled in for a seven-hour wait and parked ourselves in the main United Terminal. It was noon and hot, and we were tired from too much food, with that lazy languor that is a hangover from any vacation. I was there with my wife, two daughters, and son. We were talking about getting something to eat. I heard sirens, turned toward where they were coming from, and then, in the blink of an eye, our lives changed forever.

The Fort Lauderdale–Hollywood International Airport would be shut down for twenty-four hours by what authorities would later say was a lone gunman who took five lives and wounded six more people. Ten thousand people would be trapped in the airport for ten hours, leaving 25,000 pieces of luggage behind. It would take thirty-five buses driving continuous loops to the Everglades International Port all night to evacuate the airport. Planes trapped on the tarmac unable to unload passengers would eventually take off again for other airports. Planes in the air were routed away. People running on the tarmac would be out there with these stranded planes, and some people would be taken on board. The airport would be an *active situation* for over twelve hours, with gunshots heard after the original shooting. It was another random violent senseless act that is peculiarly American.

This is a book about the Fort Lauderdale–Hollywood International Airport shooting, told from my perspective of having been there with my wife and children. But it is also about a prototype of American shootings,

13

showing the interplay of victims, police, media, history, the shooter, and what constitutes this uniquely American form of violence. And it is also about the weaponization of returning war veterans, the failure of police and the FBI to stop this troubled young man who approached them and said point-blank that he was hearing voices telling him to kill others. The incredible fact that his weapon was taken and then given back to him, and that this was the very gun that would kill five people and wound six others and shut down a major airport in the United States, is mindboggling. The same gun that was checked through as a legal firearm and then delivered to the killer in the baggage claim, where he would stroll into a bathroom, load the Walther 9mm, and then return to start his murderous rampage.

And this is a book about questions. Why wasn't Terminal 1 locked down when the shooting began? Why did my family and I and hundreds of others run from gunshots after the initial shooting? Why the rush to declare only a single killer was involved? Many witnesses, including myself, say there were two gunmen, with multiple shots fired. But the real question is, where does this violence come from? Why is America the home of mass killers who have come to haunt us? Why do we have 5 percent of the world's population and 30 percent of the mass shootings?[1] Why, since 1949, have over one thousand people died in mass shootings in our country?[2]

These are the questions that are generated after every American mass shooting, and the answers are never enough. But, even saying that, we still have to try.

CHAPTER 1

REENTRY

January 6, 2017, 5:00 a.m.

The foghorn of the ship wakes me. I blink in that strange way that being on a vacation brings. Cruises are even more disorientating. You go from being out at sea with a fathomless black landscape pearled by a crescent moon to seeing Honduras or Cozumel appear in front of your balcony. And when it ends the shock is visceral. The orange-lit landscape of dock warehouses and ships and forklifts is at great variance from a week of five-course meals and days spent on the deck in tropical sun so foreign to our Chicago skin.

But we are back, and Fort Lauderdale streams by in the ugliness that is any transportation hub in America. We will soon be caught up in the ritual of disembarkation leading to a seven-hour layover in the Fort Lauderdale–Hollywood Airport. This couldn't be helped, with the exigencies of discounts, timing, and trying to make an expensive vacation less so at the very end. It will be a long day. The air is getting warm and very humid, and I miss the sea breeze already.

The foghorn continues its brooding lament. It is 5:00 a.m. and the *Caribbean Princess* is warning all ahead that a great presence is moving in and not to move out of the way means death.

At this time, Esteban Santiago Ruiz is already airborne, with his Walther PPS 9mm semiautomatic pistol and two clips in a protective case somewhere below in the belly of the plane. The gun is declared, and Santiago is headed for his connecting flight, Delta 1465, in Minneapolis–St. Paul, where he will begin the final leg of the seven-hour flight from Anchorage, Alaska. Santiago shuts his eyes and tries to wall out the voices telling him to kill. They are always there now. His destination is Fort Lauderdale–Hollywood International Airport. He has a one-way ticket.[1]

My son, Clay, is staring at the custom official's gun at the disembarkation point. It is probably a 9mm, but I really don't know. We are in that 66 percent of Americans who don't own a gun and don't know anyone who owns a gun. We are urbanites from Chicago who had children and moved to a near suburb and then had more kids and ended up in a far suburb. We are now a suburban family of five, with two girls—Callie, sixteen, and Careen, twelve—and our son, Clay, twenty.

Clay is naturally intelligent, had aced the ACT admissions test without studying, and had been accepted at several colleges. But like his father, who received the "gentlemen's C" in high school, he had trouble applying himself and my wife, Kitty, hacked it out with him all the way through high school to graduation. My mother did the same for me. I have often said there should be a medal in heaven for all the mothers who sit up late with their sons and daughters at kitchen tables. Clay is now a funny, serious twenty-year-old, who works a forty-hour week at a shipping company. My assumption that everyone goes to college was put to the test when Clay let us know the day before he was to leave that he didn't believe college was for him. Already my friends had adult children back at home living in their basements with $100,000 student loans, so maybe my son was onto something.

Callie, my oldest daughter, is on the cusp of sixteen, beautiful, talented, and smart. What father doesn't say these things about his daughter? She goes for extended periods without saying a word, until I lure her out with inane father antics. "You're kooky," she remarks, and then lets me twist in the wind. My youngest, Careen, is twelve, and my last life raft to fatherhood. She has yet to give up on our daughter-daddy dances at the park district, though I suspect this might be our last year. When Kitty took a nine-to-five we became even closer, having our cereal and coffee together before I ran her to school. The highpoint of my day has always been dropping the kids off at school. I know this is not the *Rich Dad, Poor Dad* motif, where I am off beating down the world for the almighty buck, but I do work at home and, besides, I like hanging with my kids.

My wife of twenty-five years and I come from different backgrounds. Kitty grew up in a small Midwestern town, where her father did hunt and kept unloaded shotguns under his bed for security. The shuck of the slide on the shotgun would supposedly send a burglar packing. Kitty remembers her father going off to hunt, and the lore is that he was hunting when she was born. But this gun culture did not transfer to any of the kids, and my wife has never personally touched a gun. I grew up on the East Coast, with liberal parents who never mentioned guns, never owned one. The only time my father ever had a gun, and I think it was borrowed, was after we moved to the Midwest and there had been a rash of murders outside of Chicago. We were living in a semi-secluded area, and one night we heard some noises outside and my father and I went to investigate. I heard the noise again and motioned to my dad, and it was then that I saw him struggling with something in his pants pocket. He finally pulled out the small pistol and looked faintly ridiculous peering into the dark woods, a suburban man in pajamas, wholly unequipped for the role of armed protector.

The only time I have ever shot a gun was up in the Boundary Waters Canoe Area of Ely, Minnesota. I had gone with some Chicago cops to a quarry. They brought along a small arsenal and allowed me to try out each gun and obliterate bottles, cans, and stones. I fired a .38, a .44 Colt Peacemaker, a Winchester, a 9mm, a shotgun, and even an Uzi. "Now this one has five in the grave so be careful," one of the cops told me, handing me the 9mm. I stared at the gun that had terminated five human beings in the line of duty. It's hard to believe, but that is my experience with firearms. I never had a desire to personally own a gun beyond my days with a Daisy BB gun.

I know very little about the Second Amendment except that it gives us the right to bear arms. Like most Americans, I am horrified by shootings and wonder why we can't stop them. My wife and I have never once signed a petition or contributed money or done anything to put our support behind gun-control legislation. And, like most Americans, we forget about guns when the news cycle runs out on the latest shooting. Guns simply haven't mattered in our day-to-day existence of running kids to school, concerts, sports, and trying to make a buck.

The life of a writer is a precarious roller coaster at best, and we have managed to hit a few highs in the last year after some severe lows. So this vacation has been sort of a capping off of beating the odds that a professional writer can make a living in the year 2017. We had been on the cruise ship for New Years, and Kitty and I toasted that this would be our year. This would be even better than the last year. We could see nothing that would knock us off as fireworks exploded over the soft Caribbean Sea.

We pass through customs and emerge outside the terminal disorientated, slightly exhausted, and with a mountain of luggage. The Uber driver strains under the load and chatters the whole way to the Fort Lauderdale airport. We veer onto the exit leading to the airport and are passing the outlying runways when I see a very strange sight. A large white 757 FedEx jet is parked off to the side with half the wing eaten by fire and most of the left engine destroyed. The black scorch marks reach back along the white fuselage. I don't mention this, as none of us are regular flyers and we all harbor our own secret doubts about tons of machinery and people being lofted into the air dependent on nothing more than air pushing up on the Wright brothers' vaunted wing. I turn around and stare again at the wounded beast in the rear window. A harbinger I don't want, but there it is.

"United?"

"Yes, United," I answer, turning back around and watching all the vacationers arriving, sunburnt, still in shorts, many heading back to the frigid temperatures of the Midwest.

"What time is your flight?"

"Seven forty-five."

"Oh, plenty of time."

We arrive and I get out of the car and inhale the slight diesel scent of jet fuel and car exhaust. It is warm and humid, and the air is not moving in Fort Lauderdale. We can't use the skycaps, as we are too early to check our luggage, so we move it into the terminal next to a man sleeping wedged behind the seats. I will always wonder what happened to that man. He never moves the whole time we are there, but he will eventually vanish along with everyone else. I carry in the last bag, and the kids collapse onto the benches. My son is soon fast asleep in twenty-year-old slumber. He has passed on college, but he has the college student's knack for sleeping anywhere and anytime and he can easily sleep for a solid sixteen hours. Callie and Careen have both slumped down and I am feeling the pull of the week of sunshine and too much food and the inevitable thud of returning reality. I look around the terminal. It is only just noon and our flight isn't for seven hours. A flight we will not catch.

At 12:11 p.m. Delta Flight 2182 lands, and thirty minutes later Esteban Ruiz Santiago, in a blue shirt and black pants, is walking toward the baggage claim area in Terminal 2. Terminals 1 and 2 are mirrors of each other. The baggage claim is on the lower level in both buildings. Santiago takes the escalator at the western end of the terminal down to the lower level and walks nonchalantly to the revolving carousel. He waits, and then sees the single hardened case that has the 9mm and the two ammunition clips. Santiago picks up the case and then heads toward the men's room and goes into a stall. He locks the door, opens the case, and shoves one of the clips into the gun. He puts the gun in the waistband of his pants and pulls his shirt down. He walks out of the men's room and emerges in the baggage claim area, where people from Delta Flight 1465 from Atlanta are picking up their bags. Many are headed for a cruise.[2]

CHAPTER 2

THE AMERICAN PAYOFF

Fort Lauderdale is the jumping-off point for many of the largest cruise lines. People fly into Lauderdale and then take a cab or a bus to the International Port, where they embark on a generally seven- or ten-day cruise. Our preconceptions of cruisers involve senior citizens toddling around with trays of food in front of a sunset mirroring the latter part of their lives. This was countered by the television show *The Love Boat* in the seventies and eighties, which managed to insert disco and bad fashion and young people into equally cheesy plots with the cruise ship as the setting. Both images are only partially true, and modern cruising bears little resemblance to Captain Stubing's ship. If anything, the modern cruise ship is designed to be a playground where passengers can enjoy the ultimate payoff for years of work.

Ocean liners gave up the ghost in the sixties and handed off the transatlantic trade to airliners. And ocean liners are not cruise ships. Liners have heavy plating for rough seas, as well as high fuel consumption, enclosed decks, and the idea of getting as many people aboard as possible—not unlike airliners, where passengers find themselves uncomfortably close to the person next to them. The cruise ship is all about comfort, on the other hand, with cabins built on top of the hull in the superstructure. No more portholes, modern cruise ships are more like floating condominiums with balconies looking out over the sea.

One-class cruising became the standard in the eighties, where everyone received the same quality of service. A floating Disney World type of environment, most cruise ships offer a casino, shops, spa, fitness center, library, theater, cinema, indoor and outdoor swimming pools, hot tub, lounges, gym, basketball courts, and tennis courts. The glass elevators rushing up and down the interior of these ships give the feeling of being in an overblown mall at times, but the atmosphere is elegant and passengers have their needs taken care of by a staff that works seventy-seven-hour weeks ten months a year, with two months off. Cruise ships are a twenty-four seven, 365-days-a-year operation. Even a week out for maintenance can result in the loss of millions of dollars. The 30 billion-dollar-a-year industry is highly competitive and becomes even more so as the baby boomers enter retirement, looking for the vaunted golden years of rest and relaxation. A cruise is the answer for many.

The five people flying into Fort Lauderdale who would die in Terminal 1 on January 6, 2017, were all headed for cruises. They were passing through the airport on their way to a week of halcyon days and luxurious evenings filled with five-course meals and walks along the promenade. This was the world we had just left. A cruise is not inexpensive. For a family of five, the trip can cost probably ten thousand dollars by the time airfare, drinks, hotels before embarkation, and miscellaneous charges are all totaled up. The cruise industry does cater to an affluent and successful segment of society. Generally speaking, many cruisers have lived orderly lives, and the cruise is a celebration of an event like a birthday or a retirement.

Terry Andres fits this profile. He is sixty-two and is going on a sixteen-day cruise with his wife, Ann, to celebrate his birthday. In the ship's dining room, you often hear the waiters singing "happy birthday" to someone during dinner. The waiters keep track of who is having a birthday, which year they are celebrating, and at what table they are sitting; Terry is slated to be serenaded. He is a big man with a cherubic face, who in his pictures looks like he will enjoy having a margarita by the pool. He had worked twenty years at the Norfolk Shipyard as a radiological control technician and is now retired. His wife is a travel agent. Terry is also an avid golfer and tennis player, and he loves having a few beers with the guys. His daughter, Ryan Kim, twenty-eight, will have the burden of telling the world about her father, a man who never had a bad word to say about anybody.[1]

Olga Woltering is eighty-four, and she, too, is headed for a cruise. She is going to celebrate her husband's ninetieth birthday. They have just marked their sixty-fourth year of marriage, and a cruise offers amenities and a low-impact way to see the Caribbean.[2] The cruise ships stop at the various islands, where people disembark for the day and return with duty-free booze, cigars, sunburns, and a new appreciation for the ship, which then sails away to another third-world island. But many like Olga and her husband will probably not leave the ship. They will see Honduras or St. Kitts or Cozumel from their balcony, and that will be as close as they get. That is fine. The constant service and unbelievable amounts of food served day and night are a senior citizen's dream. The Wolterings are from Marietta, Georgia, and are such regulars at the Transfiguration Catholic Church that everyone knows which pew is theirs. An ice storm is headed for Georgia on the day before they are to leave for Florida, and the couple makes the fateful decision to beat the storm. They move up their flight. They will arrive at the Fort Lauderdale airport on the morning of January 6.[3]

Next to birthdays, the second biggest celebrations on cruise ships are probably weddings and anniversaries. Shirley Timmons is celebrating an anniversary. One would notice Shirley; she is seventy but still carries the spark that caught Steve Timmons's eye in eighth grade. They started dating that year, and they had an All-American romance. Shirley cheered Steve all through high school as he played football for the Barnesville Shamrocks. She was Homecoming Queen, and in the 1960s she and Steven had been a part of the popular group in Senecaville, Ohio. Pictures of Shirley and Steven show a handsome couple, well-tanned and vibrant. Their house on the lake, three daughters, three sons-in-law, and eight grandchildren all speak of a life where no opportunity was squandered. The phrase "a well-lived life" comes to mind. They had run a clothing store, with Shirley doing the buying and Steve doing the books. They seemed to be a couple riding the crest of a wave. As friends said, "You never saw Steve without Shirley. . . . They were fun-loving people with a good sense of humor."[4] The cruise is a family vacation with their daughters and sons-in-law, and in three weeks Steve and Shirley will celebrate their fifty-first wedding anniversary.[5]

And some people do not go on a cruise to celebrate anything; some people are just cruisers. I met one couple who were doing back-to-back cruises and sometimes would do as many as three in a row. Michael John Oehme is fifty-seven and looking forward to his cruise with his wife, Kari. They have flown in from Omaha, Nebraska, and this is an annual event. He has left behind the cares of running his surveying company, Boundaryline Surveys Oehme-Nielsen and Associates. His daughter has long since moved out, and now it is just Michael, Kari, and their Labrador. The picture of Michael in newspapers after the shooting will show a professorial man with white hair, leaning over to his dog for a kiss.[6]

Some people see cruising as a safe way to see parts of the world they consider too rough, inclement, or inaccessible to see otherwise. They no longer have the enthusiasm of youth to go charging into a rainforest or brave the wilds of Alaska, but still their curiosity about the world remains. Mary Louise Amzibel is sixty-nine and wants to see South America and take a trip through the Panama Canal. This wonder of the modern world, built during Teddy Roosevelt's time, is not well known to most Americans and occupies only a small space in high school history books. But Mary wants to see the canal and the rainforest. A cruise ship is a wonderful way to go down into the remote corners of the world and see what you could not otherwise. The Panama Canal is a long way from Dover, Delaware, where Mary and her husband have lived since moving from Ashtabula, Ohio. She has two adult children, and she has always had an interest in traveling and seeing exotic places. The Panama Canal is on her bucket list.[7]

By 12:55 p.m., these five people will all be in Terminal 1 in the lower baggage area to claim their suitcases. The baggage claim is by the escalators and dimly lit. The main thing they have in common is that they are all going on a cruise and that they will all be in the path of Esteban Santiago, who is not there to go on a cruise. Like all people who are victims in a shooting, they have the unlucky fate of common proximity.

CHAPTER 3

FORT LAUDERDALE–HOLLYWOOD INTERNATIONAL AIRPORT

The airport of Fort Lauderdale, Florida, is located twenty-one miles north of Miami and three miles to the southwest of down-town Fort Lauderdale, positioned strategically near the cruise line terminals. It is in the top fifty busiest airports in the country, falling in at number twenty-one, and it's the fourteenth busiest in international flights.[1] The airport is classified by the federal government as a "major hub," and in 2016 more than 29,205,000 people passed through the gates on their way to other countries, sunny climes, or while returning to their homes in other parts of the United States.[2]

The airport was originally called Merle Fogg Field, and before it was an airport it was a nine-hole golf course. On May 1, 1929, the new airfield opened, and in World War II it was taken over by the Navy and renamed Fort Lauderdale Naval Air Station.[3] Airplanes were refitted for service overseas, and the station became a training base for young pilots getting used to flying torpedo bombers, specifically the TBM Avenger. The site would take its place in conspiracy history when five TBM Avengers took off in December 1945 and never returned, after straying into the Bermuda Triangle.[4]

After World War II, the airport closed for several years as the country adjusted back to a peacetime economy, and the Navy transferred control of the site to the county. Broward County International Airport began commercial flights to Nassau in 1953, and five years later Eastern and National airlines began domestic service.[5] Seven years after that forty airlines operated out of BCIA, and low-cost traffic boosted flights in the

1990s with Southwest, Spirit, and JetBlue opening hubs. The airport was closed in 2005 for forty-eight hours during Hurricane Katrina[6] and then for five days during Hurricane Wilma when eighty-mile-an-hour winds damaged jets, broke windows, and destroyed canopies.[7]

There have been more than a few accidents at the airport over the years. An Eastern Airlines McDonnell Douglas DC-9-31, on May 18, 1972, had a landing gear fold down on landing and the tail section tear away, igniting a fire. There were no injuries, and the crew and passengers evacuated safely.[8] Then, on July 7, 1983, a passenger handed a note to a flight attendant aboard an Air Florida flight, claiming to have a bomb and directing the pilot to fly to Havana, Cuba. The bag the passenger was carrying proved to contain no bomb, and the passenger was taken into custody in Cuba, where he spent five years in prison.[9]

On November 19, 2013, a medical transport Learjet 35 crashed into the ocean after takeoff, on the way to Cozumel, Mexico, after a distressed Mayday. The four people on board died, and the investigation concluded the crash was due to engine failure and human error.[10] There were also two fires on board aircraft at FLL, with one on October 29, 2015, which occurred when a Boeing 767's left engine caught fire from a fuel leak. Seventeen passengers went to the hospital, and operations at the airport were stopped for three hours.[11] The other fire occurred on October 28, 2016, when FedEx flight 910, a McDonnell Douglass MD-10-10F cargo plane from Memphis, landed at Fort Lauderdale–Hollywood. As the plane touched down, the left gear collapsed and fire broke out in the left wing and engine.[12] The crew was evacuated without injuries, and it was this plane that I saw on my way in to the airport. The burned hulk was resting beside a hangar like a junked car. I am surprised the airline didn't hide the plane away from passengers as it confirmed every person's worst fear—that these planes are still, at the basic level, mechanical contraptions with which things can go horribly wrong.

If you read *Wikipedia*, airport security is defined this way: "Airport security attempts to prevent any threats or potentially dangerous situations from arising or entering the country. . . . As such, airport security serves several purposes: To protect the airport and country from any threatening events, to reassure the traveling public that they are safe and to protect the country and their people."[13]

It is to this end that we have to take off our shoes, belts, and watches, and remove our phones, keys, and change, and even then we might still be "wanded" or pulled off for separate screening. After 9/11 we became obsessed with stopping anyone with a weapon from entering a plane, and rightly so after men with box cutters commandeered commercial planes and destroyed the World Trade Center in New York City. Fort Lauderdale and other airports use metal detectors, explosives-detection machines, X-ray machines, and explosive trace detection portal machines. Innovations include backscatter X-rays that can detect a hidden weapon or an explosive on someone. A single backscatter scan hits an individual with between 0.05 and 0.1 microsieverts of radiation. A chest X-ray will give you a hundred times that amount.

The whole airport security setup is positioned around a gated or "secure" or "sterile" area. On one side there is potential danger, and on the other are people who have been deemed to not possess a weapon or anything that could bring down a modern jetliner. The entire system is based on the idea that danger is *coming from outside* the airport and that inside the airport all is secure. People who get off planes are deemed safe or sterile because they went through the security process before getting on the plane at a different airport. The system has no defense against a weapon coming from *inside* the safe area. That would go against the basic assumption that danger is coming from the outside and not from a plane.

Fort Lauderdale–Hollywood International Airport (FLL) is divided into four terminals. Terminal 1, which is referred to as the "new terminal," was built and opened between 2001 and 2003. The other three terminals were built fifteen years before, with Terminal 4 known as the International Terminal and Terminal 3 as the Main Terminal. Terminal 2 is simply the "Delta Terminal" and is used exclusively by Delta.

Everyone flying in on a Delta flight goes to Terminal 2 and makes their way downstairs to pick up their baggage. The other terminals have a similar layout, with the baggage claim on the lower level. United Airlines uses Terminal 1, and one could walk out of that building and look down the sidewalk to see Terminal 2. A brisk walk of five minutes is all that separates the two baggage claim areas.

If someone were to fire a gun in Terminal 2, the people in Terminal 1 would not hear it. They would still be drinking coffee in Starbucks or getting a breakfast sandwich or whiling away the time, waiting for the hours of their ridiculously long layover to pass, the way we were. In fact, complete carnage could occur in one of the terminals, with those in the other terminals having no clue what had happened; bustling passengers and cheery faces behind ticket counters would continue conducting the business of a modern airport without concern. The only sign that anything was amiss would be the rushing lights and sirens of police and EMTs going by outside, and if you had already gone through security you might not even see that.

We are in Terminal 1 and unware of Terminal 2's close proximity. The kids are getting hungry, and like most people we are fixated on our own situation and oblivious to what could be occurring elsewhere in the airport. But in reality hell is about to break loose in Terminal 2, and we are a five-minute walk away.

CHAPTER 4

WEAPONIZED HUMANS

Since 1989, the United States has been involved in ten wars, with one ongoing. This has created a need for constant troops and activated the National Guard units across the country. Many "weekend warriors" have found themselves in the incinerating heat of the Middle East on a twelve-month tour. Politically, the return of the draft has been a hot potato that both parties have avoided, even though our constant involvement in wars has stretched human resources to the limit. Many soldiers have done multiple tours of service in Iraq and Afghanistan. These veterans have emerged as trained killers who are then expected to assimilate back into the civilian population.

Many do adjust to life back home, but PTSD takes its toll, and veterans with post-traumatic stress disorder can find their lives spiraling quickly into lost jobs, alcoholism, violence, and drugs, with many ending up in prison or entangled in a legal system that has no capacity to deal with men and women who have experienced the horrors of combat. So they drift.

Esteban Santiago Ruiz was born March 16, 1990, in New Jersey. His family moved to Puerto Rico two years later, where he lived most of his life in the town of Peñuelas. After his high school graduation, he joined the Puerto Rico National Guard. It is hard to know what his thinking was at the time. The National Guard was usually regarded as a safe haven against seeing action in combat. Three years later, he was headed for Iraq as a combat engineer.[1]

Santiago served in Iraq from April 23, 2010, to February 19, 2011. He received a medal for serving in a combat area. And it was here that

Santiago's life veered away from him. He was building a road when a mine went off near two friends of his. The men were killed instantly, and Santiago saw them die.[2] It is hard to know what exactly he saw. Men are blown to pieces by roadside bombs. Some have arms or legs or heads blown off. Men are burned horribly or incinerated on the spot. His aunt would later say that when Esteban came back from Iraq his mind was gone. Posttraumatic stress disorder is a term that would come now to define Esteban Santiago. He would still have his military ID when he was arrested.

In 2012, the Puerto Rican Police investigated Santiago's behavior and confiscated his weapons. The firearms were later returned to him in May 2014.[3] Also in 2012, Santiago applied for and received a Florida driver's license—which he used to apply for a gun permit—even though he had never lived in Florida.[4] He moved from Puerto Rico to Alaska with his brother and joined the Alaska Army National Guard on November 21, 2014.[5] At this point in his life Esteban had held two jobs and both were in the army. He was a trained combat engineer and, by the nature of basic training, he was a trained killer. During his time with the Alaskan National Guard he went AWOL several times and missed drills and was eventually interviewed by Army criminal investigators for what they called "strange behavior."[6] He served in the National Guard until August 2016, when he was discharged for "unsatisfactory performance."

During this time, Santiago also worked as a security guard. Other workers referred to him as "quiet and solitary."[7] He had a girlfriend in January 2016, but was arrested for assault after he broke down a door and tried to strangle her.[8] The case was pled down to a deferred prosecution agreement. In November 2016, Santiago went to the FBI field office in Anchorage and told the agents that the government was controlling his mind and making him watch Islamic videos. He added that the CIA wanted him to join the group and said he was hearing voices in his head telling him to commit acts of violence.[9]

The FBI called in the local police, who took him to a medical facility for a mental health evaluation.[10] This veteran was clearly suffering from

PTSD or worse, and he took the desperate step of contacting the FBI. The result was an investigation that uncovered no link to terrorism. The feds essentially signed off on Santiago and left the matter to the local police, who took his Walther 9mm from him but then returned it in December because he had not been convicted of a serious crime or committed to a mental health facility. Santiago was on his own again, with his gun still in his possession. He was a weaponized human being, hearing voices telling him to kill, but the FBI and the local police had determined that he was not a threat. The voices didn't stop, and he booked a flight to New York on December 31, but then canceled it. He would later say that he was concerned about the amount of police in New York City. So instead he bought a ticket for Fort Lauderdale–Hollywood International Airport in Florida.

On January 6, Santiago boarded a flight out of Anchorage and headed for Fort Lauderdale, Florida. His gun was safely checked in a locked box along with his ammo. The gun was the same one that had been taken from him twice before and given back because he had been deemed mentally competent. After the shooting he would be diagnosed with schizophrenia.

CHAPTER 5

BAGGAGE CLAIM TERMINAL 2

12:50 p.m.

Everyone is converging on the lower-level baggage claim area of Terminal 2. It is the first thing you do when you get off the plane. Get your bag and head for the shuttle bus to the cruise ship because you have a whole process waiting for you there. Cruise ships have their own security protocol, and after they check your passport the same screening of baggage and personal items, with metal detectors and bomb sniffing puffers, begins. The lines snake around and around, long and sometimes stressful. A misplaced passport means you will not get on the ship, and it will leave without you. Having all your documents is your lifeline to getting on the ship. So getting out of the airport as fast as possible is your goal.

This is why Terry Andres had reached the baggage area and had already gotten his luggage from carousel three. Olga Woltering is there as well, looking for her luggage, along with Shirley and Steve Timmons. Mary Louise Amzibel is by carousel three, and so is Michael John Oehme.[1] Everyone wants to get to the cruise ship and get checked in because then you have that first glorious moment with your piña colada or margarita in hand and you have made it and you have handed off all your cares.

Esteban Santiago has also left his plane also and headed for the baggage claim. He has claimed his one small suitcase and disappeared into the men's room. It is 12:54 p.m. when Santiago emerges from the men's bathroom with the Walther 9mm tucked into the front of his pants and covered by his shirt. He holds the case and a backpack in his left hand, and as he walks past carousel two he pauses awkwardly to pull the gun free with his right hand.

The surveillance video is hard to watch. It shows a man walking and then reaching into his belt like someone pulling out a camera. Meanwhile, Terry Andres leaves his wife, Ann, for a moment and is looking for a luggage cart. Santiago swings out his gun and starts shooting to his right, toward the window and doors. In the video he now looks like a man holding a water hose waist level. People who saw him before he started shooting said he looked very agitated, trying to get his one piece of luggage. Others said he looked almost at peace as he started to fire.

Mark Lea of Elk River, Minnesota, thought firecrackers had gone off. He was about one hundred yards away from Santiago when the shooting started, and he described what he saw: "He [Santiago] walked around the baggage claim area . . . and point and shoot; point and shoot. Anyone who was in his path of walking was shot where they were."[2] It would seem Santiago was a great marksman, but he was simply on top of people when he shot them. Soldiers are not trained to shoot to kill. They are trained to just hit some piece of the target.[3] In the fog of war, and at the long range most killing is done, solders usually fire at a shape or a muzzle flash. They are not trained to shoot people in the head or aim for the heart. The anxiety of war and senses gone haywire turn most soldiers into frenzied firing machines trying to hit anything they can. It is when Santiago gets to carousel three that he inflicts his death shots, and they are all head shots. This is not how he was trained, but this is how he kills.

Terry Andres is shot in the head and falls to the ground. Then Shirley Timmons is killed instantly with a head shot, and her husband, Steven, is shot through the eye, with the bullet going through the roof his mouth. Olga Woltering goes down next, shot through the head, and then Mary Louise Amzibel and Michael John Oehme are both shot in the head. Oehme's wife, Kari, is shot also through the neck and the shoulder. Mark Lea sees Kari screaming afterward, asking where Michael is and if he is okay: "She asked if he was still alive. . . . I saw a pool of blood and he was shot in the head. I tried to console her and tell her he was fine. He was two feet away. He wasn't breathing or moving."[4]

The area around carousel three is a blood bath, with four human beings bleeding out under the fluorescent lights. On the other side of the carousel is another body in a pool of blood. A woman behind an information counter is shot in the shoulder, and a man with two boys is shot in the wrist. Santiago drops one clip, loads another, and continues firing.[5] He is aiming between the luggage stacked by carousel three, targeting the people who are hiding. In ninety seconds he is out of bullets. A man lying on the ground swears at him.

After running out of ammunition, Santiago turns and heads back toward the other end of the terminal, dropping his gun on the way. Near the exit, between the Starbucks and the escalator, he suddenly throws himself on the floor. He is spread eagle and calmly waiting to be arrested.[6] Behind him are the dead and the dying and the wounded. It is all over in ninety seconds, but lives have been changed forever. Two deputies reach Santiago and cuff him. They hustle him away and quickly radio in. They have the shooter in custody, the area is secure. It is a lone shooter, they repeat. This is no comfort to the wounded and the dead.

CHAPTER 6

TERMINAL 1

1:06 p.m.

Nobody in Terminal 1 knows what has just happened in Terminal 2. There is no announcement. It is almost sleepy in the terminal, with a midday languor hanging over us. Initially, there is no sign anything has happened at all. It is five minutes after one, and just another day in an American airport. We have resigned ourselves to the fact that we are not leaving the airport. Anywhere we go will be expensive, with transportation and restaurants, and like most families after a vacation we have spent up to the limit. Better to stay in the airport and get some snacks. The kids join together in a single idea: we are tired and *hungry*.

"Dad, I am hungry," has become a mantra. We as parents knew this was coming. Clay announces he is going to look for food. I have already gone to a concession stand and bought a bag of granola and some vitamin water. The granola and water will remain in the terminal for days, unopened.

"Let us know what you find," my wife calls.

The man is still asleep behind the benches, wedged into a yoga-like position. Someone else might wonder if he is dead, but long layovers in airports require a different way of looking at things. A few minutes later I see the first police car zoom past the outside window. The first blue lights bring another and another and another. Even though Terminal 1 is the newest of the airport terminals, it still has the vacuous feel of a bus station. The gray carpet of the airport matches our moods. The sirens blaring by outside do not change the tenor of the moment. We are from Chicago and are used to sirens and lights. My daughters sit on our luggage, yawning.

I look up and see more police cars go whizzing by. I remember later thinking it was strange but that it was probably just a security problem. We have to get something to eat at some point and, more than that, we have to come to grips with what to do for six hours in an airport.

"We still need to get some food," Kitty murmurs, frowning at the escalators leading to the lower baggage area. I turn and stare at the now-steady stream of police cars and ambulances going by the outside windows.

A voice crackles over the loudspeaker. Something about *an event* occurring in the airport. There is no lockdown. No panic. People are still walking casually through the terminal. Skycaps are checking luggage. The people behind the United counters chat, as firetrucks, ambulances, and police cars continue to race by. Terminal 1 is still in the middle of a lazy day of travelers facing up to the reality of flying back to a winter that is giving Chicago two-degree temperatures. We are still in our shorts, T-shirts, and tennis shoes. Like most people, we are putting off the realization that we have to return to a frozen Midwest where people have been slogging through snow while we cruised around Caribbean islands.

We are still in the lull of the great American vacation and even though we have been told that "an event" has occurred, we have no sense of danger. I am not sure how we find out exactly that a shooting has occurred in Terminal 2, but we suddenly know. I think someone at the ticket counter tells Kitty there have been "shots fired in Terminal 2." This type of information moves along its own pathways, an amalgam of hearsay, fact, and the droning loudspeaker.

"There's been a shooting," Kitty exclaims, facing the windows.

I turn reflexively and watch the steady blue stream of flashing lights. Nobody is running. Nothing has changed. We have seen many shootings on television and while this one is closer it has no reality. Our kids have gone through routine lockdown drills at school. After the Sandy Hook massacre, the principal stood at the entrance to my daughter's elementary school with a police car parked in the front circle. We have seen Michael Moore's *Bowling for Columbine*, but like many suburban Americans who work in economic hubs centered around large cities we don't know anyone personally who owns a gun, and so there had been nowhere to focus our concern.

But I am concerned now.

"I'm going to look outside."

Kitty looks at me. "Do you think that's smart?"

I shrug. "I'll be fine."

I pass through the terminal doors and stand among the skycaps waiting for their next baggage customer. I turn and stare down toward Terminal 2. I see an ocean of police cars and ambulances, a wall of flashing mayhem. But Terminal 2 is a separate building, and the body language of the people around me gives no indication of danger at all. I wonder if a shooting has really occurred or whether this is rumor or false alarm. . . . Such is our reluctance to accept any type of carnage as really affecting our personal lives. I remember the statistic that puts the chance of getting struck by lightning in front of the chance of being in a mass shooting.

I go back inside and Kitty stares at me.

"What did you see?"

I shrug. "Lot of police cars. . . . Where's Clay?"

My wife turns to the escalators leading to the lower baggage claim area.

"He's still not back."

More police cars. More sirens. I turn away from the window and frown.

"I better find him."

Kitty and I look at each other. The danger is there now. It is in the air and moving like a dark fog rolling over a forest. We feel the vibration that something is terribly, terribly wrong. It is hard to know exactly when you perceive that your safety zone or sense of well-being has changed, but we suddenly both feel like we are on a dark street in Chicago. Kitty looks at our daughters and then stares at me.

"Find him!"

I take off and go down the escalator into the darkened baggage claim area. People are standing around several television monitors. I walk over and see the bright red CNN headline—"Five Believed Dead, Many Wounded in Mass Shooting, Ft. Lauderdale Airport." My heart begins to beat heavily. There are people who have been murdered not five hundred yards away. I stare openmouthed at the image of people running on the airport tarmac. People are running for their lives just outside the terminal. It is on the television, but it is also just outside this building.

We are in the lower, darkened area of baggage claim, where suitcases are revolving and passengers are grabbing their belongings and running to catch a cab or connect with an Uber. In the baggage claim of Terminal 2, people are dead on the floor or bleeding to death. I take off again, moving quickly, texting as I walk.

A text comes back—"By the Starbucks." I see the green sign and head there. People are now moving faster, a subtle uptick in the human buzz of any mass-transportation hub. The televisions are all announcing the same carnage, and people who have been in the woozy land of a tropical vacation are now unsure of their position in the universe. The danger is seeping into the terminal and senses are heightened, our breathing, heart-rates, and metabolic changes reaching back to our primitive brains that ready us for fight or flight.

Another announcement over the PA. An incident. Something about shelter in place. Yet people are dutifully standing in line, waiting for a latte or a cappuccino. Such is our reality until it touches us. I see Clay walking toward me munching on some chips.

"Where have you been?" I shout.

Clay stares at me with my own eyes, brown hair, a twenty-year-old version of myself.

"I told you I was looking for food."

My reality is not his. I am supposed to be the protector, and I feel danger all around us now. I think strangely of the time Careen disappeared on a Florida beach for a few minutes and how I ran up and down the beach thinking that would be the day my life changed forever.

"There's been a shooting in the other terminal," I say, walking toward the escalator.

"No shit, Dad."

"Let's go!"

Clay stops. "What about food?"

"Fuck the food."

This is me when I get stressed. I start cussing like a truck driver.

Clay mutters, but he now has the wide-eyed fear I am feeling. We both quick-time it up the escalators and almost run through the terminal back to Kitty and the girls. People are next to the windows watching more emergency vehicles, police trucks that look like small tanks. Some people are by the ticket counters. Others have stopped moving altogether. It is as if the terminal is suddenly filled with people who move like distressed bees, not quite sure what to do in the hive anymore.

Kitty is looking around, as I am. There is something moving out there, something dark, and we both feel it. Our daughters are both standing in their shorts and T-shirts, sunglasses and tennis shoes, and our family vacation paraphernalia suddenly feels ridiculous, as if we have been cast in the wrong movie. We should all be wearing military uniforms right now, with helmets and flak jackets, not standing here tanned, with sunglasses in our hair and sunscreen in our pockets. An alternate universe has descended and we are struggling to catch up.

"I'm still hungry," Clay says.

"Me too," Careen shouts out.

Callie is quiet, her large blue eyes staring toward the windows and the racing emergency vehicles. Incredibly, we start talking about food again. Families are always either eating, driving, going to movies, dropping people off, touring, or visiting. Motion is required lest the family dynamic turn in on itself—something that happens on rainy days when everyone is stuck inside or during a family vacation that goes off the rails with a freak snowstorm and traps everyone in a cabin. In a way, getting something to eat is a welcome diversion, and maybe the hell that is taking place in Terminal 2 will stay there and we can be blissfully ignorant and fill our time concerned only with where to get a burger and a Coke.

"We are going to get something," Kitty says, and I suddenly don't like the idea of the family splitting up.

And it is in this moment that my brain does a funny thing; it runs one moment into another one. I take a step toward my wife, and out of the corner of my eye I see what looks like a tsunami of people. In front of it are other people, and it is like a giant wave coming in, and people are running; they are running sideways, forward, straight up, and straight down. The tsunami is coming closer, and with it are screams and shouts and yelling and over top of it all is a woman's voice, and then . . . then, four shots explode in quick succession.

BANG! BANG! BANG! BANG!

The shots are metallic, like a mechanized weapon. They are four explosions of air and even then I wonder if they are from an AR-15, the gun of choice of terrorists and shooters. But this thought does not linger, or even exist, because I am running along with everyone else. My memory has it this way. People are moving sideways, lunging, twisting, like a movie freeze-framed before it is running again. Do I think? No. There is no thought now. My ancestors equipped my DNA with a fight-or-flight command that has me running in a zig-zag pattern with my kids and the avalanche of people, all of us bolting for the doors to get away from the bullets, to get away from death. Death is right there behind you, and your body knows it, and your adrenal glands have shot a stimulant into your veins, and you are now following your body, trying to find cover anywhere. The human tide demands you keep up, and later thirty people will be sent to the hospital from the stampede, but for now you are not thinking, you are just running and zig-zagging, and suddenly I am outside in the sunshine in the street with a woman and her baby in a stroller, and I am breathing like I have just run a marathon. People are running in every direction, and I see police cars speeding toward the far end of the terminal, and now I am behind a car and I am looking for my family and just like that the street is empty, with people crouched down behind whatever they can find. A man in the car I am behind is looking up at me and the woman in the stroller with the baby is asking if she can get in his car and he is staring in shock and not responding.

I hear a wheezing whistle and wonder where it is coming from, and then I realize it is my own breath. I am sweating profusely and put my head down against the car, hearing the woman asking again to get in the man's car. I don't know where Callie, Careen, Clay, or Kitty are. I don't know if my family is alive or dead. I stare across the street at Terminal 1 and see a cop pull his gun and enter the terminal. There is a second gunman. This is a coordinated terrorist attack on the airport. This is my thought. The entire airport is under siege, and I realize then that no one in Fort Lauderdale–Hollywood International Airport is safe. Anyone could be shot at any time. I am hiding behind a car in Florida in fear that any moment I could be shot dead. The questions are out there now in the shimmering hot asphalt, but it really comes down to just one.

How did we come to this?

CHAPTER 7

THE RIGHT TO BEAR ARMS

A Liberal Idea

T he right to bear arms is actually a liberal idea. I don't mean liberal versus conservative; I mean that the right to have a gun protects our Lockean rights granted to us in the Bill of Rights. Our right to free speech, our right to assembly, freedom of religion, freedom of the press, is protected *by the very arms we possess*. This is to protect us against a tyrannical government that might be set on taking those rights away. This is how it was designed and it was very progressive for the time. The individual is empowered against the forces that would seek to imprison us. So where did this come from?

Blame it all on the British. They gave us our distrust of all governments. I don't think about my right to bear arms. I don't think I am that different from other urban people in the United States who do not own guns. But I don't view the government with suspicion either, and that suspicion must be intertwined for all time with the Second Amendment. Distrusting the government is the prerequisite for fearing that the right to bear arms might be taken away any minute.

Let's throw in the whole idea that we needed guns to fight the Indians, settle the West, kill bears, and hunt for food. The Indian threat is nonexistent, the West has been settled, the bears are gone, and we all buy our meat in plastic-sealed containers. So that leaves the British. The British were coming. The patriots knew this from Paul Revere's famous night ride that alerted towns along the way. Seven hundred British regulars under Lieutenant Colonel Francis Smith were marching toward Boston.

They were headed for Lexington to destroy military supplies. They knew ammunition and muskets had been stored in root cellars and barns in the town, and they knew an unarmed militia was a militia that could not fight. The militiamen knew about the plan and moved their muskets and ammunition to different locations. At dawn in the town of Lexington, the armed patriots met the British but quickly fell back, overwhelmed by numbers and British discipline.

After the colonists retreated, the redcoats divided into groups to search for weapons caches. At 11:00 a.m. on Concord's North Bridge, not far from Lexington, one hundred Regulars met four hundred armed militiamen.[1] The colonists fired their flintlocks with sharp cracks, surprising the advancing British, who fell on the bridge. The British still believed in marching in formation, and this stopped their march onto the bridge. The redcoats fell back, with the militiamen sniping at them the whole way. The armed colonists reloaded and fired on the retreating British soldiers. The militiamen were good shots after years of hunting in the wilderness. These were people who lived by their guns for hunting, protection, and policing, and now they were using them to repel a tyrannical government. The liberal idea had arrived; freedom would be protected by force.

The British actually gave the Americans two things when it came to guns. One was an inalienable right to bear arms and the second was a reason to bear arms. The British illuminated the concept that a populace without arms was at the mercy of a tyrannical government. When James Madison sat down with others to write the Bill of Rights, the first ten amendments to the Constitution, there was nothing radical about the Second Amendment.[2] Of course people would bear arms, and the reason went back to British law.

The English Bill of Rights of 1689 allowed "the subjects which are Protestants may have arms for their defence suitable to their conditions and as allowed by law" and forbade the king to have "a standing army within the kingdom in time of peace, unless it be with consent of Parliament."[3] The English were very keen on citizenry keeping order. After the town gates were locked for the night the citizenry were the only ones between anarchy and order. The English went further and said its citizenry were to be "sufficiently weaponed."[4] When the colonists came to America, they carried with them the English Bill of Rights and had it in mind as they tinkered with the idea of revolution.

The English were not fools. They wrote laws to compel the citizenry to take up arms or to raise "a hue and cry" against all those who would threaten order. Citizens in 1285 were not only expected to do the policing but also to contribute arms for the local militia.[5] The militia men were expected to keep their weapons in good order and in private hands. And there was some "arms control" in merry old England. In 1541, a statute stated that only those who made over one hundred pounds a year could own a crossbow or a gun except in times of war.[6] The law made a connection between money and being trustworthy. But if the realm was threatened then everyone was expected to arm themselves.

At the Constitutional Convention of 1787, one objective was to give the federal government the power to raise a standing army for protection. The Anti-Federalists greeted this with alarm. Wasn't this the very thing they had fought against in the Revolution? Weren't the British the poster children for the ravages and oppression a standing army could force upon its people? James Madison countered by inserting an amendment in the Bill of Rights that would ensure militias would not be disarmed: "A well-regulated militia, being necessary to the security of a free state, the right of the people to keep and bear arms, shall not be infringed."[7]

The Second Amendment is a hedge against a centralized government and gives the people the power through arms to fight that government if it becomes tyrannical. William Blackstone, who wrote a commentary on the English Bill of Rights, explained that this power given to the people through arms was only to be used as a final solution when "the sanctions of society and laws are found insufficient to restrain the violence of oppression."[8]

Alexander Hamilton elucidated this concept of self-defense in 1788:

"If circumstances should at any time oblige the government to form an army of any magnitude that army can never be formidable to the liberties of the people while there is a large body of citizens, little if at all, inferior to them in discipline and use of arms, who stand ready to defend their own rights and those of fellow citizens."[9]

Some would argue that it is wrong to interpret the Second Amendment as a call to arms against an oppressive government, that the Constitution inserted an elaborate system of balances and checks against such power, which, more than armed insurrection, was the balance of power the framers of the Constitution and the Founding Fathers intended. But many of the debates during the ratification of the Constitution centered on the fear that the federal government might militarily take over the states and that the only protection was an armed citizenry.[10]

The Second Amendment for a lot of people came down to a point of grammar: is there an amplifying clause in the Second Amendment or a qualifying clause? Do we have the right to bear arms so we can form a militia, and so that collective right doesn't exist if we don't need a militia? That would be a qualifying clause. Or do we need a militia always, and so the right to bear arms is always necessary and inviolate? That would be an amplifying clause. It really comes down to semantics. The Right to Bear Arms through history has been interpreted as an individual right regardless of a need for a militia.

We don't trust the government. Again, blame the English. The colonists arrived in the New World equipped with a legal framework and an attitude of anti-authoritarianism that fueled the upheavals of the seventeenth century, the English Civil War of 1642, and the Glorious Revolution of 1688. It was this distrust of central power that resulted in the English Bill of Rights of 1689.[11]

When the British clamped down on the freedoms of their colonists, our English right to bear arms became our American right to bear arms. The first clause is an amplifying clause if we go with our history. We were Englishmen who needed our arms to fight our oppressor and protect our Lockean (life, liberty, and property) and God-given rights. This is where the right to bear arms becomes a liberal idea *because arms protect our Lockean rights.*[12] Every American colony did form a militia, which was then codified in 1792 in the Military Act. Essentially, we took the English right and made it our own, and our government could depend on its citizenry to look after themselves against any threats.

The tradition is one of safeguarding rights by force. The English right to bear arms was interpreted as an individual right, as was the right to bear arms in the American Constitution. It is against our oppressors we armed ourselves and still arm ourselves. The Second Amendment is the right to protect ourselves against those who would take our rights away. Americans would begin their new country as a heavily armed populace suspicious of any centralizing power. Our distrust and suspicion would become the legacy of a people with one finger always on the trigger.

The yellow "Don't Tread on Me" flags reflect this distrust. The populist movement that put Donald Trump in office reflects this distrust. The fact that the Second Amendment was used as a cudgel against Hillary Clinton as Donald Trump became the protector of the right to bear arms against all who would threaten that right shows that it is a fear easily exploited by a populace that sees black copters coming any moment. Basements are well stocked with provisions, arms, and ammo all over the rural countryside of America. The fact that the government has arms and an army and an air force makes the Second Amendment dearer to the hearts of men and women who see themselves as the last line of defense between liberty and tyranny. At last count we now have 300 million guns in America. We are a people who trust no institution and no government, and we prove it by arming ourselves to the teeth.

To say one is for or against the Second Amendment is ridiculous and shows no understanding of the Constitution. The Second Amendment is intertwined with free speech and the free press and the right of assembly. It is like saying you are for or against the First Amendment or the Third. It doesn't matter. It is here to stay. The Second Amendment protects those rights by the design of the Founding Fathers. Gun control or lack of gun control has nothing to do with the Second Amendment. If the Second Amendment were an engine, the issue wouldn't be whether to take the engine out, because then the car wouldn't run. The issue would be how to adjust the engine to run more smoothly.

CHAPTER 8

GRACE UNDER PRESSURE

1:20 p.m.

Ernest Hemingway's definition of courage was grace under pressure. This was what the matadors had, which fascinated the author so much that he described it in *Death in the Afternoon* and other books. This was what propelled Teddy Roosevelt to leave his job as undersecretary of the Navy and lead a group of cowboys up San Juan Hill in the Spanish American War. Courage goes against the instinct for survival, and courage will be demonstrated in this shooting by people who will put their life on the line for others.

We like to think that when a moment comes to test us we will have some "grace under pressure." I would have liked to have stood my ground. I have been brought up to believe that courage is a manly trait, yet I ran like the hero in Stephan Crane's *Red Badge of Courage*. The main character always wondered what he would do under fire in the Civil War and then he found out. He ran like a rabbit all the way to the back lines. This happened a lot in the Civil War as men experienced their baptism of fire. Our DNA has been handed down to us by our Stone Age ancestors, who lived by fleeing from larger or stronger animals. We come from a long line of fleers, but I still wanted to think I could have some of Hemingway's type of courage.

Ducking behind the car and staring at Terminal 1, I have only the overwhelming urge to run as fast as I can. Men who have heard gunfire directed at them in battle can overcome this, I believe, but I have never been in the military and this is my baptism of fire. I am still breathing so fast I can hear my breath outside myself and I feel sweat running off my brow and pasting my shirt tightly to my chest. My backpack, with my computer and books, is still on. I have run with a ten-pound weight on my back and hadn't realized it. Now I am behind the car in the hot Florida sun with my body still in a supercharged state.

A primitive fight-or-flight response had taken over my body at the sound of the gunfire. My body had one objective, which snuffed out my conscious thoughts with one primordial objective—survival. I was one with soldiers, victims of violent crimes, civilians caught in wars, animals that see or smell a predator or sense a life-threating situation. The body's physical reaction to severe stress can save your life. Your body pumps out catecholamines, especially norepinephrine and epinephrine, giving both animals and humans extra strength and speed to react to threats by fighting or fleeing.

I stare at Terminal 1. People all around me are crouched down, as though this were footage from Iraq or some other war-torn country. People are hiding behind cars, lying on the sidewalk, huddling against the building, or standing behind policemen, who have their guns drawn. No one knows where the shooter is. Police protocol, dictated ever since the Columbine shooting, is to go in and disarm an active shooter. The police had done this easily with Esteban Santiago, who was lying on the ground with his Walther 9mm beside him when they arrived. The police assumed they had a lone-shooter situation, and they had let the entire airport know the situation was under control. Clearly it isn't.

Though we don't know it then, the Fort Lauderdale–Hollywood International Airport, in the moment those four shots were fired, had changed into "an active shooter" situation. This means that the police don't know where the shooter is, and no one is safe. You never want to be in an "active shooter situation." It means that you could be shot at any moment. And to make matters worse, there is a high-rise parking garage at my back, with perfect sniper lairs around every parked car. In fact, many police officers are now crouched down with their guns pointed toward the garage. Many pictures will surface later showing the police crouched and staring, with guns drawn. It is the parking garage they are staring at.

The thought that this is a terrorist attack on a major American airport is immediate when the four shots went off. The CNN "Lone Shooter" that my wife and I and my kids had been depending on for our sense of safety is now out the window. This is an attack with multiple gunmen and we are all targets and I don't know where my wife, two daughters, or my son are. I take out my phone and text Kitty. It is like texting underwater. My shaking finger keeps hitting the wrong keys. "Where R U," I finally manage to text. I notice the phone isn't sending, and I flash back to 9/11 and all the other mass shootings where cell coverage is nonexistent because too many people are trying at once to locate loved ones.

I stare at Terminal 1 again, seeing the people hiding under luggage carriers and behind trashcans outside the door. The thought that my daughters, my son, or my wife could be in there bleeding to death or worse is surreal and horrible. I know then I have to go back in.

My heart rate and breathing are still that of a sprinter as I run back across the street thinking that I could be shot at any minute. I run like all those movies I have seen—bent over, zigzagging as I cross into the shade of the building and head back into Terminal 1. I go through the sliding doors and find myself in a vacant airplane hangar. That is the feeling anyway. The terminal is a silent, vast space that has been suddenly evacuated, and I am staring at a sea of suitcases, purses, shoes, flip-flops, lunches, bottled water, earbuds, phones, trash, wallets, glasses, earrings, keys, a comb, a lighter, cigarettes all scattered on the floor. Everything is left as if a ship had sunk and this was an image of the final moment. I look around fully expecting to see a shooter with a gun. The counters and kiosks are empty. The United counter is deserted. Later I will find out that people are hiding on the floor behind the counters thinking I could be a shooter. I see no one and feel relief that I have not found my family in the horrible conditions that exist one terminal over. They have not been shot in the human avalanche that carried us all outside. I look over to where we had been sitting and see our luggage piled up. I see the bag of granola and the ice water I had bought. I see some earbuds. But over everything is an eerie stillness, and all I can hear is my own asthmatic breathing, my own supercharged body still in a state of heightened awareness that will last for the next eight hours.

My phone buzzes and I pull it out, walking back toward the door. The text makes me feel like crying.

"We R OK."

"Where R U?"

"Outside . . . Do U have Clay?"

"No."

I am back out in the sunshine and SWAT teams are running toward the terminal. People are crying, swearing, lying on the ground, hiding behind poles, shrubs, barricades, suitcases, nothing. Sirens come from everywhere. I start running, looking at the people behind car doors, tires, on the curb. An Asian woman stares at me as if I am a strange animal as she sits on an overturned luggage cart. Another woman cries into her phone. Everyone is feeling the same danger, the knowledge that anyone at any time could be shot and killed.

This is the beginning of our incarceration that will last for the next eight hours. We are all trapped between Terminals 1 and 2, with hundreds of cars, police, media, ambulances, and a parking garage that now represents a shooting gallery. There is no information and there is no escape from an airport in lockdown, where every escape route represents a potential path into the sights of a shooter. Worse, if a shooter is on top of the garage with a high-powered rifle a bullet could find anyone at any moment.

We don't know it, but from the second the shots in Terminal 1 were heard we were all trapped inside the Fort Lauderdale–Hollywood International Airport. This, to me, seems to be the ultimate setup for a terrorist—bottle up the ten thousand people in the airport and begin picking them off. I finally know what the definition of terror is . . . the horror of knowing I could be killed at any second.

And at the same time I am indignant. How can this happen after

9/11? Aren't airports the one place where we are supposed to be safe? The truth is that any shooting or terrorist act of any kind in the United States relates back what happened on September 11, 2001. To this day that is the granddaddy of all terrorist acts in American, and our response to this singular event has affected our police, our politics, our sense of security, our ongoing fight over guns and rights under the Second Amendment, how we fly, our airports, our technology, the militarization of our civilian police force, our relationship with the Middle East, our immigration policies, and our election of presidents, and has led to our sense that we will forever be waiting for the next 9/11.

Every time we take off our shoes, our belts, phones, and watches, and every time we get wanded or set off a puffer because talcum powder has chemical relations with sensors designed to detect explosives or a dog sniffs our luggage, we think of that sunny day in September when the world changed, the monster in our rearview mirror that we are always trying to drive away from.

Flying would never be same after 9/11. It instantly became something we had to endure and get through as quickly as possible. We now leave hours before our flights to endure the security lines. We examine our shampoo bottles and get rid of any sort of aerosol can. Luggage will be displayed for all to see and possibly opened and manually inspected. Going to an airport now fills us with the dread associated with doctors' offices. We could be poked and prodded and examined. A plane has become a potential bomb that could wipe out a skyscraper and pilots are potential terrorists. A Muslim woman or man sometimes instills fear in us as we put our carry-on bags into the overhead compartment and wonder for the tenth time if all that technology could really stop someone who wants to do us harm. It wasn't always this way.

In the 1960s and 1970s, all aviation security was taken up a notch from what had been a system with very little security. After planes started getting hijacked, a system of X-ray machines, magnetometers, and federal air marshals was put into place, resulting in a dramatic reduction in hijackings. Then, in 1988, a bomb in the cargo hold of Pan Am Flight 103 exploded over Lockerbie, Scotland, killing 270 people. This pushed the George H. W. Bush administration to implement "anti-explosive" procedures, with mandatory X-ray screening of baggage and a one hundred percent passenger bag match.[1]

We were creeping toward 9/11 with baby steps. Responsibility for air safety and security in airports was divided between the FAA and the airlines. The Federal Aviation Administration was responsible for minimum security standards and had the power to enforce those standards with inspections and fines. The airlines were responsible for screening passengers, baggage, and cargo and for protecting the planes. Congress would create aviation security law and was responsible for funding the federal part of the aviation security system.

The biggest concern in airports up to 9/11 was keeping the planes flying and people moving through airports. Security was still secondary to getting people to their destinations quickly. There had not been a bombing or hijacking since 1991, and the feeling was that the threat to airlines had been contained. On September 11, 2001, the American security system for aviation centered on detecting the placement of explosives in baggage. The screening focused on preventing handguns or large knives from getting on airliners.

But let's say those box cutters had been detected; the rules of that time would have required the terrorists to check their box cutters in baggage, where they could retrieve them later. Much like Esteban Santiago, the terrorists would have had to wait to retrieve their weapons after their flights had landed before commencing with their carnage. This would have prevented the destruction of the World Trade Center in theory and would have left the terrorists with the possibility of attacking passengers in the baggage claim area and potentially closing down an airport. But it gets worse.

The 9/11 terrorists were known to the authorities and had been flagged as potential threats. Two of the nineteen hijackers were on terrorist watchlists, which the FAA had not been made aware of.[2] Seven of the nineteen were identified as potential threats to civil aviation based on their ticketing information.[3] Mohamed Atta, the ringleader, was singled out in the airport for extra security scrutiny, along with two others who could not answer security questions correctly.[4] Twelve of the nineteen hijackers had been identified as potential threats, and it gets worse again—three set off the magnetometers (metal detectors) in the airport, and two of the three set off a second magnetometer. Yet all nineteen of the hijackers eventually did board the planes.

We would like to think that this could never happen again. In the post 9/11 world we see airports and planes as secure areas, where an array of electronic, human, and K9 detection and apprehension keep the threats to the far side of the TSA checkpoints. On one side is the sterile world of the airport, where all screening has taken place; the odds of someone penetrating this safe zone is very low. On the other side is the dirty world where people come and go . . . and pick up their baggage.

The 9/11 commission, formed to assess what had gone wrong and what could be done to prevent future attacks, made many recommendations. The Transportation Security Administration (TSA) was formed to oversee aviation security. We are all now well acquainted with the TSA men and women at the checkpoints, who ask us to take off our shoes and our belts and ask if we have anything in our pockets.

Another recommendation of the commission was that "to enhance security and improve efficiency, explosives detection equipment should be moved from airport lobbies and placed where they can accomplish their vital mission 'in line' as checked baggage is moved from the check-in counter to the aircraft."[5] This would expand the sterile area and make sure any baggage, be it carry on or checked, would be subject to the same rigorous screening. This would not include the baggage claim area, however, which would still be outside the sterile area.

Another change that came after 9/11 involved passenger pre-screening. This had already existed to a lesser extent in the form of

CAPPS, the Computer-Assisted Passenger Prescreening System, which alerted airlines as to passengers whose bags should receive further inspection. The TSA and the airlines would consult the terrorist watchlist, the No Fly List, and the Automatic Selectee List. The people on the first two lists would not board the plane, and the Automatic Selectees would be subject to rigorous screening.

In 2004, a report by the Inspector General of the Department of Homeland Security, found a high-risk area, a hole in the security apparatus: information sharing: "Creating a single infrastructure for effective communications and information exchange at various classification levels within the Department remains a major management challenge for DHS."[6] In other words, if a man goes to the FBI and says that he is hearing voices telling him to kill, that he has been instructed by ISIS, and that he has a gun—which the FBI takes away from him and then gives it back—the agency should put that information into the database so that when one Esteban Santiago goes to purchase a one-way ticket for Fort Lauderdale–Hollywood International Airport he will be prevented from boarding an airliner with his Walther 9mm in the cargo hold.

After spending more than twenty billion dollars on aviation security after 9/11, the federal government, the TSA, the airlines, Congress, and Homeland Security couldn't stop a man who should have been watchlisted from flying with his handgun, which he was able to retrieve in the baggage claim area at his destination and then to inflict unspeakable horror and close down a major US airport for twenty-four hours. Some might call this a complete breakdown of aviation security, and then some might say that in the wake of 9/11 we are always waiting for the other shoe to drop. This time the shoe dropped inside the safe zone. Some might say you can't really stop anyone who is determined to kill.

This thought gives me no solace as I look for my family.

CHAPTER 9

ONE IN THREE HUNDRED AND FIFTEEN

1:45 p.m.

I had graduated college with a master's degree in history with the thought that I would go to law school. This was some sort of F. Lee Bailey dream that had more to do with my grandfather, who had been a highly regarded lawyer in Virginia. I had never been a great student until I could write a historical thesis in graduate school and use the power of prose to explain my arguments in exam essays. This did not help on the Law School Admission Test, which required deductive reasoning. So I sat down and wrote a novel.

Six years later I was published and had started down the high-risk road of the novelist. I married Kitty, who had been engaged to a man who promised a more stable life. I was the fun guy who took her for motor-cycle rides in the middle of the night and picked her up from her adver-tising agency at all hours of the morning. The more stable man in her life demanded an answer, and she threw over security for the unknown. "I know I will never be bored with you," she said.

I wonder now if a boring life would have been so bad. You always ques-tion your choices after a certain amount of water has flowed over the dam and that old saw that actions have consequences takes root. I have had a good career as a writer, with over twelve books, many good reviews, and even a movie-rights sale. But I've never had that out-of-the-park homerun, and so my life has resembled a high-wire act, always just one bad step from the abyss. Having kids, of course, had put that wire just a little higher.

And as I run along the outside of the terminal looking for my family in the middle of a shooting, I think about the odds. What are the odds I have played with my whole life? Would a different career have produced different results? Maybe we would not have had a layover if I had more money. Maybe we would have caught an earlier flight and gone to the beach to kill time and not been sitting in the airport. Maybe Kitty should have married that more stable man who had a more stable life. Maybe boring is alright. Maybe this is where the dice comes up snake eyes, and the odds I have played my whole life have come for their due.

The odds of being struck by lightning are about 1 in 1,000,000. The odds of being in a mass shooting are 1 in 11,125.[1] But here is the statistic that stops you cold: the chance that you will be shot dead with a firearm in America is 1 in 315. Gun violence is the eighteenth leading cause of death in the United States.[2]

This is in the realm of possibility. But none of these numbers mean a thing when you are in the middle of a shooting. You have broken the odds, smashed the roulette table, busted through twenty-one in black-jack, and rolled snake eyes. You have somehow entered the world of the unlucky and joined forces with people on television crying, bleeding, dying, and telling the world how unlucky they are. You are now officially the unluckiest person you know. Now I am running up and down like a madman trying to find my family. Oddly, I think of the time when I was a kid in Virginia and my friend showed me the room where his father had committed suicide. It was in a den, and he pointed to a hole in the ceiling. "That's where the bullet went," he whispered. "It came out of his head." I was maybe nine and didn't understand how that small hole could mean the death of a father. But bullets and guns have always been on the periphery one way or another.

Now I am running, sweating, wheezing, looking frantically for the people I would die for, and another image comes to me. Kitty and I are in a bad neighborhood in Chicago and automatic weapon fire breaks out. I push her down in the car and I try and get us out of there and

I smash into the car behind me. It is a summer night and people are running in all directions trying to get away from the bullets. We finally get out, and I go through three red lights before I slow down.

I am running across the access road bent over, with heavily armed SWAT Teams running down the street the other way. The terminal doors are propped open but it is empty and people are everywhere outside. People are still wedged under small shrubs, hiding behind cars, trashcans, poles, lying against walls and curbs. It seems everyone has a gun out. I see plainclothes policemen holding their guns, staring up at the parking garage, and that means I am completely exposed. I remember strangely the images of the people after the buildings collapsed on 9/11 running around with pictures of their loved ones whom everyone knew were gone. And I wonder if my life has changed forever. Will this be the day my life stops and another world begins? Will I now be alone in the world after the great tragedy?

We live in a mostly white suburb thirty miles west of Chicago. Yet we are urbanites who lived in the city for ten years and then in Oak Park on the edge of Chicago. We loved the progressive quality of Oak Park, but after 9/11 it changed. It seemed that the crime was coming closer. A man was mugged on our street while walking his dog. My neighbor's house was burglarized, and there were stories of a murder one block over. A man we hired to rake leaves came to my door one night and demanded money. It felt like those jets that had destroyed the Twin Towers were coming ever closer. I had studied maps of the projected blast of a dirty bomb in Chicago and decided that with a second child and our third one on the way it was time to make the final evolution to the western suburbs.

Here, crime was nonexistent. We could leave our door unlocked, our car unlocked, the bikes on our very wide front lawn. No more bikes being stolen, baby carriages stolen, garages broken into. No one stole anything. No one shot anybody. I see now that my whole life has been one of trying to mitigate the very high risk inherent in my career choice by embracing perceived safety. And of course it was an illusion. Life is risky.

I am still breathing like a runner, still frantically looking for my family.
"We R by the door."

The text comes in delayed, and I run for the door and see nothing, but then Kitty moves aside a plastic bin used for carrying luggage, and I see Callie and Kitty lying on the ground under similar bins. No one is bleeding, just lying on the ground in terror.

I glance around quickly.

"Where's Careen?"

Kitty looks to her right, and I see another gray bin, with two white Crocs sticking out from under it. I pull up the bin and Careen is lying there, crying. A long-legged twelve-year-old in sixth grade is hiding under a plastic bin afraid she is going to get shot. I pull her up and hug her for a long time. I look down to where the media trucks and police cars and ambulances are piled up around Terminal 2. To me, that has to be safer. The media trucks are large and bulky, and there are a hundred cops down there.

"Where's Clay?"

Kitty shakes her head. "I don't know."

I look again at the media trucks puffing out diesel exhaust.

"Let's go toward Terminal 2. It's safer."

Kitty shakes her head. She is trembling. "No . . . I don't want to move."

I look at the parking garage, with the SWAT teams swarming over the floors. I don't blame her. Anything in the open seems dangerous, but I think it is dangerous to stay by Terminal 1, where we heard the shots. Careen has to go with me. "I'm taking Careen down to the police and the media trucks."

Kitty looks out from her bin.

"Okay."

"I'll be back."

She understands why I am doing it. I take Careen's hand and look at her; her big blue eyes are full of wonder, full of terror.

"You ready to run?"

She nods.

"Yes."

We begin to run, and I realize that in two weeks we are supposed to be going to our daddy-daughter dance. It is a dance put on every year by the park district at which fathers get to spend a night with their daughters and eat lots of candy and warm cheese and lemonade. You watch a magician, get balloons, dance and scream, and eat too many marbleized meatballs. It is amazing, really, to see all the fathers in suits with their daughters. I used to take Callie and Careen, but Callie at sixteen feels she is too old, so it is now just Careen and me, and I know that this too will end soon. I am the dad who spends all the time he can with his kids and will be destroyed when they leave.

I have discovered that Careen has a very funny sense of humor and loves to make slime out of borax and glue. We ride our scooters around the driveway and discuss her day when she comes home from school and I am done writing for the day. Maybe it is that way with the youngest; you know that this is it, and you reach across that chasm between parents and children to stay connected as long as you can. Maybe it is because you understand it will end.

But now we are running toward Terminal 2. It is incongruous that this is the terminal where people are lying dead inside after the killer's rampage, but instinctively I am running toward the police and the media, and there are television trucks all over. We run for our lives, low to the ground along the wall, and after we clear Terminal 1 I see people out on the tarmac of the runway. There is a vast crowd of ant people, something I have never seen before. They are tiny in the distance, but I can see that they are running past the jets stopped on the runway. Chaos has overtaken the airport, and everyone is running from the unseen danger.

We reach the diesel-puffing media trucks and slump down behind a thick cement pole. Portable generators hum, along with the engines that surround us with heat and exhaust. Fear has been transmuted into a permanent adrenaline high. The fear belonged to the moment the shots rang out, and now there is just the heat and I am soaked from perspiration.

My daughter stares at me with large blue eyes. Diesel exhaust from the television trucks and the incessant wailing of the sirens are all around us. Incredibly, there are beautiful female reporters just a few feet from us, holding microphones in bright lights. This makes me feel better. If they are not worried about getting shot then maybe we are safe. They suddenly duck down, and I look back toward Terminal 1, where people are running again. It is that avalanche of humans flowing toward us like a wave. We are still on the firing line, and I remember as if in a dream that just that morning we were on a cruise. The world before the shooting is gone, and there is only this moment of survival. No one seems to know what anyone is running from. We are all running to escape an unseen terror. You have to wonder, when did mass shootings begin in our country?

CHAPTER 10

THE FIRST MASS MURDER

1949

I t had never happened before, and they didn't know what to do with him. In 1949, people didn't just kill other people for no reason. It was so rare that there was no police protocol to deal with it. It was so rare that they immediately decided the killer had to be insane and didn't even bother with a trial. They simply put him in an insane asylum and forgot about him. Prisons were for sane men, and a man who would kill multiple people was clearly insane and could not have been in control of his own mind.

His name was Howard Unruh. He was gay and a World War II vet. This was a time when it was a crime to be gay. He lived in Camden, New Jersey, in an apartment above a store. Unruh would be the first "lone wolf" killer, harboring resentment against those around him until it boiled over into a murderous rage.[1] The idea of the individual plotting revenge on those around him would become the boilerplate story for many workplace and school shooters that followed. The eerie coincidences between Esteban Santiago and Howard Unruh are striking. Both men were veterans. Unruh saw action in the Battle of the Bulge as a tank gunner, where he kept meticulous notes on the Germans he killed and how they died. He received commendations and was said to follow orders well. PTSD was a long way off as a diagnosis, but Howard's younger brother would later say that Howard was not the same man when he came back from World War II. In his Camden apartment Unruh kept German shells for ashtrays, along with pistols and machetes he had brought back from the war. He practiced shooting in the basement with a Nazi luger he had brought back with him.

Before the war Howard had been a normal kid in prewar America. His parents had divorced, and Unruh lived with his mother, who worked in a soap factory. A later psychiatric report on Unruh after the shooting would note that he had prolonged toilet training and didn't walk or speak until sixteen months, but after this Freudian stab there was nothing to say Howard Unruh exhibited anything other than normal boyhood traits.

He liked to collect stamps and build model trains. As a young adult, he didn't drink or smoke and he attended St. Paul's Evangelical Lutheran Church. His Woodrow Wilson High yearbook noted that he wanted to work for the government. After graduating, Howard worked for a printer for a while, and then worked operating a metal stamping press. And then he was drafted.

Like many returning vets, Howard Unruh had a hard time adjusting, and he ended up back with his mother in Camden. Later, a psychiatrist would write, "After WWII . . . he returned home, he did not work nor did he have any life goals or directions, had difficulty adjusting or solving problems and was 'angry at the world.'"[2] Esteban Santiago choking his girlfriend after his return from Iraq, with the resulting restraining order comes to mind.[3] A weaponized human being, still loaded to kill.

Unruh began keeping a list of those who had wronged him. The drugstore owner, Mr. Cohen, kept shortchanging him.[4] The people who lived in the apartment below his threw garbage in the backyard. A barber flooded his basement by throwing dirt into a vacant lot and blocking up the drainage. Then there was the shoemaker, who buried rubbish right next to Unruh's property line. Mr. Cohen had also called Unruh queer, and the tailor's son spread a story about him meeting a man in an alley. Howard Unruh was becoming increasingly paranoid that people knew he was gay, and this increased his sense that people were out to get him and would reveal him to the authorities.

On September 6, 1949, Howard threatened his mother with a wrench after breakfast, and she fled from the house. He then picked up his Luger and ammunition, put on a brown suit and bow tie, laced up his army boots, and left through the backyard. He encountered a bread deliveryman in his truck and shot at him, but the bullet missed. He then went to the shoemaker's store, where he shot John Pilarchik in the chest and then the head.

Next to Pilarchik's store a six-year-old boy, Orris Smith, was getting his hair cut in a barbershop when Unruh burst in and waved his gun. Clark Hoover, the barber, tried to shield the boy as Unruh shot him and the boy. Orris's mother grabbed her son and ran out into the street, screaming, until a neighbor picked them up and drove for the hospital.

Like a Wild West movie, Unruh then walked down Main Street firing indiscriminately into stores until he reached the drugstore run by the Cohens. A customer, James Hutton, fell in the doorway with a single shot, then Howard stepped over him and saw the Cohens running from the gunfire up the stairs. Unruh followed them and shot Rose Cohen in a closet but missed her twelve-year-old son hiding in an adjacent closet. Cohens mother was dialing the police when Unruh shot and killed her, finishing off Roses husband Maurice as he tried to escape onto a porch roof.

Back outside the drugstore, Unruh shot and killed four people in cars that happened to be driving down the street. He stepped into the tailor's shop, where he shot and killed Helga Zegrino, the tailor's wife, while she begged for her life. He had been looking for Tom Zegrino, the tailor. On the street again, Unruh saw movement in an upstairs window and fired, striking and killing two-year-old Thomas Hamilton. Finally, Unruh broke into a house behind his apartment, where he shot a woman and her sixteen-year-old son, wounding but not killing them. At that point, Unruh ran out of ammo, so he fled back to his apartment as the police arrived.

There were no SWAT teams in 1949. There was no protocol or procedure for dealing with a "shooter." The police were not heavily armed and they had to bring in extra weaponry. They proceeded as if at war; fifty cops surrounded the apartment and let loose with Thompson machine guns, shotguns, and pistols, endangering the crowd of a thousand people who had gathered nearby. As Unruh hid in his apartment, the phone rang. Surprisingly, Unruh answered, and spoke briefly to the editor from the *Camden Evening Courier* who had called. When the editor asked how many people he had killed, Unruh replied that he didn't know but that "it looks like a pretty good score."[5]

After the police threw tear gas canisters into the apartment, Unruh gave up and surrendered peacefully. At the police station, he described the killings in detail.

Twenty-four hours after the first mass shooting in American history, Howard Unruh was turned over to the Trenton Psychiatric Hospital. There he was committed to the Vroom building for the criminally insane. He never stood trial for the thirteen people he had killed. He showed no emotion when describing the murders, but he later said he was sorry for killing the kids.

The order of commitment states that Howard Unruh suffered from "dementia praecox, mixed type, with pronounced catatonic and paranoid coloring."[6] This meant that he was considered a paranoid schizophrenic. Experts today are not convinced the diagnosis was accurate and believe that were the incident to have happened more recently he would have stood trial. But law enforcement did not know how to view Unruh at the time, as he was so clearly outside the boundaries of even criminal behavior, and there was simply no procedure to assess the criminality of his act. He would die in the psychiatric hospital in 1988.[7]

Esteban Santiago and Howard Unruh were veterans who came home suffering from PTSD in one form or another. Both killed with no emotion, and it is telling that Howard Unruh donned his combat boots for his final tour of death. Both men had difficulty adjusting to society after serving in combat, and for a time they lived quiet lives of rage, filled with grievances against those around them. Santiago heard voices telling him to kill, while Unruh made lists of those who would die. The men are separated by almost seventy years, but the carnage created by these weaponized humans is the same. The FBI defines a mass killing as one having four or more victims.[8] Howard Unruh would go down in history as America's first modern mass killer.

CHAPTER 11

THE FEEDING FRENZY

2:00 p.m.

We are addicted to the news. CNN made us this way. Before CNN began broadcasting, in 1980, veteran CBS news anchor Walter Cronkite would sum up events for us once every evening. CNN, however, said there was enough news for a twenty-four-hour cycle, and if there wasn't they would find some. Shootings are tailor-made for networks like CNN. They are real-time crises that unfold like high-stakes dramas in front of us. The news becomes a spectacle as journalists descend on the dead, the wounded, the families, and the shooter. The line between show business and news becomes blurred.

Now that we are trapped in an airport in an "active situation" we are literally living inside the news story. The surreal is normal. Something takes over and allows us to function in extreme stress. We see this with people who have just lost loved ones; they speak as if they are talking about someone else. It is a coping mechanism. The thought that my twelve-year-old and I were running from a potential shooter does not compute. Careen and I are usually riding scooters or shooting baskets or going to Dairy Queen. We have never experienced being in a combat zone. But that is what an "active shooter situation" is: a *combat zone* where anyone can be shot at any time.

And here we are, sitting on a sidewalk in the hot sticky Fort Lauderdale air. Careen's white shorts are dirty and smudged with road grime. I am streaked with sweat, and my black T-shirt sticks to my body as if painted on. We are survivors.

I am standing up and thinking about going back for Kitty and Callie and wondering where Clay is. But of course I can't leave Careen among the fortress of television trucks and the juiced-up talking heads with their microphones. Sirens are screaming, ambulances are parked everywhere, and we are in media central. The images being pumped out to the world are coming from right here.

"I want to get out of here, Dad," Careen says, looking at me, her eyes wide.

I nod, staring at the police cars, small tanks, fire trucks, ambulances, SWAT teams, soldiers, men in dark suits, helicopters flying overhead, and buses marked Evidence. We are in a war zone, and nobody is going anywhere until the war is won. So I lie.

"We will. We just have to get everyone together," I say, standing up and looking toward Terminal 1.

Careen shakes her head. "They should have come with us."

"I agree," I murmur, looking around.

The television trucks have their antennas extended, sending out the story. The truth is, I had experienced the shooting in Terminal 2 through CNN, which had broadcasted images of people running onto the tarmac, above the bold headline "Five Dead, Eight Wounded in Shooting in Ft Lauderdale Airport." Music and graphics and cutaways resemble a movie, morphing American shootings into entertainment. One thing the networks know is that violence sells, and even better is the developing story of a real-time shooting. The Fort Lauderdale airport shooting is the hottest thing on television right now, and we are at ground zero of the media universe.

Television ushered in our current consumer-based mass culture and its adoption was only delayed by World War II, but by 1955 two-thirds of all homes in the United States had a television set.[1] The television is on for seven hours and forty minutes a day in the average American household, with an average of three televisions per home. Children consume forty hours of television per week and much of this television is violent.

A study in 1998 defined media violence as "any overt depiction of a credible threat of physical force or the actual use of such force intended to physically harm an animate being or group of beings."[2] Certainly, television coverage of any shooting falls into this category, especially now with graphic cellphone video footage being picked up by the networks.

Just after Esteban Santiago stopped shooting at the Fort Lauderdale airport, a cellphone video begins circulating online, showing the carnage in Terminal 2. The video sweeps around, and the viewer sees the dead and dying on the ground, people huddled around them. We get the horror firsthand through the grainy frenetic image. It is not polished, and this makes it more macabre. The video is already being run on television with a "graphic images" warning, which makes more people watch it.

In the sea of media parked outside Terminal 2 where Careen and I sit, the idling engines and the lawnmower sound of the generators give the area the feel of a bus depot. The danger rolls in and out like a wave as the entire airport lies under the threat of an active shooter. When the danger seems to ebb the newspeople come out of their air-conditioned trucks with microphones, ready to broadcast. They are in a feeding frenzy to get their scoop, to share this violence with the American people. And we are putty in the hands of marketing executives, who use "edits, cuts, zooms, pans and sudden noises to continually trigger our orienting response."[3] Our response comes from a primal world where we needed to be aware of any sudden or novel stimulus, allowing us to survive and to either run or fight. A mass shooting is exactly the kind of event that stimulates our orienting response—the threat of death, with the potential for real gore and real tragedy.

School shootings have been the most shocking of mass shootings, covered in the media with helicopter shots of kids and teachers running and police and SWAT teams entering the school. The line between fiction and nonfiction becomes blurred as graphics and music and interviews amplify the already-great tragedy of children and teachers being murdered. Ratings skyrocket for the stations covering these shootings, and the first network on the scene dominates the airwaves until the other networks can catch up. News coverage is often blamed for copycat shootings, in which someone imitates the crime of the initial shooter to gain similar fame. There has been talk of limiting media coverage of shootings, but this would mean surrender in the brutal ratings wars waged by television networks. No one is going to turn off their camera.

As the violent images from a tragic event are played over and over, we become desensitized; television continues the violence by replaying the shocking footage again and again. Mass shootings have left people with the impression that American society is awash in blood: "From 1960 to 1991 the US population increased by 40 percent, but the violent crime rate increased by *500 percent*."[4] In the era of mass shootings, death by gunfire suddenly seemed to be as ubiquitous as dying from cancer or heart disease. But I would find out the hard way that the media has a narrative, and they expect everyone to stick to the script. To deviate is to invite ridicule.

My interaction with the media begins as I see Kitty and Callie running up from Terminal 1 and then I see Clay coming from the direction of Terminal 1 where we had all split up. We found out later that he had been frisked by the police and then released. A photographer would later tell us she had a picture of him that she decided not to use because he looked so terrified. My family has crossed over the access road and then weaved their way through the television trucks. We are now all together and surrounded by television trucks, lights, cameras, and reporters; it is the electronic medium that has become as real as life itself for many people.

Kitty and Callie have run up and taken refuge behind a cement pole but now Kitty is lying on the ground with my children. She believes the shooter is sizing up anyone standing. Here is the insanity of our situation—some people are hiding while others are talking and laughing. The real hell is that we have no information at all. We have no idea if there are two, three, or four shooters. We are simply ducking the unseen danger that sent us running in the first place. All we know is that we heard four shots in Terminal 1 and we ran along with everyone else. This is our story.

"Get down . . . get down," Kitty screams at me.

I get down and then we all cluster around the cement pillar again for safety. I move away to get a better look at the police now moving back toward Terminal 2. A *Washington Post* photographer snaps a picture of my family huddled next to the cement pillar, and this will be syndicated and end up in many national newspapers. The photo sums up the utter capriciousness of any shooting—regular people caught up in hell. This single moment of a family in distress will be shown over and over, and this is just the beginning. I watch the television journalists standing with lights surrounding them. They are absurdly good-looking men and women and extremely young. They exist beyond the carnage of what is occurring around them. They are in the ether of a high-powered industry that allows them to float above mortals. Their images are beamed out daily, and that gives them a peculiar larger-than-life existence. Whenever I do radio or television interviews, the afterglow is one of knowing that people unknown to me have just listened to or watched me. I had floated over half the country or the state and had for a while left my terrestrial body. Or so they think. Journalists often feel a detachment because they are covering the tragedy, the shooting, the murder and not participating in the actual moment. It might be best described as a strange third-person narrative feeling of safety.

I get down on the ground with my family and lie on the sidewalk. We are a strange sight, lying on the sidewalk while others walk around us. But Kitty believes that to stand is to invite catastrophe, so we keep lying on the dirty sidewalk as the television journalists talk to their colleagues. The women are blue eyed with blond hair and dressed to the hilt. The men are in smart sport coats or bright ties. The juxtaposition of beautiful people to the people trapped in the airport, hiding, sitting, lying on the ground, sweating, worrying, caught up in a vortex they cannot escape, is startling.

We have now become the subjects of the news, the people who will tell their story. My son will tell his story about how he ran from the shots and tried to get in people's cars, offering them money to let him in until the police detained him and frisked him. He is tall and lanky and wears his hair short, and like most twenty year olds he has been stopped by the police a few times. Callie and Careen will describe how they hid under the bins, afraid they could be shot any minute. My wife, Kitty, is so scared she is lying face down on the sidewalk. I do not share her fear, but I don't know if that is because of stupidity on my part, a lack of being in touch with my feelings, or the adrenaline ride I am on.

"Don't get up," Kitty pleads with me.

"Okay," I say, listening to her for now.

She has always been the pragmatic one. Kitty worked in the rough-and-tumble world of advertising on Michigan Avenue in Chicago for years. She was an account executive and developed a very hard shell and a real ability to drill down to what was really the essence of a problem. If a creative director had a problem or a commercial shoot ran into an issue, Kitty had to intercede and solve the problem when no one else could. She is not subject to flights of fancy the way her writer husband is, who sees villains lurking over the next hill. She is fact driven and solves problems logically. So to her the situation is very simple: survival means staying flat on the sidewalk with her children. If her idiot husband wants to walk around and get shot, there is not much she can do about it. And if the police want to claim there was only one shooter, there is nothing she can do about that either. "I know what I heard and so did everyone else who ran out of that terminal," she would say later. "There was a second shooter."

There is a photo I saw later of people hiding under cement stairs next to officers with their pistols drawn, crouched in a shooting position. The people were under those stairs, behind cement poles, and hiding behind anything they could find for one reason—the second gunmen. The reason people were turned out onto the tarmac of the airport, literally running around planes that were taxiing and some being picked up by those planes, is because of a second gunmen. The SWAT teams were searching the garages, the cars, people, and luggage because of this unknown assailant. The reason the FAA ordered a ground stop and closed the airport and trapped ten thousand people was because the situation was active and that meant somewhere there was a potential shooter.

Kitty later put it this way: "I ran for my life when those shots went off. My son ran and pleaded with people to let him in their cars. We pleaded with people to let us in cars after we got up from hiding under the luggage bins and then we lay on the ground in fear, in the dirt, on sidewalks. There were shots. I have been on this earth for a long time and have never run like that before. My daughters heard the shots. An airline pilot heard the shots. The people around me heard the shots. And we all ran the same way away from the shots. We ran toward Terminal 2 because we heard shots in Terminal 1. So why didn't the police hear the shots . . . ? I have no idea."

Kitty's father is a German engineer who made his money from designing candy factories from the first bolt to the last processing machine that would wrap the candy bars. She is grounded, whereas I am prone to imaginative leaps. She is methodical while I am intuitive. She will do the heavy lifting while I will find the shortcut. She follows procedure while I look for the easy way that will assure me that I am smarter than everyone else. Kitty is smarter than everyone else but doesn't care. So her reaction was different than mine. This is how she put it: "When I heard the four shots my thought was to hide. I am a fleer so I hid behind that large pole in the terminal. The shots came from the south end of the terminal and everyone was running from that end to the north. So Callie, Careen, and I hid behind this pole. We might have still been there when you came back looking for us."

I asked her what she heard after the shots.

"Nothing. We heard nothing. But there was a Japanese woman by us on her phone, and a man began swearing at her, saying we all were going to be shot if she didn't shut up. He began to threaten her, but she kept talking in Japanese. Finally, we realized we were the only ones in the terminal and decided to leave. I think Callie said we should leave. We assumed the shooter was in the other end where the shots came from. I mean that is how you know there was a shooter. No one said anything. Everyone just started running the same way."

Kitty ran out of the terminal with the girls and picked up the luggage bins to put over them. "A man looked at Careen and said that will not stop a bullet," she explained later. "I don't know if she heard him but my thought was, 'My God, we are talking about my daughter getting shot.' So we put the bins over us and hid with everyone else. Everyone was hiding because everyone heard the four shots. The police were running, too. They were running into the terminal and the SWAT teams were running into the garage across the street. So, we lay there and that's when I texted you and then you picked up Careen and took her down to the media trucks. Callie and I lay there and then we decided to go down to where you were."

Kitty and Callie crossed into the street but realized they were exposed to the garage. She later told me, "I realized then we could be shot by anyone in that garage and so we asked a man if we could get into his car. He stared at us and said he had stuff in his back seat. We just wanted to get out of the line of fire that we felt could come from anywhere. So we went to the next car and the man didn't say anything. That was when we crossed over to the media trucks and saw you. I lay down on the ground with the kids and that's where we stayed. I felt we could be shot at any moment because it was obvious the police did not have control."

This is where the photographer from the *Washington Post* took the picture that shows a family on the sidewalk in utter fear. What most people don't understand is that the fear came from *a second series of shots* that had nothing to do with Esteban Santiago. Kitty summed it up this way days later, "I mean why didn't they lock down Terminal 1 when those people were killed in Terminal 2? Everything was perfectly normal until shots went off in Terminal 1," she pointed out, pausing. "Then they did a lockdown. They did that lockdown because of the second shooter they said didn't exist. The police should have locked down the entire airport when those first shots were fired . . . and they know it. Whoever fired those second shots is responsible for the airport closing and they got clean away."

CHAPTER 12

FIFTEEN MINUTES OF FAME

2:30 p.m.

I am staring at three cameras. Andy Warhol said we would all get fifteen minutes of fame. He was referring to the evolving media universe, with its roving eye searching for anything deemed newsworthy. Warhol said this before the internet, which really now should translate the idea to fifteen nanoseconds of fame. Such is our attention span these days that most of us will not be able to get our full fifteen minutes and will have to settle for a few nanoseconds. I am about to get mine, and it comes on the back of a national catastrophe.

The sweat stings my eyes. The air has grown even hotter. Stress makes us perspire. We have been under stress now for several hours, ready for fight or flight. The camera lunges over another man's shoulder. I am facing three cameras and three microphones. Word has gotten out that I was in the shooting. I am news fodder for the live breaking news. The microphones edge closer. No book I have ever written has garnered this much immediate attention. Celebredom is coming in a sound bite and the quicksilver fame of bad luck. The lights flip on, and I am blind as a woman fills the space below my mouth with a large spongy microphone.

"You were there in the shooting? Tell us about it. Jim, you want to get this?"

The camera lights are still blinding and I am speaking to a woman with absurdly blue eyes. "We were on our way back from a cruise and waiting for our flight when we heard the shots—"

"You mean in Terminal 2?" she interrupts.

I shake my head.

"No, in Terminal 1."

She bobs the microphone.

"There were shots in Terminal 1?"

"Yes," I nod. "Everyone ran. Three or four shots. That is how we ended up out here. This is why they closed the airport."

Now there are three more cameras on me and microphones reaching over shoulders. So you heard the shots? *Yes.* How many? *Three or four.* You are sure you heard shots? *Absolutely.* The police are saying there was only a lone gunman. *I don't know about that. All I can tell you is that we were in Terminal 1 when the shots were fired and everyone ran and Terminal 1 emptied out.* The cameras suddenly pull away, and I can hear people talking. "I don't know if he knows what he is talking about," I hear someone say. I turn, and a man with blond hair looks at me.

"Do you mind if I ask you some questions?"

He looks vaguely familiar, and I am sure I have seen him on the news. He is in front of a Fox News truck. I stare at the truck and its dark interior with multiple computer screens. The warm humming electronics smell soothing. It looks safe in there. I turn to him.

"Can my family sit in your truck?"

The man stares at me and shakes his head quickly.

"No. We are going live on a nationwide feed." He brushes back his hair, stares into the camera, and holds the microphone just below his mouth. "Are you ready?"

"I guess so," I reply, feeling strange about becoming part of the media show.

He is getting a count from a producer. A mass shooting is an event that networks and cable news shows cut away from the regular programing to cover. This is how we become part of the narrative of the Fort Lauderdale shooting, and this is how our friends and family will find out we are there. Media comes like a wave, washing away all prior notions of who we are. I wait, listening to the count, and feel strange now about these interviews. I feel like I am pushing a book again. The media juggernaut has me right now, and I know from experience that the wave will pass quickly, but right now I am caught up in that wave. The lights come up.

"I am standing here with William Hazelgrove who was in Terminal 1 when shots were fired. . . . Tell us what happened."

The microphone is below my mouth. I want to wipe my face but I don't dare. "Well, I was there to catch a plane with my family in Terminal 1, in the United Terminal, when at about one o'clock we heard four shots and everyone started running."

He frowns. "So you are saying this is not in Terminal 2 but in Terminal 1?"

"That's right."

"So you are saying there is a second gunman?"

"All I can tell you is that I have heard gunfire before and everyone in that terminal started running for their lives."

"Then what happened?"

"Then we ended up here where we thought it was safer."

"Everyone in your family is safe?"

"Yes."

The lights flick out and I turn away. I feel used up and a little shoddy for talking to the media. Should one talk about almost getting shot and sell it like a pair of shoes? Media demands that you be complicit in selling the product, and the product is sensational news. The man is already walking toward a press briefing by the sheriff. I didn't know it then, but I had just gone out live on Fox News to the world and declared that there was a second shooter at the Fort Lauderdale Airport.

Another woman asks me for a quick interview. I repeat what I had said. I turn away and my son is there. Clay and I are then both interviewed about what happened in Terminal 1. The journalists point out that the police have said there is only one shooter. I shrug and look at my son. We both heard it and we both ran. The cameras go away again. Then a man from CNN asks if I will go on camera.

I have a funny feeling about this one as he prefaces my interview for the audience. "We don't have confirmation of a second shooter but we have a man from Chicago who says he heard the shots." And then I am in front of the camera. "Tell us what you heard."

"I was in Terminal 1, the United Terminal, and a little after one I heard four shots. My wife and my two daughters and my son heard the shots."

"And what did you do?"

I look at him. "We ran for our lives out of the terminal and became separated."

The journalist, who has close-cropped hair and dark eyes, stares at me. "You are aware there is no other shooter. That the police have said there is only one shooter."

I shrug again. "This is what I heard. I heard four shots and so did everyone else who ran out of Terminal 1."

"Well, I think you are wrong," he says flatly, and I realize then I have been set up. "There was only one shooter, sir. You were mistaken. The police have informed us there was only one shooter. So there you have it. A father who is mistaken on what he heard."

And then I am off camera. The objective of this interview was to tell the world there was one shooter. I had been brought in to be confronted on live television and positioned as either a liar or someone hearing something go bump in the night. This narrative of one shooter has already taken hold, and the media is there to confirm the narrative.

I wander away from the lights feeling foolish. It is my own fault. I should not have taken any of the interviews. But I have spent many years chasing media for coverage for my books, and I was not used to the pursuer becoming the quarry. One never really wins with a medium that holds all the power. I notice a large news conference gathering not ten feet away. I walk over and stand at the back as the lights come on. There are ten cameras, with many more microphones. The sheriff begins to speak, surrounded by police and officials from the airport and the city. My fifteen minutes are over and television has won again; but, then, the medium has far more experience than I do with shootings. The first televised shooting had been in Texas and after it nothing would be the same again.

CHAPTER 13

THE TEXAS TOWER SNIPER

1966

On August 1, 1966, Charles Whitman took a footlocker filled with ammo, guns, water, and food up into the clock tower at the University of Texas at Austin, to the twenty-eighth-floor observation deck. It was a sweltering 98 degree day. Whitman was another weaponized human being. He had earned a sharpshooter badge and a Marines Corps Expeditionary medal. He could hit 215 out of 250 shots on marksman tests, excelling at shooting rapidly over long distances and hitting moving targets.[1]

Born in 1941, Whitman had an above average intelligence, with an IQ of 139. His father grew up in an orphanage and was able to become a successful businessman. Violence emanated from the man, however, and he demanded perfection from his wife and children. When Charles came home drunk one night, his father beat him and threw him in the family swimming pool. Charles Whitman's father was also a hunter and a collector of guns, who took his son hunting and taught him to shoot. He was proud of his son's natural marksmanship, commenting, "Charlie could plug a squirrel in the eye by the time he was sixteen."[2]

From a young age, Charles Whitman was deadly with a rifle. He joined the Marines after high school without telling his father. There, he excelled in a Marines Corps scholarship program and was allowed to transfer to the University of Texas at Austin. He studied mechanical engineering and received mediocre grades. Another student, Francis Schuck Jr., remembers Whitman staring at the clock tower and saying, "A person could stand off an army from atop of it before they got to him."[3]

On August 17, 1962, Whitman married Kathleen Frances Leissner in Needville, Texas. She was two years younger and an education major. Things seemed to be going well at first, but Whitman's grades fell and his scholarship was revoked. He finished out his tour with the Marines at Camp Lejeune, where he was court martialed for gambling and threatening another Marine. He spent ninety days doing hard labor before being discharged from the military in 1964. He then returned to the University of Texas at Austin to study architectural engineering. His parents divorced and he went to help his mother move out, requesting that a policeman be present in case his father showed up.

His mother took an apartment near Whitman, who was beginning to experience bad headaches and had started taking amphetamines to get his work done. He went through a series of jobs, as a bill collector, then a bank teller, then a traffic surveyor for the Texas Highway Department. His wife taught at Lanier High School.

On July 31, 1966, Whitman bought a knife and a pair of binoculars and typed a suicide note. In it, he complained of unusual and irrational thoughts and requested an autopsy after he was dead. He said he wanted to save his wife and mother the embarrassment of his actions.[4]

Whitman then went to his mother's apartment and stabbed her in the heart, leaving another note. He wrote that he hoped his mother was in heaven and that he loved her with all his heart. Then he drove over to his apartment and killed his wife in the same way while she slept. He left another note with instructions on his life insurance policy and requesting that his dog be given to his in laws. He phoned the workplaces of both his wife and his mother and said they would not be in.

After this, Whitman loaded up his footlocker with a plastic container of gasoline and a high-powered rifle with a telescopic scope, along with pistols, ammo, and canned food. He drove to the University of Texas at Austin campus, and carried the footlocker into the thirty-story university clock tower. There, he took the elevator to the twenty-seventh floor, which was as far as it went, and then dragged the footlocker up two flights of stairs to the observation deck. He killed Edna Townsley, the reception in the observation area, and dragged her body out of sight. When a group of tourists arrived, he shot at them, killing two and injuring two more.[5] The uninjured tourists were looking for help when the elevator arrived on the twenty-seventh floor again, carrying Vera Palmer, who was coming to relieve Edna Townsley. One of the men looked at her and said, "Lady, don't you dare get off this elevator."[6]

At 11:48 a.m., Whitman began firing from the clock tower, aiming at people walking across the campus below him.[7] University police received a call that something had happened in the clock tower, and two unarmed security officers arrived to check it out. As they started up the stairs to the observatory, they saw bodies and then heard the shots.[8] They went back down and called the police. Whitman had begun firing from all sides of the tower with his three rifles and two pistols. People were shot and killed and lay in the 98 degree heat. Armored vehicles were later used to pick up the wounded and the dead, since many of the people who first tried to help were also struck with bullets. With the high-powered rifles, Whitman was able to kill people up to two blocks away.

The television cameras showed up. The grainy black-and-white images on the film shot that day show puffs of white smoke, with the crack of the rifle heard a few seconds later. Bodies lay out in the open on the concourse.[9] This was the first time Americans witnessed the carnage from a mass shooting as it was dumped into their living rooms. This was the first time children watched real-time violence. Parents were surely caught off guard as cartoons were interrupted for bodies lying in the sweltering heat of Texas, the rifle cracks of death erupting from small speakers on televisions all over the country. One reporter interviewed a Vietnam veteran who was breathing hard and covered in sweat. He had just run out into the open and carried a person to safety. The second person he went out for was dead.[10]

This was carried by network cameras and beamed to antennas poking into suburban American skies. People were not familiar with wanton carnage. Vietnam was about the Communists who had to be stopped. Those bodies meant something in the war against Communist aggression. This meant nothing. These people were not dying halfway around the world but right here on a safe college campus in Texas. And they were dying as dad came in from cutting the lawn and mom made a peanut butter and jelly sandwich. They were dying between episodes of the *Dick Van Dyke Show* and *Leave It to Beaver* or *The Beverly Hillbillies*. Television had gone from entertainment to a portal into a strange dark world where wanton death was displayed in the safety of the home. You can only imagine moms reaching for the plug on televisions all over America, or sitting down to watch in horror, in fear, in amazement.

It is the ultimate voyeurism to watch other humans die while you sit in the safety of your own home, through a device that allows us to be there in mind but not in body. Television is the peeping Tom who not only looks at naked women but, worse, looks at dying humans shot for no reason at all. And the new twist, the joker in the deck, is that the show has no end time. *Gilligan's Island*, *Green Acres*, and *Dragnet* all end after thirty minutes, but this new show could go on for hours because it is live television. All bets are off, and no one knows how it will end. Will the good guys get the bad guy or will the bad guy just keep killing people? . . . Stay tuned.

The police returned fire but were pinned down by Whitman's precision shooting. Whitman picked off a boy on a bike and then an Associated Press photographer who was running. He shot a pregnant woman, then a student crossing the campus. No one was safe. The police hired a plane with a sharpshooter to try and get a shot but Whitman drove the plane off with a burst of rifle fire. The police had no SWAT Team to call in. They had no plan for how to take out a man with high-powered rifles and a sniper's precision. It would come down to beat cop Ramiro Martinez. Martinez was grilling in his backyard when he heard about the shooting. He left his steak on the grill, put on his uniform, and drove to the campus. He crawled to the clock tower's main entrance and handed a rifle to Allen

Crum, an employee of the university bookstore. Together they made their way to the observation tower, followed by George McCoy, who had a shotgun loaded with deer slugs.

Martinez turned the corner on the observation tower and saw Whitman. He fired his revolver and Whitman retuned fire. Ramiro then emptied his revolver as McCoy burst onto the platform and let loose with his shotgun. Martinez's bullets smashed into Whitman's rifle and one hit him in the neck. McCoy put a deer slug between the sniper's eyes, and Charles Whitman fell back dead.[11]

Thirteen people were dead and thirty wounded. Whitman was quickly dubbed the "Texas Tower Sniper." America had watched from their living rooms as a man indiscriminately killed other humans. Mass shootings from this point on would be media events, shown to people who had never seen a gun or a dead body before. This became part of the horror beamed out across America and would begin the modern era of mass shootings, where television presented the faces of the killer and the victims to the world.

Charles Whitman would be found to have had a brain tumor after his autopsy. No one could say if this was the cause of his murderous clock tower rampage, however.[12] The Texas Clock Tower Shooting was the first intersection of mass communication with a mass shooter, and it would be the jumping-off point for televised carnage. Domestic abuse, a floundering young man looking for his place in the world, a military-trained killer, a familiarity with weapons, a hatred of his abusive father . . . this is the stew that would be served up again and again in the new televised culture of violence and mass murder. Shooters would relish the moment when they became famous, as television itself sometimes became another reason to kill.

OUTSIDE TERMINAL 2

3:00 p.m.

Heat becomes the enemy. We have one bottle of water and nowhere to get more. The heat is becoming more and more oppressive. There is no breeze, and the stress combined with the heat makes us all lose water quickly. Callie is the first to succumb. We are still by the cement column that has become a base camp of sorts. We are flanked on one side by the television trucks and on the other by a low cement wall. It is probably as safe as we can get at the moment. But Callie is unusually white. She does not look well, and she is not talking.

One time when we were on vacation in the Boundary Waters of Minnesota my wife and Callie wanted to go hiking. There were blueberries and trails and possible bear sightings out in the forest that called to the city folks from Chicago. On vacations I always bring big fat biographies to read. Vacations in my family growing up were always read-a-thons at the beaches of Kitty Hawk, North Carolina. My parents would plop down their chairs and read the entire time, so I took on their habits, and when I had my own family vacations I always looked forward to having long stretches of time for losing myself in Hemingway, Jefferson, Mark Twain, Jack London, or Custer, anyone who I could sink into in a one-week vacation.

That morning I had made my coffee and positioned my book and was about to sit down when I was confronted by a little girl in a bathing suit, wearing Nemo flip-flops and holding a blueberry bucket. Her hands were on her hips, while Kitty and I argued about going on a hike.

"I just want to read," I declared, feeling like I was already losing vacation time.

"I thought we said we were going hiking this morning."

Clay had not even gotten out of bed, so he wasn't going. I wanted that freedom now. I wanted to read. I faced Kitty and Callie and stood my ground.

"I'm going to read."

Callie took a step forward, her blue eyes narrowing, her bucket out to her side. "Dad! We are going on a hike!"

And then with perfect aplomb she stuck her tongue out and made that sound that is every kid's defense. I stared at the my seven-year-old daughter and realized I was beat.

"Okay. We are going on a hike," I muttered, grabbing the baby monitor so we could hear when Clay woke up.

And now she is sixteen and still has the same funny sense of humor and the ability to say what is exactly on her mind. Bird of Joy is a name a teacher gave Callie in elementary school and it stuck. I can't remember ever having a cross word with her and sometimes I wonder if I should be more strict because it doesn't feel like parenting, just a great long ride of pleasure. But now we are down behind the cement pole and Callie, who has been stoic through all of this, is starting to breathe heavily.

"Here, let me cool you down," I say, grabbing the one water bottle the newspeople had given us. I begin sprinkling water on her forehead.

"I'm alright," she says, but she is not.

Her breathing is increasing and she is pale. I am wondering about shock when Kitty murmurs that Callie is hyperventilating. Stress or intense anxiety can bring on hyperventilation. Being shot at would probably qualify, and the stress has been intensified by being in an "active situation," where the shooter is thought to still be out there. Under the circumstances, and the prolonged adrenal ride, it is no wonder that Callie's body has started to break down. I myself have been riding for hours on some weird high that I know is brought on by coursing adrenaline. I am ready for fight or flight, and I have really decided that if I hear shots again then I am going to run toward them and not away from them. It's something about having been scared to death once and being really pissed about it.

But right now Callie is breathing like she is running a marathon, and she's perspiring. I am putting water on her frantically. She needs to be cooled down and, more than that, she needs to get to safety. Her body needs to get off the fight-or-flight merry-go-round. I stand up and look around and see the Fox News truck. I had already asked the talking head if my daughter could take refuge there and his answer had been an empathetic and curt no. So much for the press. I see the very nice woman who had earlier taken a picture of my son but said she would not use it. I look down and Callie is worse. She has her eyes closed and she is very white. I look for EMTs or an ambulance—anything to get her out of here, because being in this situation is not working for anyone anymore and we really have to get the hell out of here. I walk up to the photographer.

"My daughter is hyperventilating. Do you think she can sit in your car?"

The woman turns, dreadlocks swinging, her cameras slung around her neck. "Absolutely. Where is she?"

"Let me get her," I say, running to my daughter. "Callie . . . this woman is going to let you stay in her car."

She holds up her hand. "I'm fine . . . I'm fine."

But she is wobbly and we lead her over to the sedan parked in the street, the press credentials in the window. I put her into the air-conditioned car and the woman gestures to Kitty and Careen.

"It's okay if your wife and other daughter want to stay in there, too."

Compassion in hell. "Yes. Thank you."

They get in the air-conditioned car and I slam the door. It is a sturdy car with tinted windows. They are out of the firing line. They are out of the heat. For now they are safe. I feel much better and go back to Clay by the cement column. I look down at him and see the same road grime that is smudged over all of us. We are all hot and sweaty and dirty and, worse, we are imprisoned in an airport with no escape and a shooter on the loose. I look at Clay.

"You want to get in there, get in the car?"

He shakes his head. "No."

"You sure?"

"I said no."

I nod and I slide down against the pole and sit in the puddle of water we were using to cool Callie down. It feels good in the heat and I lean my head back and for a moment nod off. I open my eyes and stare at the brightly lit television trucks.

"What a fucking day," I mutter.

Clay holds his hands together over his knees. He looks at me sideways from his number-four haircut that is just a shade above a marine cut. It is the current style. He squints, holding his hands up in front of him.

"Did stuff like this happen when you were a kid?"

I shake my head, thinking back on my childhood in the seventies and eighties.

"No. It didn't. The world was different then."

But I am wrong. It did. I just didn't know about it.

CHAPTER 15

CHICKEN NUGGETS

The McDonald's Shooting

1984

When I was in junior high I used to ride with a friend to McDonald's on our bikes and buy two Big Macs. We would eat them sitting outside by our ten speeds and then turn around and bike the two miles back home. A red-faced Ronald McDonald clown had marketed the McDonald's corporation to us, and a hundred different commercials had positioned McDonald's as the all-American fast food restaurant. I grew up in a family that always had McDonald's fries decomposing under the car seat—although they did not actually decompose and my father would murmur about the preservatives used to keep that fry looking good.

Everyone loved McDonald's, and if you were going to launch an assault against the very culture of America then McDonald's was a ripe target.

James Huberty didn't care for McDonald's. He was born in Canton, Ohio, on October 11, 1942, and he had contracted polio when he was three years old.[1] He didn't end up paralyzed like many victims but he walked with a strange gait for the rest of his life. His father bought a farm in the Ohio Amish country, taking young James and his sister to the country. His mother had no interest in farming, and she abandoned the family and moved out west to become a missionary. After a brief stint studying sociology at Malone College in Canton, Huberty ended up studying embalming at the

Pittsburgh Institute of Mortuary Science.[2] In 1965 he married Etna Mark-land and later received his embalming license. He worked for two years at a funeral home before leaving to become a welder.

The couple had two daughters, Zelia and Cassandra, but life wasn't good for the family. James Huberty had a predilection to violence and Etna liked to manipulate his paranoia.

Huberty became a survivalist with deep suspicion of the government. He believed the "black copters" were coming and blamed the US government for his failures. He began to collect weapons and believed the right to bear arms was under assault by the government, that international bankers were controlling the Federal Reserve, and that Soviet aggression was everywhere. Huberty stocked up on food and more weapons with the belief that a great conflagration was near, with either nuclear war or the breakdown of society. He always had a gun within arm's reach. He complained that the country was abusing working people and was out to get people like him.[3]

A move to Tijuana, Mexico, in the fall of 1983 did little to improve his situation. He put most of the family's belongings in storage but took the arsenal with him. His wife and daughters seemed to acclimate to their new surroundings, but Huberty became withdrawn. After only three months, they moved just across the border to San Ysidro, California, a suburb of San Diego, where Huberty was able to find work as a security guard.[4] The family was cramped in a two-bedroom apartment. A car accident not long before they had left Ohio had left Huberty with neck pain and shaking hands. He was depressed and began hearing voices.

Finally, in July 1984, James was fired from his job. He called a mental health facility and complained about having strange thoughts. When the facility didn't return his call, he told his wife he was going to hunt humans and left with his Uzi, an automatic pistol, and a shotgun. The first automatic weapon used in a mass killing would make its debut at a McDonald's.

Huberty drove down the hill to the San Ysidro McDonald's that was visible from his apartment. It was July 18, 1984, and Huberty was about to enter history as the worst mass killer in the United States at that time. He entered the McDonald's carrying the 9mm Browning semiautomatic pistol, the Uzi carbine, and a Winchester 12-gauge pump shotgun. He had a brown bag full of hundreds of rounds. There were forty-five customers in the McDonald's when Huberty entered. He told everyone to lie down on the floor.[5]

James Huberty aimed his shotgun at a sixteen-year-old employee, John Arnold. The gun didn't fire and assistant manager Guillermo Flores shouted, "Hey John, that guy's going to shoot you."[6] Everyone thought it was a joke until Huberty raised his Uzi and shot manger Neva Caine dead with a bullet entering just under her eye. Huberty then got his shotgun working and shot at Arnold. Screaming that the people in the restaurant were dirty swine, Huberty shot Victor Rivera fourteen times with the Uzi when he stepped up to reason with him.

Huberty then turned his attention toward six women and children huddled together near the counter. He shot and killed eighteen-year-old María Elena Colmenero-Silva with a single gunshot to the chest. He killed nine-year-old Claudia Perez with a spray of bullets from his Uzi, wounding Perez's fifteen-year-old sister, Imelda, in the hand and eleven-year-old Aurora Peña in the leg. Aurora was partially shielded by her pregnant aunt, eighteen-year-old Jackie Reyes. Jackie died as Huberty shot her forty-eight times with the Uzi. Beside his mother's body, eight-month-old Carlos Reyes sat screaming. Huberty shouted at the baby to shut up and then killed him with a single pistol shot to the center of his back.

Huberty shot and killed a sixty-two-year-old truck driver named Gus Verslius, before targeting families who tried to hide under tables, shielding children with their bodies. Blythe Regan Herrera had crawled under a booth with her eleven-year-old son, Matao, while her husband, Ronald Herrera, went under the booth opposite with Matao's friend, twelve-year-old Keith Thomas. As Huberty opened fire on them, Thomas was shot twice, in the shoulder and arm, but was not seriously wounded;

Ronald Herrera was shot eight times, in the stomach, chest, arm, and head, but he survived; Blythe and Matao were both killed, struck with multiple gunshots.

Twenty-four-year-old Guadalupe del Rio and thirty-one-year-old Arisdelsi Vuelvas Vargas hid under another booth with their friend Gloria Soto Ramirez. Guadalupe and Gloria lay against the wall, while Arisdelsi huddled in front of them. When Huberty fired under the booth at them, Gloria was not hit, while Guadalupe was struck in the back, abdomen, chest, and neck but was not critically injured. Arisdelsi, however, was shot in the back of the head. She lived long enough to make it to the hospital, but she died there the next day.

Teenage employees died as they tried to escape. Forty-five-year-old banker Hugo Velazquez Vasquez was killed with a single shot to the chest. Huberty shot three eleven-year-old boys riding into the parking lot on their bicycles; two of them died there, while the third lay in his own blood for an hour before he could be pulled to safety. An elderly couple were gunned down as they started to enter the restaurant. A family of three were caught in their car and sprayed with bullets, critically injuring the parents and the baby girl.

Seventy-seven minutes later, the carnage in the McDonald's ended when a police sniper shot Huberty through the heart. The killer's body lay sprawled on the floor of the restaurant next to his victims.

The restaurant was later razed and replaced with a monument to the twenty-one people murdered there. Police were criticized for not entering the restaurant fast enough. The police complained they had been outgunned by Huberty, and police departments as a result began putting together special teams who were trained to use high-caliber weapons and respond to situations like the one that had unfolded at the San Ysidro McDonald's.[7] Huberty's widow would later sue McDonald's claiming it was Huberty's meal of chicken nuggets loaded with monosodium glutamate that made him go on his murderous rampage. The suit was thrown out.[8]

The San Ysidro McDonald's shooting was the worst mass shooting at the time. The juxtaposition of the cultural icon of America's favorite restaurant—where the Ronald McDonald clown welcomed families and kids—with mass murder was jarring. The kids who were gunned down while riding to get a burger reminded me of my own many journeys to McDonald's. I don't know why I was unaware of this shooting at the time, but one has to wonder if it was pushed down under the juggernaut of McDonald's advertising. It is just incongruous to think that people died for nothing more than going to get some fast food.

Mass shootings were still unique in 1984. They were freak accidents that should not have occurred, and so our national consciousness pushed them back into the category of plane crashes and towns struck by tornados. It was just really bad luck to be in a mass shooting in a McDonald's, and most people soon forgot the event, aided by the million-dollar advertising campaigns that branded McDonald's as the safe playground of middle-class families. James Huberty's name faded quickly from the public awareness, but the multiple gunshot wounds he inflicted and the number of people he killed and wounded attested to the firepower of the Uzi. Huberty claimed he had seen action in Vietnam, but he actually had never served in the military. Mass shootings had now taken a deadly twist in the United States. A shooter armed with an automatic weapon had the fire power of a battle squadron and in minutes could murder over a hundred people. In the end, James Huberty was a paranoid, failing white man who saw the government and others as conspiring against him. His moment in history collided with a clown named Ronald McDonald who quickly trumped our cultural recollection of a loner who gunned people down in a fast food restaurant in 1984, a rampage that his wife ultimately blamed on chicken nuggets.

Only in America.

CHAPTER 16

SHELL SHOCK

3:30 p.m.

Everyone is running again. It is like the sea, and the wave begins at one end and sweeps across to the other. The stampede of people comes toward the media trucks and then slowly dissipates again. Nobody knows anything. A bullet traveling a mile a second is the unknown. People can be shot from a mile away with rifles, and no one wants to be in that unlucky statistic. Word passes through the media that the police are going to detonate a bomb they've found and not to panic when it goes off. This does nothing for our nerves.

The press conference held by the Broward County sheriff and the FBI has done nothing to alleviate the stress either, or the feeling that no one is control. The FBI drones on about their investigation while the sheriff fields questions. A reporter asks Sheriff Israel about the shots in Terminal 1.

"There were no shots," he responds.

"But then why did you shut down the airport?" she persists. "You only did that after people were running out of Terminal 1."

Sheriff Israel frowns and repeats his mantra that they are only being thorough and that there is only one shooter but that they have an "active situation," which everyone knows is code for there still being a shooter out there somewhere. Other questions come about Terminal 1 and all the witnesses who heard shots. The sheriff repeats that there was only a lone gunman, Esteban Santiago, and that they have him in custody. Someone asks about the victims, and the sheriff says they are still trying to identify the victims.

The truth is that the victims are still inside Terminal 2 and the family members will not be notified for a long time. Many will not get the news until the next day. I am standing with the reporters and newsmen outside Terminal 2 on the rim of the press conference. I feel I should blurt out something, say that the sheriff and the FBI are wrong and that there were shots in Terminal 1, but I have been cowed by the skeptical CNN journalists who implied that I had either imagined it or lied. I didn't want all those cameras swinging around a second time toward the author who craves publicity. That is also pinging around—that somehow I am doing these interviews to push my books. It is something all modern authors have to deal with now to sell books, walking the line between being a monk and an aluminum siding salesman. So I say nothing.

And now we are beginning to wonder about our luggage. It is among the twenty-five thousand pieces left by people running for their lives from a gunman the police say never existed. But I am standing in the exhaust of media trucks in the hot humid Fort Lauderdale night watching SWAT teams with submachine guns and shotguns at the ready. Something happened, and the media can only catch a piece of it. The real story is that ten thousand people are stuck in a major American airport in an active shooter situation. They can't know that my daughters are now sitting in a car with their mother because of the heat and the fact that outside there is a chance of getting shot.

The photographer with her vest and multiple cameras hanging off her shoulder saved my daughters. I think about getting us out of the airport. We are stranded like ten thousand other people, and no one has any information. There have been rumors of buses being brought in but no one knows for sure. But I know I have to get our luggage back, or at least try to get it. My thinking is that we will rent a car and drive home, as the thought of getting on a plane is blasphemous. We will escape somehow and get away from the madness.

I stand up and look at my son. I have to do something. I am tired of sitting and feeling like I am helpless against a tide of events that seem only to bring danger. I want to start trying to get out of the Fort Lauderdale Airport, and the first step toward that is getting back the luggage we left in Terminal 1.

"I'm going back to Terminal 1 to look for the luggage. You want to go?"

Clay stares at me with big dark eyes.

"You are going back there. Are you crazy?"

I shrug and turn toward the terminal. "I have to get our luggage or at least try if we want to get out of here."

He turns away and watches a SWAT team pass by.

"Screw the luggage. I'm not going anywhere near that terminal," he mutters.

I find out later that not only did Clay hear the shots, he also saw smoke from the gunfire in the terminal. He is right to not want to return and I don't blame him. Fear affects us in different ways and all my life I have always been scared and then brave. Once when I was ice skating with a friend we were confronted by some boys who claimed the pond for their own and chased us away. The fear grabbed me and we left, but then I drove back ready to fight the boys. They were gone of course, but there has always been a delay like that with me. The shots were terrifying but now I wanted to go back and face whatever or whoever had made us all run for our lives.

"Okay. I'll be back," I say, not feeling good about heading toward the shooter.

Clay shakes his head. "You're crazy."

I can't disagree but I start back toward Terminal 1, passing men ready for battle. They are everywhere now, and I wonder about all those returning soldiers like Esteban Santiago who were changed forever from the war. In the early days people had no idea what was happening to these men. Something affected men in the trenches in World War I after long bombardments with shells landing around them and shaking the earth. No one knew what a shock wave was. No one understood what we are just beginning to figure out from dead NFL players, who have concussive injuries that make men lose their memory and then their minds.

Early doctors had no idea that one hundred years later people would watch grainy digitized films of men who could not control their limbs, their mouths, their tongues; men who could no longer speak, walk, or think, and study what they then called shell shock. That was the first term they came up with, and they sent the men to hospitals to doctors who had no idea what to do. The phenomenon began to be noticed in World War I, although there must have been cases in the Civil War. World War I was the first mechanized war in history, and soldiers went into it not understanding the horror of machine guns, mustard gas, tanks, flamethrowers, and, most importantly, high-explosive shells. A man sitting in his trench could suddenly find himself buried by an exploding shell weighing as much as a small car.

Ernest Hemingway in *A Farewell to Arms* would describe such a moment in this way: "I heard a cough, then came the chuh-chuh-chuh-chuh—then there was a flash as when a blast furnace door is swung open, and a roar that started white then went red. . . . I felt myself rush bodily out of myself and out and out and out . . ."[1] Hemingway would never recover psychically and would revisit this moment in the character of the damaged soldier in novels such as *The Sun Also Rises*, *A Farewell to Arms*, and *For Whom the Bell Tolls*, along with short stories such as "A Way You'll Never Be," "Soldier's Home," "A Clean Well-Lighted Place," and "In Another Country."

Hemingway, like many others of his time, could find no way to escape the memories of war but through drink or suicide. Tragically he would eventually commit suicide after drinking for decades. Some would say that suicide and depression ran in his family and that Hemingway was merely succumbing to a stacked deck. But the truth is that he probably suffered from shell shock in one form or another going all the way back to being wounded by a mortar shell in World War I. He would never be diagnosed as suffering from PTSD or shell shock, but we can connect the dots left by his long literary trail and his history of habitual self-medication.

There were few answers at the time when Hemingway was buried by a high-explosive shell. The British Expeditionary Force had to come to grips with the mysterious ailment afflicting the soldiers. After intense bombardments, soldiers reported an inability to sleep, walk, reason, or even talk. Their nervous system seemed to be under assault. Film taken of the first shell-shock victims of World War I show men convulsing, trembling and shaking uncontrollably, falling down, or staring into space for hours at a time. Clearly something had happened to these men, even when they showed no outward sign of injuries. The term "shell shock" was born, referring to a psychological injury.

These early victims were treated as cowards. The soldiers were coming back from the trenches blind, deaf, mute, paralyzed. Shell shock was thought to be the cause, the theory being that the concussion of the exploding shell was literally shocking their brains. This would be borne out one hundred years later in Afghanistan and Iraq, where road-side bombs like the ones Esteban Santiago was exposed to created the same type of brain changes seen in NFL players with multiple concussions.[2] But the British soldiers in World War I showed something else as well. Soldiers who had not been near the bombardments and had not been blown up were also suffering from the symptoms of shell shock. The term shell shock was coined by medical officer Charles Myers and would become *combat stress* in World War II and then post-traumatic stress disorder.[3] These terms would define a broad range of symptoms resulting from the horror of war and the human body breaking down under the stress.

By the end of World War I, 20,000 men were still suffering from shell shock. This was not something that went away with the end of the war. During the war, in 1916, over forty percent of casualties were from combat-related stress.[4] Britain could not provide enough mental institutions, spas, country homes, or insane asylums to handle the massive amount of shell-shocked men. Many soldiers never made it to hospitals and were court-martialed for cowardice, while others were executed for desertion.

The treatment for many was as bad as the cause: solitary confinement, disciplinary treatment, electroshock treatment, shaming, re-education, and emotional deprivation. The medical community had no answers for men who had been altered by war. Many were returned to the front and the British High Command banned the use of the term "shell shocked" at the Battle of the Somme.[5] The trickle of men coming back from the front permanently damaged turned into a flood that threatened the army. The British decided that the mention of shell shock could infect the entire army and that no one would be left to fight. Men were sent back to fight or were shot for cowardice. It was left to private-sector doctors to find a cure for the soldiers who came back as shadows of their former selves.

Arthur Hurst pioneered a cure for soldiers at a hospital in Devon.[6] He would take the men out to the peaceful rolling hills of the Devon countryside. The men would work the land and then they would talk about their war experiences. Therapy and writing exercises would follow as the men improved. But the bulk of World War I vets were left to deal with shell shock on their own.

By the Vietnam War, the term post-traumatic stress disorder (PTSD) would be used to define any type of stressful life-threatening situation. The wars in Iraq and Afghanistan created a new definition of PTSD. The random roadside bombs would create shell shock symptoms and soldiers going over with National Guard units would find themselves putting a soldier in a body bag on one day and on the next lighting the candles on their daughter's birthday cake. Jet travel had compressed time so that there was no period of readjustment at all for modern soldiers doing tours of duty in the Middle East and then returning to American life. For Esteban Santiago and the two mass shooters in New Jersey and Texas these adjustments were compounded by failure and resentment.

Anger and rage are the salient emotions of PTSD shooters. Post-traumatic stress would be spread far and wide over the people in the Fort Lauderdale airport who could not leave except by climbing over fences or running though adjacent fields or trying to get into the one of the planes on the tarmac. The victims of mass shootings who survive have psychological wounds that often never heal. They have more in common than we would think with those British soldiers coming back from the hell of trench warfare. Shell shock is a distant country that many enter and few return from.

It would be easy to pin mass shootings on shell shock or PTSD if all the shooters were veterans, but there is something much more sinister out there pushing people to kill large groups of people. The NRA says that guns don't kill people, people kill people. This may be true, but the invention of the gun changed the art of killing forever.

CHAPTER 17

A SHORT HISTORY OF THE GUN

When I was a kid I used to make gunpowder. I had a chemistry set and in it was powdered iron, sulfur, and powdered charcoal. I was missing potassium nitrate, or saltpeter as it is commonly known. Saltpeter was long rumored to have been given to troops in their food at various times in history to keep them from fornicating with prostitutes, since it supposedly kept men from getting erections.[1] The drugstores in Baltimore when I was growing up sold saltpeter.

So I went to the local pharmacy, run by two brothers. One of the brothers was high up behind the pharmacy counter and looked down at me when I asked for a bottle of saltpeter.

"Do you know what this is used for?" he asked me.

"Yes," I answered. "To give to animals." I knew farmers used saltpeter to keep some animals from copulating. "They use it for cows," I added.

The brother stared at me and shook his head. He disappeared and then came back with a round flat container of saltpeter. "I know what you use it for. Just don't blow yourself up," he said, taking the two dollars I handed him. He knew I was making gunpowder. When I returned home I quickly mixed the saltpeter with the sulfur, powdered iron, and powdered charcoal. I had borrowed one of my mom's mixing bowls, and the gunpowder looked gray against the white porcelain. Then I went outside and made a long line of gunpowder on the sidewalk. I struck a kitchen match and touched it to my creation. The gunpowder burned like the Fourth of July with fiery sparks and blue smoke. *Pssssit!* It had burned so fast all I was looking at was a black line. But it had worked, and I had created the propulsion behind every bullet that has ever killed a human being.

I never put my gunpowder into a gun. I had other ways of demonstrating the basic mechanics of a gun though. I had been collecting the tennis-ball cans that my dad discarded. I had three, and I taped them together to create a long tennis-ball-can bazooka. Then I stole the lighter fluid for the grill from the garage and took a tennis ball that my dad wouldn't miss. The cans were open end to end except for the last one, which I had covered with the plastic top that came with it. I had poked many holes in the top and then taped it on securely with masking tape.

I was about to demonstrate the basic principal of a gun. I opened the lighter fluid and squeezed some drops down in the mouth of the open tennis-ball can. The lighter fluid vaporized and then I shoved a tennis ball down my cannon and looked around. Our yard was bordered by high shrubs, and so no one could see the boy about to shoot off a tennis mortar. I had my dad's lighter and I struck it several times before it lit. I positioned the can to the sky with one hand and touched the lighter to the holes in the tennis can's plastic cover for just a second. There was a loud *thunk* and the tennis ball blew out of the can and became a small dot in the sky. Smoke wafted out of my cannon and I shouted in victory. I had just built a gun.

A gun is a normally tubular weapon or other device designed to discharge projectiles of other material. The projectile may be solid, liquid, gas, or energy and may be free, as with bullets and artillery shells, or captive as with Taser probes and whaling harpoons.

Or it may be a tennis ball. My gunpowder was lighter fluid, my bullet was a tennis ball, and all I needed was another tennis ball and a few drops of lighter fluid and I would be ready to fire again. If I had put gunpowder in the end of the tennis-ball can there is a good chance I would have blown myself up, as the thin tin or aluminum of the can could not have contained the combustion. That would be more of a cannon, and I actually had one of those as well.

Believe it or not Big-Bang Cannons were sold to kids and you can still buy them on the internet today.[2] My cannon was green and made of heavy cast-iron metal. I had a tube of Bangsite, which is made from calcium carbide, the same chemical miners used for their lights in the early part of the twentieth century, known as carbide lamps. But I had a real cannon and all I had to do was take some calcium carbide and dump it in the breech of my cannon, which was filled with water. Calcium carbide produces highly flammable acetylene gas when it meets water. When I replaced the breech I counted to three to let the gas form, and then I pulled back a flint plunger much like the one on my dad's old lighter and rammed it forward.

Boom. Fire shot out of the cannon and there was a deafening boom. This was my go-to toy, as I realized quickly At the time, I could put things like corks, wadded paper, or a rubber stopper in the end of the barrel and shoot them across the yard. This is even closer to a modern gun. My gun had the sparker, which was the equivalent of a percussion cap in the center of a bullet. The gunpowder was the calcium carbide. The bullet itself was whatever I could find to stick in the end of the barrel. Gun technology has not changed much since the musket loaders of the Revolution. I had one of those, too.

My musket loader was a rifle and, like the Revolutionary soldiers, I had to load my musket from the end of the barrel. The soldiers' bullets were made from lead and mine were made from cork. Each of my bullets was a small cork ball and, like the Revolutionary soldiers, I had a plunger to push it all the way down the barrel. Another difference between my rifle and that of the Revolutionary solider was that before the soldier could put in his bullet he had to tear open a paper cartridge with his teeth, put some gun powder in his priming pan, pour the rest of the powder into the barrel, and then shove the musket ball down.

I had to do something extra, too, and that was to pull back the trigger, the hammer, and put a cap on the anvil. The anvil had holes that led to the barrel and this would allow the explosion of the cap to propel my cork mini-ball out of the barrel. It didn't go very far, but neither had the colonial's bullet that he fired at the British—about eighty yards. That was it. After eighty yards the patriot could not be sure he was going to hit anything because all accuracy went out the window. Like my cork ball, the lead ball came out of the barrel and would veer off. It was hard to hit your target with an eighteenth-century musket and the best way was for the soldiers to fire en masse and hope the volley would hit as many people as possible.

In 1855, a new discovery changed guns forever. It was called rifling. The barrel was grooved, and "these grooves guided a lead ball or other projectile to spin as it exited the barrel ensuring a straighter line shot."[3] This made all the difference in the United States' wars against the Native Americans, who still had smooth bore muskets and so had to get within eighty yards to hit the soldiers. The rifling caused the lead ball to spin, and this spinning kept the bullet straight and allowed a shooter to be much farther away from his target. The combination of this improvement in accuracy with higher caliber bullets (larger lead balls) led to the horrific carnage of the Civil War.

Soldiers still had to load their weapons like I loaded my musket loader, but the rifled musket changed tactics on the battlefield. Armies no longer had to fire en masse to hit their target. They could sharpshoot and fire individually and cause much more damage. The defenders now hid behind rocks or trees and picked off the advancing troops with deadly accuracy. Even though military leaders knew this new accuracy made troops in the open vulnerable they still marched across fields, with the most famous of these open charges being Pickett's Charge at Gettysburg. The dug-in Union troops destroyed Pickett's regiment five hundred yards out and the stragglers who made it to the line were butchered. Still, loading was slowed by shoving a bullet down the barrel, and it wasn't until the breech loader of the late nineteenth century that this changed. I had one of those, too.

The breech loader took what we now call a modern bullet. My breech loader was a toy shotgun, if you can believe it. I cracked it open and put in two plastic shells that were actually the bullets. But I put them in from the *rear of the barrel*, much like the breech-loading muskets. A soldier now put in a bullet composed of a metal jacket filled with gunpowder and a percussion cap, or small explosive charge, in the center. The lead bullet was fitted to the cartridge. When the hammer fell on a breech loader, the percussion cap exploded inside the bullet, which ignited the gunpowder that burned and exploded, transferring the expanding energy to the bullet that flew out of the rifled barrel.

I had percussion caps, too. My friend reloaded his own ammo, meaning he had boxes of percussion caps and a container of gunpowder and shot (small BBs). He reloaded his shotgun shells and was nice enough to give me a fistful of percussion caps to take home. Once home I took a hammer and hit the percussion caps, which blew up like mini bombs not much bigger than a firecracker. I also would throw them on the garage floor, where they would sometimes detonate. Such was the all-American boyhood of the later twentieth century.

After the invention of breach loaders, soldiers could reload rapidly, but they still could only load one bullet at a time. Enter Samuel Colt. Colt came up with the idea for a revolver in 1836 while on a ship.[4] The early revolvers had to be loaded like a musket from the front of the barrel up until breech loaders, but this was only a single shot mechanism. The Colt revolver could be fired multiple times. This meant that when the shooter pulled back the trigger the next cylinder advanced and a person could shoot six shots in succession. The famous term "six shooter" was born.

Then Colt made his classic breakthrough, namely the Colt .45. This revolver was loaded from the rear with a cartridge and fired as fast as the hammer could be pulled back. A double-action revolver was offered later, in which the cylinder was advanced by the trigger, but it was slower. Americans know the Colt .45 or the "Peacemaker" from every Western that was ever shown in a theater. Every gunfight, every showdown in a dusty old town, was a showdown between two Colt. 45s.[5]

I had a metal Colt .45 that fired caps. The barrel did not revolve, but later I got a blank gun with plastic blanks that were loaded into the cylinder just like real bullets. This gun fired like a Colt with the barrel rotating up each blank to the hammer. Then much later in life I was able to shoot a real Colt .45, one that a gun enthusiast owned. He warned me that the accuracy was terrible. I shot six bullets at a far target and when it came back without a single hole I knew he was right.

The truth is, cowboys mostly missed each other and rarely did men face off on Main Street. But gunslingers in the West did have revolvers tied to their legs and many ended up in gun battles. The black powder used at that time created so much smoke that no one knew who had been hit until sometime after the shooting. Usually men in the West fought spontaneously and many times no one hit their mark.[6] Bullets were expensive and not many cowboys had time or money for practice. The Colt and the Winchester dominated Western gun culture.[7]

The Winchester rifle was a short-barreled repeating rifle that was useful when shooting from a horse. As fast as a cowboy could cock the rifle, he could fire the Winchester with a much higher accuracy than a Colt. But most cowboys did not want to get in a gunfight, and the majority of Colts and Winchesters were used for hunting and deterrence. A man's reputation for killing was much stronger than his actual use of the gun. Still, if there was a golden period for American guns it was during the period after the Civil War up until 1890, when the frontier was declared closed. Cowboy culture has been handed down ever since.

The twentieth century brought some improvements in guns, but the big step forward belongs to General John T. Thompson, who wanted a more efficient gun to kill Germans in World War I. He had wanted to upgrade the Browning automatic and came up with a machine gun that used the force of the bullet to eject the shell and chamber up another one. All you had to do was pull back the bolt the first time. "Once you pulled the trigger, the twenty-round clip or fifty-round barrel fed the bullets into the firing pin like a frenzied creature spewing fire and death. Thompson came up with the name the Annihilator."[8]

The general thought he would sell his machine gun to the army for "trench sweeping" in World War I. The problem was that the war ended two days after Thompson had gotten the bugs out of the gun. The only bullets that worked with the Annihilator were the armor piercing .45 cartridge. Some of the soldiers who did use the gun later felt it was too heavy and the larger fifty-round barrel was hard to load. The British complained about the rattling noise of the trigger mechanism. But everyone loved the way it fired. Two men with Thompson machine guns had the firepower of nine. The US post office bought some after a series of robberies but General Thompson was disappointed with initial sales. The Thompson machine gun cost two hundred dollars and this was at a time when the price of a Model A Ford was four hundred dollars.

But gangsters loved the Thompson machine gun, or what they called the tommy gun. General Thompson had unwittingly provided outlaws with the perfect gun. When Al Capone's car and driver were riddled with bullets while he was inside a restaurant, he studied the bullet holes and knew the game had changed. A man with a Thompson could decimate a couple of cops. He could riddle their car with holes in seconds, and if the cops weren't running for cover they were dead. The gun was compact and could be kept under an overcoat until you were ready. Then you pulled the bolt back and you could simply *annihilate* somebody with the gun. It fit weirdly into a violin case and many gangsters looked like they were going to a recital before they wiped somebody out.

The Thompson was also perfect for firing from a car into a store that hadn't paid for protection or didn't want a gangster's booze. The machine gun wasn't accurate, but it didn't matter; the Thompson literally sprayed bullets, and it wasn't uncommon for someone to have fourteen bullet wounds. Hit men liked it because they could be sure their man was dead. The St. Valentine's Day Massacre in Chicago would make the Thompson world famous. Nobody could survive a Thompson onslaught; General Thompson's Annihilator always lived up to its name. And the two hundred dollar price tag was not an issue. The only drawback to the Thompson was that it kicked back and bruised the shooter's ribs.

The Thompson would eventually lead to semiautomatic weapons that would later became assault weapons, which would lead to a short-lived ban on these type of weapons.

The Assault Weapons Ban was a direct result of the actions of Patrick Edward Purdy and George Hennard. Purdy was an abused child left homeless at thirteen, who entered into a life of crime on the streets of San Francisco.[9] He then lived with his father and entered high school, where he drank and became addicted to drugs. His father was killed by a speeding car and Purdy was homeless again at seventeen. Eventually he was placed with a foster mother in Los Angeles. He was arrested for prostitution, drug dealing, possession of an illegal weapon, and armed robbery. He spent thirty-two days in county jail and tried to commit suicide twice. A psychiatric report found him mildly mentally challenged.[10]

He then drifted across the country working as a welder and doing menial work. He ended up as a boilermaker in Portland, Oregon, and lived with his aunt in nearby Sandy. In August of 1988, he bought an AK 47 from the Sandy Trading Post.[11] Not long after this he moved to Stockton, California. In December he purchased a 9mm Taurus pistol at the Hunter Loan Company in Stockton. Friends said he was frustrated at not being able to make it on his own and was angry about everything.

On January 17, 1989, he set his car on fire behind the Cleveland Elementary School in Stockton, using a Molotov cocktail. He then went to the playground of the school and began firing with his AK 47 at the Cambodian and Vietnamese children who made up the majority of the school's enrollment. Purdy fired 106 rounds in three minutes and killed five children, wounding thirty others and one teacher. He then shot himself in the head.[12] The question as to how Purdy could buy automatic weapons with a criminal record sparked a debate on banning assault weapons in Washington.[13]

Then, two and a half years later, a thirty-five-year-old merchant mariner, George Hennard, who hated black people, gay people, and women, would finally push the ban through. George Hennard's father was a surgeon and his mother a homemaker. He graduated high school in 1974, joined the Navy, and was discharged three years later. He then joined the Merchant Marine but was busted for pot and discharged. His parents divorced in 1983 and George moved to Henderson, Nevada, with his mother. In 1991, Hennard bought a Glock 17 and a 9mm Ruger P89 pistol at a gun shop in Henderson.[14]

Hennard was a misogynist. He sent two sisters in his neighborhood a menacing note and called them "treacherous female vipers."[15] A store owner said later he would push women out of the way to buy his soda or cigarettes.[16] Others said he spoke little and was prone to wild outbursts and rants about people he hated, calling women snakes.

On October 16, 1991, Hennard drove his 1987 Ford Ranger pickup through the front window of Luby's Cafeteria, where about 140 people were eating lunch. He jumped out and yelled, "It's payback time. Is it worth it?"[17] He then opened fire, killing twenty-three people. Hennard reloaded three times and shot people in the head, walking between the tables to shoot more.[18] He called women bitches before he shot them and passed up men to kill more women. When the police arrived, he fired at them, but he was wounded and retreated to the bathroom, where he shot himself in the head. Twenty-three people were killed in the rampage, with another twenty-seven wounded.

The time was ripe for a federal assault weapons ban that would prohibit the manufacture, transfer, and possession of semiautomatic assault weapons. The ban passed in 1994 and was set to expire in 2004.[19] The NRA launched numerous challenges and lost in court each time. Studies following the ban could find no link between the ban and a reduction in crime, but these were countered by a report from the Brady Center citing a three-percent reduction. No study centered on mass shootings specifically and the use of automatic weapons. The ban expired on September 13, 2004.

President Barack Obama made reinstituting the Assault Weapon Ban permanently one of his priorities.[20] After the Sandy Hook Elementary School shooting, a new version of the ban went up for a vote in Congress and was defeated forty to sixty in the US Senate in April 2013. Efforts to prohibit high-capacity clips, which allow mass shooters to not waste time reloading, were also defeated in Congress.[21]

CHAPTER 18

RETURN TO TERMINAL 1

4:00 p.m.

I'm making my way back to Terminal 1 for our luggage. Florida is a hot, humid glove now. We have been under a lockdown situation since 1:30. It is not so much a lockdown as a lock-in. No one can leave the airport grounds. We have talked to media people and asked if we might get a ride out but they are going nowhere. The story is still developing as there is an active shooter somewhere, but here we get lost in semantics. The police chief has called it an "active situation." If you look up "active situation" on the internet, it is all the same—an active or fluid situation means that the police do not have the area under control. It means anyone could be shot at any time.

This is the paradox of ten thousand people being stranded in a major American airport. We are here because of a shooter the police say does not exist. When Esteban Santiago shot and killed five people and wounded thirteen others there was no lockdown. Terminal 1 was calm. People went about their business and the airport was open. People were arriving for flights and being picked up. It was only after the four shots rang out in Terminal 1 and the ensuing panic that the airport was closed and the situation declared active. That is when the SWAT teams swung in.

I am walking through what looks like a third-world country now, with soldiers and police holding guns at the ready. People are sitting, lying down, hiding, staring, some crying, a woman is strumming a ukulele. I stop to watch her. She is walking back and forth along the curb and singing. It is so out of place, yet I know why she is doing it. She is young and pretty and she is trying to get away from where she is. She wants to leave the unreality of our situation, where anyone can get shot. The SWAT teams are armed to the teeth and then some. They have shotguns, automatic weapons, and pistols. I find out later that SWAT teams must outfit themselves. If you get the SWAT manual off the internet, a good deal of it is about the equipment, and it is all optional. In fact, the SWAT team is just a group of police officers with more intensive training.

The SWAT teams are walking by me in Kevlar vests, holding shotguns, submachine guns, 9mm handguns. They are wearing helmets. Pistols are strapped to their legs and shotguns are at the ready. Some of their helmets are ill-fitting and slide around at funny angles. They are looking at the parking garage; some are looking up, many just have their guns in the ready position with their fingers on the triggers. I wonder then if there are many accidents? Do these guns go off accidentally, and what is the protocol when they do? It would seem that with this many guns, accidents are bound to happen. Actually, they do, with tragic consequences.

A man who was suspected of gambling illegally was shot and killed in a botched SWAT team operation in the middle of the night. The man mistook the SWAT team for an intruder and went for his gun and was shot dead.[1] A woman whose son was wanted for marijuana thought the SWAT team kicking in her door in the night was an intruder.[2] She, too, went for her gun and was shot dead. Students in high schools who have been suspected of possessing drugs have been made to kneel with guns to their head.[3] The problem with SWAT teams is that they are paramilitary with a minimum of training. Until there is a need, the SWAT member is the cop pulling you over for a speeding ticket. He or she has bought a lot of gear on the open market and much of it is overflow from the defense department. They keep it at home and, when called, quickly change into the gear and become a SWAT team member.[4] They are part of an aggressive paramilitary unit possessing overwhelming firepower. They are let loose on an unsuspecting populace that is not used to seeing heavily armed men and women out in public. The sight of them conjures up images of a military dictatorship or a coup.

I am now getting close to Terminal 1. I should at least try to get our luggage before we try to leave the airport. One advantage we have is that our luggage was not processed and is still on the baggage cart. If we had checked our baggage, we would be like thousands of other people who left behind the 25,000 pieces of abandoned luggage. Many will not get their luggage or belongings for days, and there are people who don't have their wallets or phones. Some who were going through security don't even have shoes. Everyone left their belongings behind as they ran from what they perceived to be a possible coordinated attack on the airport. That had been my first thought. There was a 9/11-style attack under way in the terminals and Terminal 1 was next. Esteban Santiago had just been the first of many.

This thought is on people's faces, and the thousand-yard stare is there. Americans do not have a fountain of knowledge to pull from for events like these. We have not been invaded since the War of 1812, when the British burned Washington, DC. Our oceans have generally kept us safe.

Most Americans in the twenty-first century live in urban and sub-urban areas and don't have guns. One-third and falling is the statistic of gun ownership that is batted around.[5] The gun culture has been in decline for some time. The NRA will point to the increase in gun sales, but these guns are bought by the *same one-third* who are stocking up against a pos-sible war with the government.[6] This was accelerated under the Obama administration when many thought the Second Amendment was in danger of being repealed. Gun owners could not buy enough guns and ammunition. They could not dig enough shelters, stock up on enough water and canned goods, or buy enough ammo.

The general populace is not composed of hunters or gun owners, and most have no acquaintance with the hunting-gun culture that goes all the way back to the pioneers. The NASCAR-watching, beer-drinking, pickup-driving image of the gun owner with a Confederate flag waving in the back is the stereotype many urbanites have of those who own guns. It is as false as the latte-drinking liberals who want more gun control. There are some who do fit these descriptions, but people have a nasty habit of jumping out of assumed groups.

The truth is that most Americans are too busy raising their kids, paying their mortgages, sending their kids to college, and trying to squirrel away something for retirement to worry about guns or gun control. Most people live in suburbs around large economic centers or major cities and plug into that economic grid to make a living. Having a gun or not having a gun does not come up in conversation. If you want to have a gun then have one. If you don't, that is fine, too. Most people are not joining the NRA because they believe the Second Amendment is under siege and most people are not signing petitions to control guns. Getting to a son's ballgame or a daughter's play and keeping food on the table occupies three-quarters of Americans.

So when a shooting occurs, we are in alien territory. The thought that one could be shot at any minute is impossible to square with our day-to-day lives. Hearing shots is terrifying and foreign. Seeing bodies is horrifying and unreal. Seeing SWAT teams dressed up like combat-ready soldiers makes no sense. Why am I caught up in this? Maybe I am closer to the one-in-three-hundred-and-fifteen odds that I will be shot with a firearm.[7] But none of this helps. Our psyche is not equipped, and PTSD will affect all involved to some degree or another.

I am still walking through the swirling lights of police cars, ambulances, and firetrucks when I see Terminal 1. I recognize two women I saw in the terminal before the shots. I see a man in bright red coveralls with long gray hair, a beard, and a dog. He was there, too, and I wonder then about the man sleeping behind the benches we were sitting on. I have already blotted out parts of what happened and I wonder if this is the brain's way of dealing with what is too horrible. The two women are standing outside the door.

"Are they letting anyone in?" I ask, looking into the terminal.

Both women have gray hair cut short, and they remind me of many teachers I had in grade school.

"No," one replies. "It's full of soldiers."

I stare and see SWAT teams with dogs walking inside the terminal. There is a beefy SWAT member standing guard at the door with his automatic weapon at the ready.

"Everything we had with us is in there," the other woman says.

I am still sweating and I step back and try and see over to where we were standing with our luggage. I turn back to the women.

"You heard the shots?"

They both nod.

"Of course. There were four of them," the one with reading glasses replies.

I nod slowly and look around. People are milling about and some are still hunkered down behind barriers or poles. I then see the woman who wanted to get in the car with her baby. I walk toward her. She is pretty with red hair.

"You tried to get in a car . . . I was there," I say loudly, feeling like we are veterans of some sort of past battle.

She stares and then smiles. Her blouse is practically open and I don't know if it was torn or whether she just wears it that way. My own clothes are torn and dirty and sweat soaked.

"Oh, yeah. Can you believe that asshole wouldn't let me in?"

I shake my head and it seems what we are talking about occurred days ago. All sense of time has gone out the window. There was only this moment now, and it will be impossible to access what has happened to all of us until we are out of the airport and away from the danger. The woman leans over her baby again.

"Did you hear the shots?"

She shakes her head. "I didn't . . . I was just running because everyone said there was a shooter."

We talk some more and then we part. We have been together in a terrifically dangerous moment, but that is long gone now. She is trying to find a way out of the airport as am I. We are still both trying to survive,

SHOTS FIRED IN TERMINAL 2

and survival is preeminent in this moment. I look back into Terminal 1 and it is as if I hear the shots again. There are explosions, concussions, and then I am running again This is not actually happening but I have been reliving the moment all day and seeing Terminal 1 brings it home.

I start back toward the media trucks where my wife and two daughters are waiting in a car and my son is sitting behind a thick concrete pole. More SWAT teams jog down the arrival lanes, and I remember reading somewhere that when SWAT teams arrive they have operational control. It makes sense. They have all the gear and short of bringing in the army they are the closest thing we have to soldiers.

I feel the weight of my backpack again. During all of this I have had my backpack on, filled with my computer and books. Never once have I taken it off and it has adhered to my back from perspiration. In all the television interviews I am there in my black Brooklyn T-shirt and backpack—the writer caught up in the extraordinary situation. Already my phone is blowing up with people who saw me on Fox News. People I have not spoken with for ten years are calling me, and this feels strange. I have crossed the Rubicon into the other world where tragedy befalls people, and I am on the other side of the television and unable to get out. We are all caught up in a drama we can't escape, and I wonder if this will be the fork in the road of my life. Will bad things continue to happen? Will bad luck plague me now? Being in a mass shooting is the worst kind of bad luck. You are simply in the wrong place at the wrong time and the roulette wheel in the sky has deemed this might be your final moment. It is terrifying if you think about it too much.

Two weeks ago, we were celebrating Christmas in the Midwest. One week ago, we were on a cruise bringing in the New Year. Now we are at an airport with five dead people inside a terminal and a shooter who could pop up anywhere and at any time. And the worst thing is that we can't leave. You think there is a grand plan in these shootings, with the police running the show. But the truth is that chaos and violence go hand in hand and no one has anything under control. The airport is closed and there are ten thousand people stuck in it and there are men with guns everywhere and there still might be a bullet out there with your name on it. These are the incredible thoughts that go through my mind as I weave my way back through the military junta of third-world America and head for Terminal 2 again. Guns are everywhere, and you have to wonder, were we always like this? But I know the answer, because I have been around guns all my life.

We all have.

CHAPTER 19

COWBOYS AND INDIANS

I t started all the way back with Charles Dickens, who was fascinated with American gun culture, so much so that in 1844 he wrote *Martin Chuzzlewit* based on his visit to America. In the book, Hannibal Chollop, an American, carries "a brace of revolving pistols in his coat pocket," and says, "It ain't long since I shot a man down with that sir."[1] Dickens's Chuzzlewit exclaims, "What an extraordinary people you are.... Are pistols... and such things Institutions on which you pride yourself? Are bloody duels, brutal combats, savage assaults, shootings down, and stabbing in the streets your Institutions?" The answer would seem to be a resounding yes.

The United States is the only industrialized nation that maintains a gun culture. It began early in rural America with a boy being given his first gun usually before he turned twelve; the passage to manhood was equated with the ownership of a weapon. America was born with a rifle in its hand but the truth is the early colonists did not have many guns. Author and historian Garry Wills, reviewing Michael A. Bellesiles's book *Arming America*, wrote, "A Colonial historian at Emory University, [Bellesiles] . . . while searching through over a thousand probate records from the frontier sections of New England and Pennsylvania for 1763 to 1790 . . . found that only 14 percent of the men owned guns, and over half of those guns were unusable."[2] The guns were not reliable and the musket was ill-equipped for hunting, being inaccurate and scaring away game. It was the native-born Americans who fomented the gun culture.

The long gun put food on the table and defended the pioneers and later settlers against wild animals and in their wars with Native Americans. Frederick Jackson Turner's famous frontier thesis of ever-expanding

Westward boundaries was backed up by the armed frontiersman.[3] We had different needs than the Europeans from the beginning. The colonists in Massachusetts and elsewhere needed smooth bore, lightweight weapons with high accuracy. The musket would not do because of its inaccuracy. The Pennsylvania rifle was born around 1720 and would make its mark later in the Revolution when the British would comment on the deadly accuracy of the "American rifle."[4]

History being what it is, the Pennsylvania rifle was turned into the Kentucky rifle by Daniel Boone, who made it famous in his exploits while exploring Kentucky. When Americans headed out onto the plains, however, the rifle showed its deficiencies. It was a single loader and this would not do in the wide-open plateaus where a buffalo could charge or escape while reloading or worse an Indian could attack while the pioneer jammed a bullet down the barrel. The buffalo didn't have a chance when gun manufacturers produced the Winchester, the Henry, the Sharps, the Spencer, and the Hawken. There were sixty million buffalo in the early 1800s. By the 1880s the buffalo were practically extinct. People from trains mowed them down. Professional hunters mowed them down. The telegraph companies shot them because they knocked over the telegraph poles. By the time Theodore Roosevelt went on his famous Buffalo hunt in 1883, he had to search for a week to find one buffalo to shoot.[5]

The introduction of the Winchester meant the beginning of the end for the Native Americans. This repeating high-caliber weapon could easily be carried and fired on horseback, destroying the Indian strategy of waiting for a solider to fire before releasing an enfilade of arrows.

In the 1850s the derringer was the gun of choice for many Americans in rapidly developing urban environments. It was the gun that John Wilkes Booth would use to kill Abraham Lincoln. The gun was "light and palm size . . . it was the tiniest handgun yet made."[6] The derringer was the Saturday night special of its day, being accurate and deadly at short range as well as easily concealed.

But the Colt revolver would push the derringer aside and become the most famous gun of all in American history. There is not an American boy who does not carry some trace of the gun that "won the West" in manner, dress, or just cultural shadow. The .45 caliber six-shooter did not have to be reloaded after every shot like the derringer. Samuel Colt invented the first six-shooter in 1830 and improved on it with each passing year. The Colt is really the first modern handgun that "brought convenient ultimate violence within everyone's reach by supplying a dependable easy-to-carry, ever-ready destructive device."[7]

Too big and clunky for urban environments, the Colt was ready-made for the West. The heavy .45 caliber "peacemaker" on the thigh of any man in the West made him the equal of any other man. The cowboy had his gun and outlaws abounded—from Billy the Kid to the James Brothers—with men pulling their pistols on each other with little provocation. The West had few lawmen and so the law depended on whoever drew first. Writers of dime novels back in the East and later moviemakers in Hollywood had their greatest setting, and the gun-dominated Wild West would live on long after the frontier was declared closed in 1890.

Gun culture was preserved through the cultural bonanza of selling the West, something that had been going on since 1865. I recently published a book on Teddy Roosevelt, in which I concentrated on the time he spent out West. Roosevelt managed to squeak in three years in the Wild West before it was declared settled in 1890. Historian Fredrick Jackson Turner made this declaration based on census data that, to him at least, showed that the West had been mostly settled.[8] More importantly, Turner came up with the Frontier Thesis, which said that American democracy came from having a wide-open frontier that allowed people to go out and find democracy in great expanses bereft of churches, government, and law. It was here that the American traits of rugged individualism and liberty grew, nourished by the availability of free land and a spacious frontier that allowed people to continue migrating to the West and creating communities based on democratic ideals, backing up the word of law with the gun. American violence came from the West, where people were armed and settled disputes with bullets and six-shooters. Turner believed the American penchant for violence began out on the frontier.[9]

When Teddy Roosevelt went out to find his bit of the West in 1883, he adopted the cowboy ethos for his own and faced down a few men, risking being shot himself. Teddy's identity at this time was wrapped up with an ability to kill with a gun. He proved himself time and again, shooting buffalo, grizzly bears, and just about anything that moved. He would not actually kill another human until the Spanish American War but his reaction was the same as killing an animal. He felt the glory and the victory over the dead creature at his feet. Shooting animals or men was honorable and proved one's manhood in the late nineteen and early twentieth centuries.

Another early-twentieth-century writer, Ernest Hemingway, would stretch the gun ethos into literature, with characters who fought in wars and killed many animals on hunts. The gun and the man were intertwined in Hemingway's personal life, with a father who was known to have incredible vision and who could pick out the eye of a squirrel at five hundred yards.[10] Hemingway's early short stories have him hunting with his father or cleaning a shotgun, and his later stories of loss in war and on safari would have the gun become the final solution for a man in decline. Hemingway would kill himself with a shotgun blast from a prized weapon.[11]

After the Civil War ended, writers discovered that people in the East could not get enough of cowboys and Indians and guns. *The Great Train Robbery* was filmed in 1903 and was probably one of the original Westerns. It was shot in New Jersey, but Hollywood would not let go, and classic Westerns such as *Stagecoach*, *My Darling Clementine*, *Red River*, *The Gunfighter*, *High Noon*, and *Gunfight at the O.K. Corral* set the bar. Not to be outdone, the East created its own form of Westerns with gangster films, which were really just Westerns with urban characters. The 1920 gang wars during Prohibition gave Hollywood another gift, and Humphrey Bogart, James Cagney, and Edward G. Robinson gave boys another gun-swaggering character to emulate. Television cemented gun culture and introduced American children to violence. Guns have been made for children for more than 150 years, as toys and as training tools for boys who would follow their fathers into hunting.[12]

Even though my family never had a "real" gun in our house doesn't mean I didn't come from a gun culture. All boys in America are steeped in gun culture, as are many girls. In the pre-videogame era it began when I was given cap guns and blank guns. My friends and I would blast away at each other, choosing who would be a cowboy and who would be an Indian. My first BB gun was given to me when I was in sixth grade. It was a Daisy BB gun, and to this day I can remember the feel of the stock and the oiled smell of the steel BBs. Hitting cans and bottles in the backyard was something my dad and I could do together. We bought paper BB targets with bullseyes, and I remember vividly running to get the target and counting the perforations from the BBs.

My first Daisy was replaced with a larger BB gun modeled after a Winchester. This gun could shoot farther and didn't require the repeated cocking that would pressure the spring in the gun. This BB gun was a single action in which you would cock the gun once and then squeeze the trigger to hurl the BB toward the target. One day I was home by myself after my mother had called me in sick from school. I took out my BB gun and pointed it toward a car parked by the curb. My thinking was that it would make a small hole in the window. Really I wasn't quite sure what it would do, but I wanted to find out. I stayed low in a crouched sniper position and aimed the rifle at the center of the driver's side window. I fired and saw the BB arc through the afternoon light and strike the window dead center.

There was a crash, and in horror I watched the window shatter into tiny squares of safety glass. What I didn't know was that car windows are designed to shatter at impact into these small squares to lessen the chance of someone being cut to ribbons. This didn't matter to me. I ran up to the attic and hid my BB gun behind some Christmas boxes. I then pulled down the shade and saw police detectives examining the window and turning to my window as they examined the trajectory. I spent the next week in cold fear and never took out my BB gun again. We were living in the city and I rarely had a chance to shoot it anyway. I ended my gun collection with a pellet rifle that had more power and could perforate a can or shatter a bottle. But sports and girls and school supplanted any continuation of my journey into the land of guns, and my pellet and BB guns mysteriously disappeared.

My mother had never liked them. She was one with the mother in the film *A Christmas Story*—"You'll shoot your eye out."[13] I am sure she disposed of my rifles, and I never bothered to ask. Guns were something for kids and I was now a young adult, but the gun culture had affected even our liberal family. The scene in the movie where the father, played by actor Darren McGavin, says that he had a gun when he was kid to explain why he bought Ralphie a gun is a perfect example of how gun culture is handed down through the generations. "Oh I had one when I was a kid," he explains to his wife. I would imagine video games and Xboxes supplanted a lot of this with the middle class, but the feeling is still there.

I had plastic machine guns, bazookas, plastic grenades, pistols, muskets, cannons, cap guns, blank guns, guns that fired plastic bullets, squirt guns, ray guns, holsters, armor, rifle slings, targets, model rockets, water rockets, and a very realistic M16. These were all toys and I didn't end up a "gun nut." But I fantasized about shooting people with my toy guns. I didn't fantasize about shooting animals, though I did take shots at squirrels and birds with my BB guns. I ran around pulling my toy gun out and blasting away at my friends, parents, and neighbors, and no one thought anything of it. Why should they? The Westerns we watched showed men proficient with guns, and Clint Eastwood was an urban version of a tough guy who dispensed the bad guys with his .44 Magnum.

I doodled incessantly in my notebooks and drew soldiers firing machine guns, hiding behind hills. In my doodles people were always getting shot. I ate my cereal imagining violence of all kinds. The news was on in our house a lot; there was constant footage of the Vietnam War, and it was the era of assassinations. I was in Indian Guides and Boy Scouts, in which playing cowboys and Indians was standard, and if we didn't have plastic guns we used sticks. Someone was always dying. *You're shot! You're dead!* Many arguments would break out over who was dead and who wasn't. Sometimes the dead would stomp off in protest saying they wanted to be the shooter and not the victim. All in all I was a normal American boy of my time; little did I know that I was merely the product of a nation with a long history intertwined with guns.

I did see myself as a cowboy, and to this day when I take the trash down our long driveway in the darkness and go down a small grassy incline, I see myself on a horse. This comes from hours and hours of watching men with guns bulging out of holsters and rifle shucks crossing the frontier with their horses. A cowboy is self-reliant, independent, takes nothing from any man, is a dead-eye shot, and, more than all that, he is a man who backs up what he says and banishes enemies with his guns. It is no coincidence that our Western states are the most heavily armed, with pickup trucks replacing horses and automatic weapons replacing six-shooters.

The gun culture was given over to the military in World War II, with GIs finishing off Germans and Japanese with machine guns, M1s, pistols, grenades, bazookas, or fifty-caliber machine guns. The good guys were armed to the teeth again, except this time we were not just saving our country but saving the world. Hollywood had a field day.

Now boys were running up hills with guns to knock out the Germans or the Japanese. The duck and cover of the movies translated to boys diving behind hills and looking over to take a shot. One of my favorite toys was my GI Joe doll. You could buy all sorts of weapons for him, and this was long after World War II had ended. Our collective memory of that war was kept alive through movies and television shows, and action films of amped-up police and heavily armed bad guys kept the gun culture alive.

The Matrix and Quentin Tarantino's films would take guns and American violence to its next logical step, with orgies of murderous mayhem, guns front and center. Video games have taken over a lot of the cultural mores presented in movies, only now the viewer is able to participate in the carnage. Even at a time when rural culture is in decline, we cannot escape the heritage of the gun and hunting ethos that belongs to our rural traditions. Modern mass shooters live out their gun fantasies by taking action. They are already well schooled in American gun culture going all the way back to cowboys and Indians. Add a touch of mental illness, PTSD, or psychopathic tendencies, and they take that next step in our gun-laden history and consummate their affair by killing prodigiously. They are the cowboy gone bad.

CHAPTER 20

NO ESCAPE

5:00 p.m.

I learn later that some people do try to get out of the airport. They hop fences, cross access roads, or head across fields, only to be met with the raised guns of a SWAT team. The pictures show people with hands raised marching toward what look like soldiers. They are then frisked, questioned, and have their IDs checked before they are turned back and returned to the airport. The police have no way of knowing who is a shooter and who is just someone caught in the airport when it was closed. So we all become suspects and I receive more than a few suspicious glances from gun-toting officers.

I feel like we have all been parked, like that burned-out 757 I saw on the way in. We have all been affected by the initial shooting and after the second shooting we have all become potential terrorists. The police are still checking parking garages and combing through the airplane hangars. All anyone wants to do is leave. We want to get away from the police, the ambulances, the SWAT teams, the television trucks, the people sitting on the curbs, on the sidewalks, clustered around buildings, the people out on the tarmacs, the jets that cannot fly, the jets that cannot land. We are all in a state of suspended animation with just one overriding thought, common to all refugees—escape and get away from the lurking danger.

I make my way back toward the media trucks. The swirling lights and the people sitting everywhere give the world a surreal quality. The media people are still looking for stories and I see other "witnesses" getting their fifteen nanoseconds of fame. My phone is still ringing with people who saw me on television and want to make sure I am safe. My father has called several times but I can't seem to get through. The cellphones are still acting strange and I don't know if this is because of the media antennas or the fact that ten thousand people are stranded in an airport with nowhere to go and all trying to call loved ones on their cellphones to let them know they are alright.

I see Kitty and the girls are still in the reporter's car. I see other journalists in the street doing live feeds. Kitty holds her finger to her mouth motioning to a man in the front seat phoning in a report. I go back over to Clay, who is sitting on the ground looking stressed. I sit down next to him and he looks up.

"What did you find?"

I shake my head. "Nothing. They wouldn't let me in."

Clay nods and stares off. He was to go to college last year and at the last minute—and I mean the last minute, the car was packed—he said he didn't want to go. He had scored very well on the ACT exams but decided he wanted to hold off. Clay has taken a nine-to-five job at an import-export company and likes it, but I know there are times that he wonders about the path not taken and thinks he should have gone to college. I get it. We all wonder about that path not taken and now we are pinned down in an airport and we question the twists and turns. Had I been a business man we would not have had a layover in the airport. We would have gone to the beach for the day or we would have flown out earlier. But a writer must watch his money, and I have been thinking like a writer for so long I don't know how to not think about money. But isn't this unfair to my family? Shouldn't I have chosen a path less risky, something not so close to the edge of the cliff? Because right now we are all on the edge of the cliff. Maybe Clay would have taken a different path if he had grown up seeing a father with a steady nine-to-five instead of an overeducated man who lines his mantle with books and his office with signing posters.

My son might then have found my routine in his and school would have not been such a burden. Even I know this is ridiculous, but this must be *someone's fault*. Why did we stumble into a shooting? Why did we run for our lives? Why might my kids now have PTSD or some other psychological stressor when others breeze through airports all the time and nothing happens? The kicker is, we never fly. Writers go on driving vacations. This was a treat and now we are in an airport being searched by SWAT teams, with five dead people in a building just a few yards away. The hell of it is those bodies will be there for a while as evidence is gathered, and family members will not be informed for too long. The forensic teams will have to have their time, and identities will have to be confirmed while the families wait. In Columbine and Sandy Hook family members would have to wait until the next day for confirmation that their loved ones had died.

Clay and I sit in silence. We are in one of those sidebars of family life where there are no markers. We have joined forces with families caught up in wars, hurricanes, tornadoes, freak floods, and blizzards. There are the strange stories of families being swept off a road by a deluge or running out of gas in a desert with the father setting off never to be heard from again. Or the families murdered in their homes by unknown assailants. When I read *In Cold Blood* I always marveled at that 1950s Kansas family that had it all and then had the incredible bad luck to end up with two killers in their house. This is all in that other world of existence, and all you can do is endure and try to get to the other side and get the hell out and never look back. The thought of our home with the fireplaces waiting in a snow-crusted landscape seems like a Carrier and Ives scene, something out of a Christmas movie where there are no guns and no death.

Like most fathers and sons, Clay and I were close before he hit adolescence and then our relationship got lost under the pressure of school and growing up. Now I wish I had been able to break down those walls. A phrase stuck in my head long ago—*the silent shame of fathers and sons*. We are always careful around each other. We both have a temper and are careful not to set each other off, so real talk is sidelined and instead we talk about the Cubs or the Bears or food. Chicken wings are our mutual favorite and we have frequented Yak-Zies next to Wrigley Field, which has the best wings. Many times I look for topics that we can both enter into but come up short.

"This really—"

"This sucks," he says, looking over defiantly.

"Yes," I say, nodding.

He pauses then looks down. "I hate it that you did those interviews," he mutters.

I nod slowly. I know what he is talking about; Dad the whore. The media whore selling himself because maybe it will sell a few books. This thought has crossed my mind. I have been selling books for so long I don't know how not to. I have a media persona and it turns on like a light when the camera or microphone swings my way. It comes from an early realization that being a good writer with awards and great reviews is not enough to sell books in the age of the internet. You have to make noise, and noise is not pretty. It is countless hours of social media badgering and grabbing any mainstream media you can lay your hands on. I had a fantasy, as all writers do, that my career would follow the Fitzgerald–Hemingway arc, where my books would magically sell and I would be sipping absinthe on the Left Bank of Paris. I was quickly disabused of that myth. Hemingway married well and Fitzgerald was almost destitute at the end.

It is with shock that all writers realize they are on par with a man selling insurance once a book is finished. The crass economics of selling books to make a living requires the development of another side of the writerly world. My father is one of the best glue salesmen in the world while my mother was a writer and a painter. I do have both sides and people don't recognize the salesman writer barnstorming bookstores and popping up on television or invading their morning drive time. He is one with that man setting out with glue pails in the back of his car. The thoughtful, hidden-away writer has left and will not reappear until another publishing contract appears on the horizon.

But my son sees none of this. Dad disappears into the room over the garage to write and then appears in newspapers, as a voice on the Chicago radio, signing an occasional movie deal. But he doesn't see the gritty sweaty pushing that is so awful that it makes me cringe when people block the social media posts that dun them to death. It is in a way horrible. And so when the camera turns on I don't shrink away. Even when it concerns death because, of course, death sells more than anything else.

"I know. It looks bad to you," I begin.

His eyes are red. "No one is going to buy your books because we're on television."

I nod again and look at him. "I know . . . that's not why I did it. I was there and people should know there was a second shooter."

He looks at me and shrugs. "Yeah. Whatever."

This is where we are. I am not sure what a man who writes books can say to his son who is not big on the life of the mind. He aced his ACT without studying and he has the cerebral horsepower, but I just don't think he sees a need to read books or sit in a classroom. He hated his classes in high school and I suspect there were other things he hated there as well. But these are the things we don't talk about so I founder again.

I nod slowly and see another crowd of journalists gathering as the governor of Florida walks up to the microphone. I stand up and, like all fathers the world over who don't have easy answers, I change the subject. Sons and fathers are better doing things together—eating chicken wings, going to a ballgame, or going to a press conference.

"Guess I'll see what the governor has to say."

Clay looks over, then stands up. He sees the suits walking up to the lights. His eyes grow. "That's the governor?" There is awe in his voice, and a dad-son adventure beckons.

"Yes, I have never seen a governor. . . . You want to check him out?"

Clay gets up and nods. "I'm not doing anything here. I'll go with you."

"Good," I say, as we walk over to hear the governor.

Governor Rick Scott is surrounded by a crowd of security guards, media, and his own entourage. They move as one and approach the microphone. Clay and I are on the outside with the cameramen and the reporters are closer in. The governor says to pray for the victims and the wounded. He is asked how he got there and says he flew in to Executive Airport, which is about fifteen miles away. "What do you think about guns in airports," a reporter asks. The governor ducks and says this is no time to get political. He says he has the National Guard on standby. I wonder about this. The National Guard is on standby when the police have declared there is a lone shooter? Clearly, he knows more than he is saying. He brings up the National Guard several more times while taking questions. He has talked to President-Elect Trump but not President Obama. Several reporters question why he has not talked to the president. He says he has a personal relationship with Donald Trump. The governor looks small and pale and is in a drab suit. Television will fill in the rest for America and colorize the incident.

The truth is, there are a lot of media trucks and police cars parked all around with a large number of people doing nothing. There is not a lot to do and the interviews have tapered down. Clearly Governor Scott flying in and telling everyone to pray for the survivors and letting people know he can bring in the National Guard at a moment's notice is the main event. Clay and I stand as the only non-journalists inside the media pool around the head of state. I am amazed that no one has asked us to identify ourselves, but the sheer amount of law enforcement has created a perceived safety zone.

The National Guard is only called out for true emergencies: floods, rampaging fires, riots, epidemics, threats of invasion, threats of terrorism, and the like. They have never been called out for a mass shooting, but the airport is closed and the planes are being diverted, with ten thousand people stranded in an area that is considered an "active situation." You would only bring out the Guard if you believed the breakdown of order was at hand or that the airport was under siege. The police story is at odds with the governor's having the Guard on standby. Cleary there is another threat that could bring in the tanks and armored vehicles and soldiers.

But the press conference is over. Clay and I go back to our cement column and sit down. My son shakes his head.

"You know what I don't get?"

"What's that?"

He holds his hands up. "Why don't they just get rid of the fucking guns. Just tell people they can't have them?"

This is the reaction. It is the thought you have when confronted with murdered people and the breakdown of order. There is something wrong and if you have a problem, you want to solve it. Why can't we all agree that guns are not doing us any favors? Why can't we just say, as people of the twenty-first century, that it doesn't work anymore to have armed people in our society. Clay stares at the cement wall that goes along the sidewalk. Beyond the wall is the tarmac where people are standing out by 737 airliners because they don't know if they will get shot or not.

He turns to me. "Why is that, Dad?"

I look over and see that he is a stressed-out twenty year old with day-old stubble and airport grime smudged on his face from lying on the sidewalk with his mother and sisters. The thought that we are prisoners waiting to be released or sent to our doom is inescapable. The governor can leave the airport but normal people are trapped along with any terrorists, shooters, psychopaths, deranged boyfriends, or pissed-off coworkers, all of whom could be carrying an automatic weapon capable of murdering a hundred people in minutes. These guns can be bought in department stores all over America or on the internet. They are as easy to get as buying a loaf of bread. And one might ask: if one were trapped in a major airport shut down for the next twenty-four hours because of people with guns, why it is that we cannot do anything to curb this national health problem? Because, ultimately, human health is the opposite of human death. So my son's question is dead on. Why can't we just get rid of the guns?

"It's complicated," I offer up.

He screws up his face in twenty-year-old indignation. "What's that mean?"

"I mean . . . it's complicated."

"Dad. It's not complicated. It's a question. Why can't they just get rid of the fucking guns?"

I turn and stare at him.

"The NRA for one."

He frowns and asks . . . the question.

"Who the fuck is the NRA?"

CHAPTER 21

A SHORT HISTORY OF THE NRA

I don't know anyone in the National Rifle Association. I see the red stickers on the back windows of pickup trucks or on a bumper. They are sometimes joined by yellow "Don't Tread On Me" stickers. I have seen Wayne La Pierre give a speech surrounded by armed men after a horrific shooting where he says the only way to stop a bad guy with a gun is to give a gun to a good guy. I have seen Conceal and Carry Class signs on the side of the road. I have seen presidents complain about the NRA and I have heard of senators forced out of office because they voted for gun control. I saw a tape of Donald Trump speaking to the NRA in which he said Hillary Clinton wanted to take away everyone's guns. I have heard that gun sales went through the roof when Obama was elected. But as an urban/suburban American I have had no direct contact with the National Rifle Association or anyone who is a member.

The history of the National Rifle Association is actually very different from its image today as the hard-charging political organization that will cut down anyone who opposes them. The NRA was actually born of necessity. Union soldiers just couldn't hit the Confederates. They fired one thousand bullets for every Confederate shot. The problem was that nobody understood the new rifle barrels that could actually be aimed at a soldier. They still fired large-volley enfilades as though they were using smooth-bore muskets. This concerned Captain George Wingate as he considered it in 1871, after the Civil War had ended. How could there be a national army for defense if no one could hit the broadside of a barn?

Wingate sent men to Europe to learn how they trained their troops, and on November 16, 1871, he and *Army and Navy Journal* editor William

Church organized the National Rifle Association in New York.[1] They elected Union general Ambrose Burnside as their first president. They immediately set up shooting ranges to start instructing soldiers on how to shoot and hit their targets. Even though the Civil War was over, General Wingate believed it was better late than never. He wrote the first marksmanship manual in the United States on how to shoot a rifle and hit the target. Small clubs started to spring up in other states. For the first time, there was a civic organization to teach soldiers how to shoot a rifle. Wingate's manual turned into the United States' marksmanship instruction program.

This was first time anyone had taken on the lack of training with modern weapons in the United States military. General Ulysses S. Grant served as the NRA's eighth president and General Philip Sheridan as its ninth. The organization was strictly intended to improve the use of firearms to protect the country. The headquarters was located in Washington, DC, with a connection to the military occurring through the Civilian Marksmanship Program that would train civilians who might be called to service.

The first link between the firearms industry and the NRA began in 1910 when the Springfield Armory and Rock Island Arsenal manufactured the M1903 Springfield for members of the NRA. Soon after this, the director of Civilian Marksmanship began to have M1911 pistols made for members. Beginning in 1903, the government provided money for shooting tournaments, ammunition, and targets for NRA members.[2] It made sense at the time that the government would support an organization that helped men shoot straight and hit their targets. This went back to the English, who wanted citizens to be well-versed in the handling of weapons so they might aid in policing and defense against attack from another power. The same attitude prevailed in 1776. The nascent government wanted the citizenry to be well armed to protect the rights granted in the fledgling democracy.

So in the early twentieth century, ammunition, targets, and specially made weapons were a small price to pay for an army that could at least hit the enemy. The legislative branch of the NRA would not come until 1934, when the first gun-control legislation was passed in the United States. The National Firearms Act (NFA), passed in 1934, was supported by NRA president Karl Frederick. In hearings, he said, "I have never believed in the general practice of carrying weapons. I seldom carry one.... I do not believe in the general promiscuous toting of guns. I think it should be sharply restricted and only under licenses."[3] So here we have a very different NRA. The NFA of 1934 and the Gun Control Act (GCA) of 1968, which created a system of licensing gun dealers and restricted certain weapons, were both supported by the NRA. The truth is that the NRA was not interested in opposing gun control and was in fact an organization of hunters and sportsman. The role of training soldiers to shoot had been taken over by the army, but after the GCA of 1968 a new type of gun-rights activist came on the scene with the establishment of the lobbying arm of the NRA, known as the Institute for Legislative Action.

A political action committee, the Political Victory Fund, followed and was used against perceived anti-gun candidates in the 1976 election. The NRA permanently changed their course at the 1977 convention in Cincinnati when activists took over with an agenda of strict adherence to Second Amendment issues. The transformation from a gun club to a political organization aligned with conservatives and Republicans had been mostly completed by the eighties. The NRA was considered the most powerful lobbying organization in the United States by 2001.[4] Eighty-eight percent of Republicans had received a contribution in some form or another in 2001.[5] Political candidates were scored from A+ to F for how strongly they supported gun issues in national elections, and millions of dollars were pumped into elections to defeat those in favor of gun control. At the same time, the NRA claimed to be the "oldest civil rights organization in America" but this claim can be disputed as they did not aggressively push for gun rights until 1934.[6] The protection of the Second Amendment, the right to bear arms, therefore is deemed a fight for and about civil rights.

So what happened? How could an organization devoted to target practice turn into this virulent machine that cuts down any type of gun-control legislation? In 1968, the United States was in the middle of a cultural revolution. The *silent moral majority* was a term coined by President Richard Nixon and described as a force to be reckoned with. We had had the Democratic Convention protests in Chicago. We had Woodstock, the Beatles, the Rolling Stones, drugs, protests against the war in Vietnam, civil rights unrest, and those long-haired bearded bums. All this contributed to the feeling that core American values were under siege. And one of those core American values is the right to bear arms.

In the most turbulent year of the sixties, 1968, the NRA veered into the "you are either for us or against us" mode and never looked back. Violence in America was making people question the legitimacy of owning a gun in an urbanized country. Handguns were viewed as a scourge. At the same time that the gun culture was waning, the NRA stuck a spike in the side of the mountain and basically said it would be relevant and preserve that traditional piece of the American way of life. And any attempt to abrogate or infringe any aspect of gun ownership would be viewed as an assault on the Second Amendment. To give an inch would be to give a mile so the inch would not be given. Stopping someone's right to own an assault weapon will lead to a corrosion of the basic right to bear arms, according to the NRA, and this will lead to an assault on American freedoms. Guns protect our rights and so guns must be protected fiercely, and those who want to abrogate or modify or adjust that right will be given no quarter. This has led to political cryogenics on gun control. No one wants to take on the NRA.

The first presidential candidate endorsed by the NRA was Ronald Reagan in 1980. Donald Trump's bid for the presidency was the first time the NRA endorsed a candidate early in the election process. The NRA spent over fifteen million dollars in the 2012 election targeting Barack Obama to steer votes away from him.[7] The NRA routinely sues American cities that have gun-control legislation on the books, forcing cities like

Chicago and San Francisco to repeal gun legislation. They successfully fought the implementation of the Assault Weapons Ban when it expired in 2004[8] and they are in favor of conceal and carry laws in all public places in the United States. Wayne La Pierre, the NRA's current president, began as a lobbyist for the NRA and is the face of the *not giving an inch or they will take a mile* attitude that prohibits gun control in any form.

Few can forget the face of the NRA when Wayne La Pierre's answer to Sandy Hook was armed guards in every school and at the same time fighting off any curbs on assault weapons, including any restrictions on high-capacity magazines.[9] The actor Charlton Heston made history by holding up a musket at the NRA's annual convention and declaring they would have to take it from his "cold dead hands,"[10] invoking patriots of the Revolution from Patrick Henry to George Washington.

A major victory for the NRA was the passage of the Protection of Lawful Commerce in Firearms Act during President George W. Bush's administration. This made it impossible for victims of shootings to sue the manufactures of weapons used in those shootings. The Sandy Hook parents took a run at this law and are still litigating, saying that the AR-15 was marketed as a weapon designed to kill humans.

The NRA sued San Francisco over its restrictive gun laws and had the city pay $380,000 in legal costs as well as forcing the abolition of Proposition H, which banned ownership and sale of firearms.[11] The NRA sued New Orleans when guns were confiscated during Hurricane Katrina. The city was forced to return all weapons to their owners.[12] Chicago was next to be sued by the NRA, this time over handgun laws. The city was forced to repeal the laws restricting the use of handguns.[13] The State of New York was then forced to repeal a law restricting the size of magazines for automatic weapons.[14] Pittsburgh, Philadelphia, and Lancaster all were sued and forced to repeal gun legislation.[15]

The National Rifle Association had begun as an organization to help soldiers shoot straight and hit their targets after the Civil War. It had then morphed into an organization promoting gun safety and training. It later morphed further into a civil rights organization that was solely concerned with protecting the right to bear arms under the Second Amendment. And it transformed yet again into a political organization that joined forces with conservative coalitions to choose candidates friendly to the issues the NRA supports, which are those of the Far Right.

In the year 2018, the NRA continues as a political lobbying organization fighting any type of gun-control legislation in the United States. Over 72 percent of NRA members support expanded background checks for gun purchases and common-sense gun laws. Esteban Santiago broke no laws although he had been deemed mentally ill.[16] He was given back his gun twice, even though he told the FBI he had voices telling him to kill. He then boarded a plane with his gun and ammunition in a protective case and flew to Fort Lauderdale to shoot as many people as he could. Those early patriots, who created the National Rifle Association so a man could aim at the side of a barn and not miss, would have been appalled.

CHAPTER 22

CASABLANCA

7:00 p.m.

T error is something you have to experience to understand the word. It is uncertainty, fear, and stress, coupled with a feeling of impending doom. It is the unknown that grips you, and we are not a people equipped to handle this new emotion. Middle-class people mostly live lives that follow patterns and these patterns give us expected results: school, college, work, family, retirement, dying only of disease or natural causes. The pioneers were much more experienced with terror. They experienced the terror of Indian attacks, starvation, bears, freezing to death, disease, dying from lack of water and shelter, even loneliness. The people who settled America knew life was short and terror sat at their elbow. Many would leave their bones on the plains after starvation, exposure, or Indian attacks robbed them of their lives. The unexpected was expected.

Corporations have given Americans a model to plug into, and risk aversion has become a way of life. Terror for modern people belongs in the television. Our terror is confined to doctor visits where unknown diseases lurk. So when we are confronted with terror, be it through a shooting or a bombing, we aren't quite sure what to do with this catastrophic anxiety. Our only response is to get as far away as possible and that is our focus now—to escape from the Fort Lauderdale–Hollywood International Airport.

We hear rumors again that buses are coming but no one confirms this. Kitty, Callie, and Careen are still in the car, but the photographer lets us know she will be leaving soon and she can't take anyone with her.

The police are trying to contain the ten thousand people at the airport with the idea that a shooter still might be hiding out somewhere. People who have tried to escape the airport by climbing fences or running across fields are frozen in time by photographers taking pictures of them with their hands high in the air as heavily armed SWAT officers intercept their flight.

The bottom line is that we have to be ready to go at a moment's notice. All our energy is focused on escaping the airport. The airport is danger. The airport is uncontrolled and the atmosphere resembles a battlefield, with SWAT teams wandering around, not sure where the next shot might come from. I notice that the governor has quickly departed after giving his news conference. The media men and women are hanging around with their microphones ready. I have fielded more than a few calls from radio stations asking for a live interview. One woman is going to call me back and interview me when I know when we are leaving.

A central problem is that we still have no luggage and all our clothes and belongings are back in Terminal 1. Irrationally, I feel that if I could retrieve our luggage then I could take back some control and this would lead to escape. All day long we have been swept up in events that have left us powerless and in danger. I feel that if I could get our luggage then we will be closer to leaving and getting to a place of safety. I think of that old movie *Casablanca* where everyone is hanging around trying to get a flight to America while the Nazis close in. The people sitting, lying, sleeping, and staring remind me of those trapped people during World War II. It is hot, still oppressive. Everyone in the film wants to get out of Casablanca and escape to America; our hell is that this *is* America.

"I'm going back to try and get our luggage again," I declare, standing up. "We need it to get out of here."

Clay stares at me shaking his head.

"You want to go?" I ask him.

"No!"

"Okay . . . I'll be back."

I walk over between the police cars, ambulances, fire trucks, and armored SWAT vans and rap on the photographer's car window. Kitty lowers the glass.

"How's everyone doing?"

Kitty looks at the girls, who are both on their phones. Normalcy to some degree has returned to their little oasis, but I know it is temporary. I bend down closer to the window.

"I'm going back to Terminal 1 to get our luggage."

Kitty gives me the same look that Clay had. "Are you sure you want to do that?"

"I have to. We have to get the fuck out of here and we need our stuff." I look up as a bus roars by. There are lots of buses but no one knows where they are loading and when they will be leaving. There are lots of rumors "Eventually, they are going to have to get us out of here and I want our luggage so we don't have to come back. We'll rent a car and drive home. All of this will be behind us. Fuck this airport and fuck flying home."

Kitty nods. "Sounds good to me."

We both have been thinking of driving home. I have already worked out that we are not coming back once we get out of the airport. People have been shot and died here. It is not a place I want to come back to. Escape. Escape. Escape. This is all I am focused on. Once we get clear we will rent a car and drive back to Chicago. The cost is no longer important; what is important is getting home safely. It is luxurious to think of the privacy and safety of a car trip right now. Anything is better than hanging around a hot sweaty airport with constant fear gnawing at us like a metastasizing disease. I want to be away from the airport, where armed men look for another armed man.

Kitty squeezes my hand.

"Be careful."

"Absolutely."

I begin to walk back toward Terminal 1 again. There are big police vans all over the place. I assume they contain some sort of evidence-gathering equipment. I weave through the media lights and the people who had interviewed me. They say nothing and laugh and talk among themselves. They have some sort of psychological armor that allows them to interview people whose husband, son, wife, or daughter has just been shot and killed and not to feel the pain. They are on a different level in a different world where they are untouchable. The rest of the world is ugly, tired, and used up. They are young, handsome, beautiful, and, what's more, they are on television.

I clear the media trucks and pass the Japanese woman who had stared at me before sitting down. She stares at me now with blank eyes that say nothing at all. The woman with the ukulele is sitting on the curb still picking out songs. Other people just stare out into the early darkness with the thousand-yard stare of soldiers. Everyone has been revved up way too long. We have all been in danger and our bodies are tired of being ready to run or fight. And those of us who have heard the shots know someone is still out there with a gun.

I see Terminal 1 and the door is open. There is no one there and, without thinking, I walk in and am met by a tall armed SWAT officer. He has an enormous jaw and a helmet on. He stares at me with his rifle at the ready. The terminal is littered with the belongings of people who have run for their lives—purses, phones, wallets, drinks, food, shoes, socks, strollers, diapers, bottles, beach towels, sunglasses, Band-Aids, Chapstick, makeup, and hundreds of pieces of luggage. The silence of the terminal is startling. People had dropped everything and ran when the shots went off. The SWAT officer speaks without taking his hand off his gun.

"You gotta leave."

The voice is deep, authoritarian, and very close. I turn and see a man dressed for combat, wearing camouflage and holding a big ugly rifle. The solider is standing to my left and just then I see our luggage cart. Some of the luggage has fallen out but I count the six suitcases and two carry-on bags. Everything is there. He points to the door.

"You gotta leave . . . now!"

That's what the soldier says to me. I know I have one chance to get our luggage back. I don't know there are 25,000 other pieces of luggage that will remain unclaimed until the next day. No one is getting back anything, but I have to try.

"That's my luggage," I exclaim, pointing to the luggage cart. "I just want to grab it and go."

He turns, keeping both hands on his rifle. "That's your luggage?"

I nod. "Yes. That's my luggage. All I need to do is grab it and I'm outta here."

He look at me, a man with red hair, blue eyes, shorts, sunglasses, baseball cap, and backpack. Yeah, a dad. A middle-class man from the middle of the country. He rolls his shoulders and takes a chance.

"Get it and get the fuck out of here."

I run to the luggage cart and throw the pieces that have fallen onto the top. I see the granola I bought and the vitamin water. I see ear buds on the ground, flip-flops and tennis shoes. The terminal is frozen in the moment when my family started running from the shots. I throw the carry-on bags on top as well and start to push the baggage cart toward the door. The solider watches me as the carry-ons fall off. I throw them back on and keep pushing and I am outside.

Sweat cools all over my body as I begin pushing my leaning luggage cart. I am one with the homeless pushing their earthly possessions in shopping carts. I push the bumping cart back toward the media trucks. The luggage keeps falling off and it is slow bumping over cables from the trucks and down sidewalks. People watch me like I am some curious circus that keeps falling apart as I keep throwing the luggage back up and continuing. The Japanese woman watches as all the luggage falls out of the cart and I run around stacking it again. Her expression doesn't change. I am wet with perspiration as I inch to where Clay is sitting against the post. He turns and then a glimmer of a smile crosses his mouth. It is the first time since the shooting I have seen the expression of impending doom leave his face.

"You got it!"

It is a victory of sorts on a day of horrible defeats. I nod, coming to a halt and wiping my face with my T-shirt. Kitty, Callie, and Careen walk up, and I know the sanctuary of the photographer's car is now gone. It is time to get the hell out of Dodge.

"She had to go," Kitty explains, before I asks. "You got the luggage."

"Yes. I got the luggage."

"Buses are coming to take us out, so it's good you got it."

I nod and turn, seeing a line of Greyhound-style buses approaching. We are finally getting out of the Fort Lauderdale–Hollywood International Airport. Hallelujah. Callie is staring at the luggage and I realize in that moment she isn't wearing her glasses. She turns to me, her blue eyes picking up the media glare.

"Dad . . . did you see my glasses?"

I frown. "No . . . did you leave them?"

Callie nods. "Uh huh."

I stand up and stare at her. "Shit."

Her glasses cost six hundred dollars and she is nearly blind without them. We are getting some semblance of our lives back, and the pieces of family life hinge on phones, glasses, wallets, and keys. Her glasses are a piece to be retrieved. Callie shrugs.

"It doesn't matter."

In a way it *doesn't* matter, but suddenly I am pissed. I am pissed that we are about to be victimized *again* and my daughter will be without her glasses and we will have to pay six hundred dollars to replace them. We have been victims all day and I am tired of being a victim.

I breathe deeply. "Where did you leave them?"

"By where we were sitting."

I turn back to Terminal 1 and stare at my nightmare. I breathe heavily again. I want to wrestle something back from this beast who has turned our lives upside down and terrified us all day.

"Stay right here . . . I'll be back."

"Are you sure?" Kitty calls out.

"Yes! Stay there!"

I take off, and this time I run. I want to get back before the buses come, and I weave my way back through the media trucks and sprint up the slight incline to Terminal 1. The door is still open and I go in again and this time no one is there. I run into the semi-darkened terminal and realize I am pushing my luck. I half expect to meet the second shooter in that cavernous space. Instead, I meet the SWAT man again.

"Hey . . . what the fuck are you doing?"

I turn. He looks really pissed.

"My daughter left her glasses," I shout, looking around frantically.

He points to the door. "You have to get the fuck out of here!"

His hands are still firmly on his rifle. I nod and stare at where we had been sitting. The glasses aren't there. I am about to turn and go when I see a thin pair of glasses on the floor. They are just sitting there in the open . . . a young girl's glasses with an arabesque design on the frames. I grab them and a pair of earbuds that I think might be hers as well.

"I'm good," I shout back at the man with the automatic weapon.

I run outside and now I am sprinting because the buses are filling with people and the one thing I do not want is to be left behind. I run past the Japanese woman, the woman with her ukulele, the people sitting, lying down, the SWAT officers, the cops, the FBI men in suits, and I reach Terminal 2. My family is still huddled around our luggage. Callie turns and smiles.

"Here," I say breathing hard, handing over her glasses.

"Yay! You got them."

A small victory. Callie puts them on and I realize it is the first time we have put some things back together all day. We had our luggage and she had her glasses.

"Let's get going," I say, pushing the luggage cart toward the curb where the buses are lining up.

I look at Careen, who is staring at her phone. She does not seem fazed at all by what has been going on. I mention this to Kitty later and she shrugs. "Well, they have been training for this for years in school on lockdowns. It is part of their world more than ours."

This is true. They have been going through lockdown drills ever since elementary school. This is part of their life: training for the shooter who might come into their school. They have grown up in a post-Columbine world where the television images of people running out of that fortress school in Colorado still haunt the internet. School shootings happen in their world, and every time I am buzzed through locked doors after staring into a concave lens confirms it. School kids all over America practice hiding under desks and locking doors and teachers are trained to minimize slaughter by sheltering in place. That had all started with a school in Colorado and two seniors named Dylan Klebold and Eric Harris.

CHAPTER 23

COLUMBINE

1999

E ric Harris and Dylan Klebold were seniors and they were brains. Eric was handsome and Dylan was tall, angular, and geeky. Eric had spiky hair and listened to industrial rock and got lots of high school girls. Dylan was six-three and 143 pounds and didn't have the success with girls, but he had a date for prom and Eric didn't. None of this mattered. They were going to kill people, lots of people. They called it "Judgment Day" and it would begin with a holocaust of exploding propane tanks they had learned how to detonate from *The Anarchist Cookbook* on the internet. Then, after the fireball had incinerated hundreds of students at Columbine High School, the real killing would begin with an Intratec TEC-DC9 and sawed-off shotguns while they tossed portable explosives from a duffel bag loaded with ordinance. Their long trench coats would conceal their weapons and add to the swaggering Western gunslinger motif. In their words, this would be fun.[1]

Columbine was not the first school shooting. Many preceded it. But it was the most deadly school shooting at that time; the mother of mass death in a school. When you read the book *Columbine*, by Dave Cullen, you have a deep revulsion that two humans could do this to other humans. Thirteen students plus the shooters were killed in the Columbine shooting and twenty-four were wounded.[2] Columbine would become the face of all school shootings until Sandy Hook for the deadly cold-blooded planning and the detached way the two shooters murdered teenagers in the school library.

Video games would be examined. Bullying would be examined. Police tactics would be examined. The culture would be examined. Books would be written and FBI reports complied. In the end, there are still the questions of what drove Eric Harris and Dylan Klebold to murder their fellow students using automatic weapons, bombs, and sawed-off shotguns. It is sadly the monument to all school shootings before and since. The worst of American school carnage related to firearms and children. Even Sandy Hook would not approach the sheer cultural impact that Columbine would have at the time and still does. Many lockdown procedures, security procedures, zero-tolerance policies, shooter profiles, intervention programs, and bullying programs have a blood trail leading back to Columbine. The shooting ranks up there with the great calamities of the late twentieth century.

I don't remember how I found out about what had happened on April 20, 1999. I know I saw it on television, with the aerial shots of the helicopter showing a fortress of a school in Columbine, Colorado, surrounded by police cars, with students running in small lines. A memorable scene was a bloody student dropping from a window that turned out to be an escape from the carnage of the school library and the CNN red letters above images of police crouched behind their cars with guns drawn while the shooters inside massacred students.[3] This approach of not going into a school where a shooting was taking place would be forever dumped into the ash heap of police procedures in exchange for an immediate entrance policy that recognized that shooters were not hostage takers but killers.

Most people would never know the real horror of Columbine. When you read about it, though, you recognize the cold-blooded horror inflicted by two seniors in Columbine High School. Gun-control laws would come out of Columbine, along with movies, games, and subcultures that worshiped the nihilism of Eric Harris and Dylan Klebold. Michael Moore's film *Bowling for Columbine* would become a staple for gun-control advocates. It is the two killers of Columbine who are responsible for my children knowing how to duck and cover in lockdown drills in their elementary schools and high schools. And it all began with a website on America Online.

Eric Harris created the website to vent his hatred of his teachers and fellow students. Then came posts about how to make bombs. There were death threats to students at Columbine. The video game *Doom* played into it, with Harris designing new gaming levels for his friends. The Jefferson County sheriff became aware of the site when the mother of Brooks Brown discovered it after Eric had made death threats against her son many months before the Columbine killings occurred. The Jefferson County sheriff investigated with an affidavit created to secure a search warrant. The affidavit was never filed and the warrant was never obtained, which would later become the center of an alleged cover-up by the Sheriff's Department and would become the great "might have been" of Columbine. If the search warrant had been issued then the worst mass school shooting in history might never have occurred. Eventually, Harris deleted the site from AOL.[4]

Eric Harris grew up on military bases and loved playing war with his brothers. His father, Major Wayne Harris, was a stern taskmaster and discipline was handed out quickly. Eric attended five different schools as the family moved around from base to base. His childhood photos show a normal clean-cut kid. He wrote later that he loved guns and loved playing war, always playing a Marine. His father eventually retired in Colorado in Jefferson County, and Eric started attending Columbine High School.

By that time he was very into the video game *Doom*, which gave him a virtual reality for his war fantasies. When writing later about his childhood, he said he remembered the Fourth of July most vividly. He loved explosions.

Dylan Klebold, on the other hand, liked school. He was in the Challenging High Intellectual Potential Students, or CHIPS, program. His parents named him after Dylan Thomas. He made a pine wood derby car in Cub Scouts and earned merit badges. He had a great pitching arm and in Little League loved to strike out the batters. He was competitive and really hated to lose. His parents were liberals, intellectual, and loved taking the kids into the woods in Colorado. One time on a trip to a creek he fell in the mud and went berserk when his friends started to laugh at him. His mother had to take him away to calm him down. A neighbor noted that he seemed to just blow up at times.[5]

Harris and Klebold acquired their weapons from a "straw buyer" at a gun show and a friend whom they paid five hundred dollars. They constructed pipe bombs, most of which would never go off, and propane tank bombs.[6] They sawed off the barrels of the shotguns to increase the power and make them easier to conceal and loaded up their vests with ammo on the morning of April 20, 1996. They drove to the high school and attempted to set off the propane tank bombs. None exploded, however. Eric Harris carried a 12-gauge Savage Springfield 67H pump action shotgun and a Hi Point 995 Carbine. Dylan Klebold had the 9 x 19mm Intratec TEC-9 semiautomatic handgun and a 12-gauge Stevens 311D double-barreled sawed-off shotgun. They loaded their weapons by their cars, hoping the propane tank bombs still might go off. Harris saw fellow student Brooks Brown in the parking lot and told him to go home and get away from the school.[7] Locked and loaded, they walked toward the school cafeteria. They wore their long trench coats and referred to themselves as the Trench Coat Mafia. The two high-school students kept their shotguns low inside their coats.[8]

Rachel Scott was eating her lunch outside the cafeteria with her friend Richard Castaldo. Harris shouted *"Go Go"* and they raised their weapons from their trench coats. They began firing and Rachel Scott was hit in the chest and head and instantly killed. Dylan shot Castaldo in the torso and arms, hitting him eight times with the nineteen-cent Kmart bullets from the TEC-9. The gun tended to spray bullets, and the fact he was hit so many times indicates the rapidity of fire. Rachel Scott was shot four times.[9]

Harris lost his trench coat as he and Klebold approached the stairs leading to the cafeteria. He let loose with his 9mm carbine and shot Daniel Rohrbough, Sean Graves, and Lance Kirklin, who had been walking up the stairs. They at first thought Harris was holding a paintball gun until he fired shots into Danny's knee, chest, and stomach. Danny hit the concrete hard, and Lance tried to help him. But Danny was dead and Lance was shot in the chest, leg, knee, and foot. Lance blacked out and when he came to Harris was standing over him. Sean Graves was shot in the back.

Many students in the cafeteria thought the shots were part of a senior prank. The shooters fired at some other students sitting outside and wounded them before descending the stairs to the cafeteria. They stepped over the boys they had just shot. Lance Kirklin lay on the ground, pleading for help. He tugged on someone's pants leg, but Klebold sneered, "Sure I'll help you," and shot Lance in the face.[10] Harris shot and paralyzed Anne-Marie Hochhalter, who was trying to escape. The two shooters then headed toward the west entrance of the school and fired at Patti Neilson, an art teacher, who thought at first that it was either a prank or a movie. When the glass shattered in the door, she ran to the library, telling students to get under their desks. She then dialed 911.

Deputy Neil Gardner had received a call that there was a shooter in the school. At 11:22 Gardner spotted Eric Harris outside the school, and Harris fired ten shots at him. Gardner leaned over the top of his car and fired off four rounds. He didn't have his prescription glasses and his bullets didn't strike anywhere close to the shooter. Harris then fired several more rounds and disappeared into the building. The killers began moving down the hallway of the school. The police were beginning to arrive, but Harris and Klebold still had the school to themselves as the police wouldn't enter for over an hour.

Columbine was the Wild West for Harris and Klebold, or they were characters in *Doom*, as they threw pipe bombs, shot out windows, and gunned down fellow students. Stephanie Munson was shot in the ankle but managed to hobble out of the school. Science teacher Dave Sanders was spreading the alarm and had been evacuating students from the cafeteria. He moved through the school with a student, trying to get as many people out as possible. They turned into the main hallway and saw Klebold and Harris at the other end. The shooters opened fire and Anderson was hit twice in the chest. He fell as Klebold passed him and went after the student. They were hunting humans in a large mazelike building similar to every American high school. It was very much like a video game in which bad guys were popping out around every corner.

Dave Sanders dragged himself toward the science lab, where he was pulled inside by a teacher hiding with thirty students. He was bleeding heavily and one of the student put a sign in the window reading, "Bleeding to Death," so that rescuers would come to that classroom first and get Sanders out. Those in the lab applied pleasure to Sanders's wound while students called the police from the classroom with their cellphones.[11] The students and teacher used their shirts but Sanders was bleeding out fast. He would not make it, but the most depraved part of the Columbine massacre was about to begin in the library.[12]

Fifty students were hiding in the school library, which made for a contained and target-rich environment. The two shooters entered while Patti Nielson was on the phone with 911. Eric Harris's command "Get Up" was recorded on the 911 tape. Then, "All jocks stand up, we'll get the guys in the white hats." A tradition of the jocks wearing white hats had made them a target for the socially ostracized Harris and Klebold. When no one stood up, they began shooting anyway.[13]

What followed then was on the level of war-crime atrocities. Kyle Velasquez was hiding under a computer desk, and Klebold shot and killed him first. A girl was asked if she believed in God and then was shot. An African American student was taunted and called racial slurs and then murdered. The two shooters went to the window and fired at police, then returned to their duffel bags to reload and continue killing. A girl under a desk was killed with a single shot to the head. Klebold fired his shotgun under desks without looking. The recoil of the sawed off shotgun caused the gun to kick upward into his nose and blood gushed from it. A girl who was shot in the neck cried out and Harris snapped, "Quit your bitching." Harris walked around the library shooting sixteen- and seventeen-year-olds with his shotgun. He killed students instantly with shots to the head and the back while Klebold fired with his TEC-9. The carnage was surreal, and in the end the list of the dead and wounded read like battlefield horror.

Kyle Velasquez, age sixteen, died from gunshot wounds to the head and back. Patrick Ireland, age seventeen, was shot in the head and foot. Daniel Steepleton, age seventeen, was shot once in the thigh. Makai Hall, age eighteen, was shot in the knee. Steven Curnow, age fourteen, was slain by a shot to the neck. Kacey Ruegsegger, age seventeen, was wounded in the shoulder, hand, and neck. Cassie Bernall, age seventeen, had her life ended by a shotgun wound to the head. Isaiah Shoels, age eighteen, was killed by a shot to the chest. Matthew Kechter, age sixteen, was also murdered with a single shot to the chest. Lisa Kreutz, age eighteen, was wounded in the shoulder, hand, arms, and thigh. Valeen Schnurr, age eighteen, took bullets in the chest, arms, and abdomen. Mark Kintgen, age seventeen, was wounded in the head and shoulder. Lauren Townsend, age eighteen, was murdered with gunshot wounds to the head, chest, and lower body. Nicole Knowlen, age sixteen, was hit in the abdomen. John Tomlin, age sixteen, died with shots to the head and neck. Kelly Fleming, age sixteen, was hit with a shotgun blast to the back and died. Jeanna Park, age eighteen, was hit in the knee, shoulder, and foot. Daniel Mauser, age fifteen, had his life ended with single shot to the face. Jennifer Doyle, age seventeen, was hit in the hand, leg, and shoulder. Austin Eubanks, age seventeen, was wounded in the hand and knee. Corey DePooter, age seventeen, was murdered with gunshots to the chest and neck.

Less than an hour later, Eric Harris and Dylan Klebold committed suicide using one of the shotguns and the TEC-9 The police did not enter until after the shooters were dead. Police tactics would forever change after Columbine, however. Instead of waiting to enter, police in active-shooter situations would go in and pursue the shooters. Charlton Heston would lead an NRA convention a week later in Colorado and would famously hold a musket over his head, proclaiming, "From my cold dead hands."[14]

Victims' parents would be among the demonstrators protesting the NRA outside the convention and calling for gun control. The only change to come out of the Columbine shooting, though, was Kmart banning the sale of handgun ammunition in its stores, and this only happened after Michael Moore took two Columbine survivors to the Kmart headquarters and filmed the encounter for his movie *Bowling for Columbine*. Moore also visited Heston and confronted his support of the NRA in the wake of Columbine. The old actor stopped the interview and shuffled off, while Moore trailed him with a picture of a girl shot by a six-year-old who had found his stepfather's gun and brought it to school.

Metal detectors and lockdown procedures for high schools across the country would be implemented after Columbine. Lockdown drills would become part of everyday school life in America. There would be copycat murders and plots that echoed Dylan Klebold and Eric Harris's rampage.[15] The rock singer Marilyn Mansion would be blamed for influencing the two students, along with Goth culture and video games.[16] The seminal book on the shootings, *Columbine*, by Dave Cullen, would come out ten years later. The bullying of Eric Harris and Dylan Klebold would be cited and some would say that such a thing was bound to happen when students are ostracized.[17]

Harris and Klebold would be studied intensely, with psychiatrists labeling them as psychopaths in waiting without a lot of the classic symptoms of full-blown psychopaths.[18] That seemed the only diagnosis that might explain why two normal American young men would plan and carry out such cold-blooded murders. Basically, psychopaths have no empathy at all, no normal human response to the suffering of others. They have iced-over emotions that don't spark, and so one theory has it that they are forever looking for what will stimulate them.[19] Any thrill ride, any adrenaline ride that might allow them to feel something could be seen as acceptable, including killing multiple people. Because of their failure to feel anything, psychopaths don't tend to examine their motives or their actions, instead seeing themselves as superior. To the psychopath, other human beings are an oddity, and they might well ask why people feel anything? Meeting a plea for help with a shotgun blast is a perfectly normal response for a psychopath.

But of course all these psychological explanations fall apart when reliving the carnage that Eric Harris and Dylan Klebold inflicted on that day. All theories about why two young men would murder their fellow students would be discounted and there would be the implementation of security cameras and the turning of schools into locked-down institutions. Does it matter that Eric was on Zoloft and in therapy and so was Dylan? Does it matter that Dylan made a copy of Heinrich Himmler's famous speech to Nazi SS leaders in which he justified the slaughter of human beings.[20] The video tapes from the security cameras show two lanky young men strolling around the lunchroom with their weapons. On the six-month anniversary of the shooting, 450 kids would call in sick at Columbine because they were afraid it might happen again. A friend of Dylan and Eric's had said he was going to finish the job; he was arrested and held on $500,000 bond.[21]

Twenty years later, my kids would be buzzed into their kindergartens, elementary schools, and high schools and would go through drills for active shooters. The high school and elementary school principals would stand guard. There would be several real lockdowns implemented when suspicious characters entered the school. The Trench Coat Mafia would live on through the internet. Dress codes would be recommended that would prevent students from concealing weapons in bulky shirts or pants.[22] Columbine High School would require a 1.2 million dollar remodeling.[23] Murder in high schools by heavily armed intruders would become a cultural part of American life after Columbine. The shooting in Colorado would stand as the worst school shooting in American history—until the Sandy Hook Elementary school massacre. Colorado would close the gun-show loophole that allowed people to purchase guns without a background check.[24] No significant national gun-control legislation would be passed in Congress because of the Columbine school shooting.[25]

The sad legacy of Columbine lives on to this day. On May 18, 2018, Dimitrios Pagourtzis walked into Santa Fe High School in a small Texas city with a sawed-off shotgun concealed under his trench coat and murdered ten people and wounded thirteen others. It was a violation of the school dress code that had forbade trench coats ever since Columbine.[26]

CHAPTER 24

ESCAPE FROM FLL

9:00 p.m.

Getting out of the airport consumes us. Leaving means safety. Leaving means getting away from the possibility of a shooter taking a random shot. As long as we are in the airport there is a possibility of danger. The news trucks have not budged. The newspeople still look amazingly fresh and beautiful. There is a story lurking out there somewhere and no one wants to miss it. We have seen the buses coming to take everyone out and then there are rumors that we have to get to a disembarkation point to catch the buses.

A SWAT team officer points down the road. "You have to get down to the end of the airport to catch the buses," he says, holding his submachine gun with one hand and pointing with the other. I look at our luggage. We have seven bags and five people. I will carry two and Clay can carry two. I turn to Kitty.

"What do you think?"

We hear the rumble of diesel engines as the buses started to roll by. They come one after another and show no signs of slowing down. It is the first glimmer of hope that we might get out of the airport. Kitty's clothes are black with grime and her hair is stringy and frizzed from the humidity. We all look like we have been through a war.

"I say let's go," she says, watching the buses.

"You have to walk down on that side to catch the buses," the SWAT officer continues, pointing to a narrow walkway on the far side of the street.

"Thank you," I shout, getting everyone situated with a suitcase. For some reason, I have this vision of *Dr. Zhivago*, the David Lean film, in which Zhivago and his wife and child are forced to leave Moscow to get away from the Bolsheviks who are coming to arrest him. We are refugees and we join a long line of people walking on the narrow walkway as buses hurtle past. The oppressive heat comes back and I realize we have had hardly any water and no food for over seven hours. Dehydration is a real issue.

"Everyone stay to the inside of the sidewalk," I yell back, watching the dangerously close buses. It is even hotter and the air is stiller, if that was possible. We have the grim determination of people who just want to reach a place where a shower and a bed will be a reality. So we begin our trek. Fort Lauderdale–Hollywood International Airport is very large and I have no idea where we are supposed to end up to catch the buses. But for the first time we are going somewhere with a purpose instead of waiting and hiding from unseen shooters. The police cars and ambulances roll past and I wonder about the people shot in Terminal 2. Are they still there? Police procedure doesn't allow expired victims to be moved until all evidence is gathered. This could go up to twenty-four hours if lots of victims are involved. The stories of loved ones not getting the news about their relatives for many hours is legend.

But we are leaving. All we have to do is reach a destination point and the buses will take us out of the airport and this part of the nightmare will end. Our refugee line snakes all the way back to Terminal 1. We are all following each other blindly. We covet the return to normal life. We have not become victims. By the twists of fate no bullet has found my family. We have acted out of self-preservation and whoever was behind the shots in Terminal 1 has not made himself known to us. Esteban Santiago had not checked his baggage through to Terminal 1. But he could have. He could have taken a United Flight and picked up his bags and Clay could have been down there looking for food or I could have been looking for Clay, and once you cross paths with the terminal velocity of a killer then you have rolled the dice, you have rolled badly, and your odds skyrocket. You are no longer one in eleven thousand. You are no longer even one in three hundred. You are now one in ten or however many people are in the area. You have become that terribly unlucky person people see on the news and you might become a gruesome statistic, never knowing what hit you.

Middle-class people going through their lives never see the lightning strike. They never feel the heart attack or the train that was supposed to not be there or the freak steel beam that falls from a building. Many people in the World Trade Center died thinking it was just another day. Their cars were parked in the commuter lots and left by the trains. They didn't know they would die and they suddenly become one with the person who falls in a retention pond on a golf course or the man who is electrocuted by urinating on the third rail of an elevated train with the high voltage following the stream back.

When it happens you are the conduit for the pernicious current that runs through the universe and you are the man lighting the stove, not putting on his seatbelt, not seeing the baseball at the game that hits him in the temple. Odds mean nothing when you break them. Your odds have broken down. You *did* get struck by lightning. You *did* get the incurable disease. You *were* in the baggage claim area of the airport when the shooter opened up. You *did* get shot. You *are* dead. Once you find yourself near a shooter you play the odds with those around you. Some will die. You just don't want it to be you or your family. You are the soldier with the kill or be killed attitude. It will be either him or me, and it's not going to be me. You wish others well but you have to survive and others around you are bent on the same thing. Darwinism kicks in in its rawest form. Though there are others who push back against this like the man who threw himself over the young mother and whispered, "I will protect you," when Santiago began shooting.[1] He was a hero and those people give humans a God-like dimension. But most of us just want to live and will do anything to stay in the light.

People's lives will be altered by Esteban Santiago and by the second shooter, whose shots many believed they heard. You cannot control what is happening but you can control the outcome. You want the victim to be anyone but you. That is your thought when you run from the bullets: anyone but you because the statistics no longer matter. You have crossed the Rubicon and you are dangerously close to that statistic and you think your life will be changed forever even as you go through it.

I look over and there is that gutted white 757 behind a high, razor-tipped fence. The white soot-stained fuselage faintly glows in the night and it is a testament to all the things that can go wrong. Here is this multimillion-dollar piece of state-of-the-art technology and now it is a fire-blackened carcass parked behind an airplane hangar. It's just another piece of junk that didn't work out. Millions of hours of human design, engineering, effort, history, going all the way back to the Wright brothers went into that plane and yet it caught fire and burned and became an inert collection of steel and technology that just didn't work out. We are flawed and so are our extensions. We may be humane beings, but we have a terrible murderous side that shows itself in the one-in-a-million events that leave our most thought-out elevated designs junked on the side of the road. The randomness of the universe has its due.

I am thinking about all of this as another armed SWAT officer in full camouflage approaches with an arm up. There is an army of SWAT men and they are blocking the forward motion of our refugee caravan. "You can't go this way; you have to go back," he says, pointing from where we had come. I come to a stop and wipe my brow and stare at him.

"But we were told the buses are loading up there," I protest, pointing down the road.

He shakes his head with his hand firmly on his rifle. I am wondering when I will stop talking to men with enough firepower to go fight in Afghanistan. He shakes his head again. "I don't know anything about that," he says. "You have to go back the way you came."

I look at Kitty and my daughters. Everyone is hot, tired, dehydrated. We have no water and nowhere to get any. I worry about Callie but for now she seems to be doing alright. I look at Kitty.

"We have to go back."

Already people are turning around. Kitty is much more practical than I am. She has already turned around while I foolishly think I can change the armed man's mind.

"Let's go," she says, leading the kids.

Now I am in the back of our wagon train as we head back to Terminal 2. It does not feel good to think about this. Terminal 2 and Terminal 1 are forever linked with danger, if not death. And they are the last place we want to be but we are headed straight back into the abyss. I start thinking about *Casablanca* again and the struggle of Rick to help Victor Laszlo, and Ilsa escape before the Nazis get them. They are trying to get to America where they will be safe. Of course we are already in America and even presidents aren't safe. It would take a president getting shot to get a piece of gun-control legislation passed.

CHAPTER 25

TAXI DRIVER

1981

John Hinckley was obsessed with Jodie Foster. He followed her everywhere and had seen the movie *Taxi Driver* fifteen times. He saw himself as the taxi driver from the movie, played by Robert De Niro—the building volcano who would one day blow sensationally. Travis Bickle, the character, would try to protect the twelve-year-old prostitute played by Jodie Foster and then try to assassinate a US senator who was running for president.

Hinckley wanted to impress Jodie Foster. He enrolled in a writing course at Yale University to be near her, and he followed her around for years. He wrote her letters and called her but she was not interested. Finally, Hinckley decided that if he achieved fame equal to Foster's she would be attracted to him. He began to follow President Jimmy Carter around, wanting to follow in Travis Bickle's footsteps. He was arrested for firearms possession at the Nashville airport where Carter was supposed to stop. The Secret Service and FBI both missed the red flags, though, and Hinckley was released. A new president was elected, giving Hinckley a new target. He quit going to the psychiatrist his parents had found to help their troubled son, and started trailing President Ronald Reagan.[1]

On March 29, 1981, Hinckley took a bus to Washington and checked into the Park Central Hotel. The next day he wrote a final letter to Foster thinking that this would be the end and that he would die in the assassination attempt. He told her that he would give up his idea of shooting Reagan if she would have him.[2] He didn't mail the letter, though, and instead left for the Washington Hilton Hotel where Reagan was giving a speech. The hotel was considered safe, as it had an enclosed passageway for the president to use and there was only about thirty feet from the entrance of the hotel to the limousine, so Reagan didn't wear his bullet-proof vest.[3]

John Hinckley waited in a crowd outside the hotel, behind a rope line. The people were thought to have been screened but it was found later that they had not.[4] In his mind, this would be his moment to impress Foster and live in infamy, just like Travis Bickle. The president emerged at 2:27 p.m. and walked toward his limousine, passing right in front of him. Hinckley raised his Rohm RG 14.22 revolver and fired six times in 1.7 seconds, missing the president with all except for his last shot, which ricocheted and caught Reagan in the left side of his rib cage. White House press secretary James Brady was hit in the forehead with the first of the exploding bullets. The next bullet struck police officer Thomas Delahanty and punctured the back of his neck as he tried to protect Reagan. Hinckley shot past Reagan with his third shot and smashed a window across the street. Special Agent Jerry Parr had shoved Reagan into the limousine by this point, and Secret Service agent Tim McCarthy stepped into the line of fire to protect the president. McCarthy was struck in the abdomen with the fourth bullet. The fifth bullet lodged in the bulletproof glass of the armored limousine's open door. The sixth bullet glanced off the armored car and struck the president under his left arm, glancing off a rib and stopping in his lung, only one inch from his heart.[5]

Hinckley was quickly tackled by Secret Service agents, who protected him from the bystanders who had grabbed him and wanted to tear him apart. One agent wielded an Uzi submachine gun to deter mob violence, and Hinckley was hustled off. Authorities discovered that his gun had been purchased at a Dallas pawn shop and loaded with six Devastator bullets, which had explosive charges inside the lead. The only one that exploded, however, was the bullet that hit James Brady. Doctors wore bulletproof vests while removing the others from victims. As he was being arrested, Hinckley asked the officers if the Academy Awards would be postponed because of the shooting.[6]

Ronald Reagan survived, as did the other men who were injured in the attack, but press secretary Brady was permanently disabled and used a wheelchair for the rest of his life. He remained press secretary in name only for the remainder of the Reagan administration. Brady and his wife became advocates for gun control after the shooting.[7] John Lennon's death at the hands of Mark David Chapman in 1980 had sparked a debate on gun control that picked up steam after the assassination attempt on Reagan.[8] The Brady Bill, the Brady Handgun Violence Prevention Act, was passed into law on November 30, 1993.[9] For the first time, background checks would be required when a gun was purchased from a federally licensed dealer or manufacturer unless there was an exception—a "private sale," which constitutes an online sale or someone selling their gun to another individual. If a gun was given to someone else then it must be checked with the National Instant Background Check System (NICS).[10]

A series of restrictions in the act further tightened up gun ownership. People could no longer buy a gun if they had been convicted of a crime or were a fugitive from justice or had been "adjudicated as a mental defective"[11] (a legal term meaning a person has been determined to be "a danger to himself or to others" or else "lacks the mental capacity to . . . manage his own affairs"[12]) or committed to a mental institution. Also excluded from gun ownership are those who have been discharged from the armed forces with a dishonorable discharge, those who have renounced their United States citizenship, have a restraining order on them, or have been convicted of any type of domestic violence.

The Brady Bill was the most comprehensive gun legislation of the twentieth century. The NRA dug in to defeat the bill, taking it all the way to the Supreme Court, where concessions were given so as not to force state and local authorities to run the NICS background check (although most still do), as well as to abandon the five-day waiting period in exchange for an instant background check. By 2016 the number of background checks that had been completed under the Brady Bill reached 202 million, with 1.2 million firearm purchases blocked.[13] The most common blocked purchases were felons who had attempted to buy guns and failed the check.

When John Hinckley went to trial for his attempt to assassinate President Ronald Reagan, he was found not guilty by reason of insanity. His lawyer claimed he suffered from narcissistic personality disorder. He was released in 2016 from an institution for the criminally insane. His lawyer had petitioned for his release claiming that his mental illness is in remission.[14]

The Brady Bill is the only piece of major gun legislation that the National Rifle Association failed to defeat. It is one of the few times a shooting in the United States has translated into gun-control legislation. Such is the power of the president.

CHAPTER 26
THE WARRIORS
10:00 p.m.

I watch lots of films. Kitty goes to bed and I stay up for the quiet time and get sucked into *Double Indemnity*, *A Bridge Too Far*, *Reservoir Dogs*, any Coen brothers film, and old films from the seventies, eighties, or nineties. *The Warriors* is a film I have seen many times and rewatch whenever it pops up on cable. The premise is simple: a gang gets caught on the wrong side of town in hostile gang territory and they have to cross New York in one night to escape. By dawn they have been through hell but they make it to their side and the final shot is of them by the harbor with the Statue of Liberty in the distance.

We are the warriors now. We have been threatened with gunfire like the warriors. We have been chased like the warriors by unseen assailants. We are hungry and thirsty and sweat grimed, with our hair mussed and arms slicked. The warriors are making their way through an urban jungle and so are we, with our suitcases, along the side of the road, with cars and buses roaring past leaving us breathing diesel exhaust. The warriors were in constant danger right up to the end and so are we. Terminal 2 and Terminal 1 loom in the distance as we again pass the burned out hulk of modern aviation, reminding us that leaving the ground is no easy feat. The warriors passed the burned out cars and the burned out people of their world, too, and looked for the light on the other side of New York. We look for the light somewhere out there beyond the confines of the razor-topped fences of the Fort Lauderdale–Hollywood International Airport. We have been dragging our suitcases for over an hour now, along with thousands of other people. We are all warriors now.

The buses, police cars, armored SWAT vehicles, and ambulances whoosh by. I have lost all track of time and I feel I cannot remember ever not being soaked with perspiration. I think it is around ten o'clock at night. Kitty and Clay and the kids are behind me and no one is talking; we are just trying to get wherever we are going. It turns out that the SWAT guy had it all wrong. We are supposed to now just find a bus, any bus to get on. The buses have finally stopped and are parked in a long diesel-fuming line of blue smoke and hissing airbrakes.

"Let's cross," I shout, and we go across the access road to the buses now lined up for departure.

"What are we doing?" Kitty shouts.

"Trying to find a bus," I shout back.

But so is everyone else and the thought that there are more people than buses is evident in the people running from bus to bus. The worst thought now is not that you can't get out but that you might be left behind. There is still the possibility that any moment the shooter will emerge and start cutting people down. We are well-schooled in terrorism and we have seen the coordinated attacks on cities in France and England and the thought that this was a coordinated terrorist attack is still out there. So it is time to escape, time for the warriors to break into the light in view of the Statue of Liberty.

We cut between two buses and go to the first one. The driver shakes his head. "Can't get on this bus. It's full," he says, hooking a thumb behind him. "Go on back and see if you can find one with some room." Now we are walking back toward Terminal 2 and every bus is filled to capacity. People are in the aisles, standing in the door. People are trying to squeeze on while other people tell them the bus is too full and to go find another. This is like the evacuation of Vietnam or any movie where everyone is trying to escape but transportation is limited and they know some people will not get out. We keep walking and walking. Some buses are empty but the doors are closed and when I bang on the door the drivers shake their heads and point behind them.

"Are all the buses full?" Kitty asks behind me.

"Hope not," I shout back.

I can smell myself, the rank odor of someone who has been perspiring way too long. Everyone is going from bus to bus and banging on doors. The drivers just shrug and motion behind them.

"Dad, are we going to be able to get on a bus?"

I look back at Careen, who is struggling with one of our carry-ons.

"Absolutely," I say, with more confidence than I am feeling.

"Yeah, Dad. I mean, what the fuck? Are all the buses taken?" Clay grumbles, saying exactly what I want to say.

"No. We will find one," I say, feeling like we are on another family outing where I am promising a gas station is coming where everyone can use the bathroom and get something to drink or eat. It is surreal the way family life just continues under any situation. I am sure families in war feel this same way.

"We are never going to get out," Careen proclaims, in twelve-year-old bravado, voicing our secret fear.

"Shut up, Careen. Of course we will," Clay says, shooting her a dark look.

"I just don't want to get shot at again," she says, shocking all of us with her honesty.

"No one is going to get shot at again," I say crossly, hearing myself as if someone else is speaking.

We come to another bus. It has Reserved written on its overhead sign and the interior is semi-dark. The driver is sitting down and I am about to bang on the doors when they fold open. The young black driver stares at me as my family comes to a stop in front of him. We are tired, dirty, sweaty, exhausted, hungry, and thirsty, our clothes are soot streaked, and we are breathing heavily from our journey around the airport. The driver takes all this in as I croak out, "Can we . . . . can we get on your bus?"

He opens his hand and gestures to the cool nirvana of air conditioned comfort. "Well, come on if you are going to get aboard."

I feel the first ray of hope that there is an end to this day and that it won't end in disaster. But I am not sure I am hearing correctly.

"We can board?"

He frowns. "Hell yes . . . ain't nobody on the bus right now."

I look at the kids and nod.

"Let's go!"

We carry our clumsy suitcases into the air conditioning, which feels like cool water after the close humid air. The bus driver and I take the suitcases from the girls and put them to the side and then we go all the way to the back and commandeer the rear seats and put our remaining suitcases in front of us. People stream in, and in minutes the bus is full to capacity with people standing in the aisle. I look at Kitty and see she is thinking the same thing. We are close to getting out of the Fort Lauderdale airport and we will not become a statistic. We will not end up as another tragedy that people will talk about for years. We were in the wrong place at the wrong time but the gods or whoever did not take their pound of flesh, and, like the warriors, we are almost there.

My phone rings and I pick it up. It is almost out of power.

"Is this William Hazelgrove?"

I recognize the voice from a television station that had called me earlier.

"Yes."

"Can I ask you a few questions?"

I hesitate, feeling the strange sensation of being cold in the air conditioning.

"Sure."

"Where are you?"

"I am in a bus. We are getting ready to leave."

"How do you feel?"

I pause and look out the window and see Terminal 2 with the police still guarding the doors. I stare at the media trucks waiting for the next catastrophe, and I see the grounded airplanes out on the tarmac and the platoons of camouflaged men still searching for the elusive shooter. I look at my children—dirty, sweaty, exhausted. I wipe my eyes.

"Alive," I say.

CHAPTER 27

THE WORST

Sandy Hook

2012

The rich or the upper middle class usually escapes. They have enough money to buy the nice homes with the big yards in the nice areas where crime and lone nuts do not reside. Mass shootings fall traditionally on those in the lower end of the middle class. There is an economic component to mass shootings. Even the first shooting in 1949 was an assault against a thrifty middle class of shopkeepers, tailors, and barbers. The McDonald's shooting and those at Columbine, concerts, and theaters all hit middle-class people where they and their kids go. But those with a bit more money seemed to be able to duck most of the carnage. That is until Sandy Hook, when upper-middle-class professionals were assaulted by a brutal attack on their children in the last sanctuary of society: an elementary school.

There are shootings that have left more people dead. There are shootings where horrific moments are replayed and replayed on the internet or through witnesses recalling what happened. Sandy Hook is not the worst American shooting in terms of numbers or grotesque moments. Sandy Hook is the worst because of the depravity of murdering twenty first-grade children between the ages of six and seven.[1] The shooting was the low point for American society because, no matter how you slice it, what happened was the outgrowth of the cancer that infects our culture. This tragedy is almost indefinable.

I remember hearing of Sandy Hook. I could not get it out of my head. Nobody could. It was December 14, 2012, and Christmas was coming. I was up in my office writing when news of the shooting reached the internet. I began reading and even as I was reading I hoped Adam Lanza had restricted his shooting to adults. It is terrible to think we rate human beings this way, but Careen was seven and in first grade at the time, and this one hit close to home.

Parents all over America viscerally felt pain when they learned that Adam Lanza had gone to Sandy Hook Elementary School and targeted children. It was impossible to believe. I wrote about it on my blog extensively and then I stopped because nothing I could write would make any difference. What had happened had no parallel. We had no measure for this one and we were all left with one central question: who or what would do such a thing? Because a creature that would kill like this raised the question: Is such a creature even a human being?

Adam Lanza washed his hands continually. He couldn't stop washing his hands. He changed his socks twenty times a day. His mother was constantly doing laundry. He blacked out the windows of his basement and wouldn't talk to anyone, and he communicated through email with his mother who was still in the house. His food had to be arranged strategically on his plate or he wouldn't eat it. He was taken out of school at sixteen and homeschooled. He would not touch a door knob and went through boxes of tissues every day.[2]

Lanza was diagnosed with Asperger's syndrome and placed on antidepressants, but his mother took him off them because of adverse reactions.[3] He was diagnosed with sensory integration disorder and then obsessive-compulsive disorder. His father suspected he had schizophrenia. He was obsessed with mass shootings. He watched videos of the Columbine shooting over and over. He kept a large chart on a four-by-seven piece of cardboard where he ranked American shootings. He was antisocial and anorexic, and at six feet he weighed one hundred and twelve pounds. He played video games nonstop and loved *Super Mario Brothers*. His mother,

THE WORST: SANDY HOOK

Nancy, was a gun enthusiast who had over a dozen firearms in the house. She was divorced, lived comfortably off of alimony, and took her son to the local shooting range where she put high-powered automatic weapons in his hands. Adam Lanza destroyed the targets at the range with a Bushmaster XM15-E2S rifle designed to kill massive numbers of humans.[4]

On the morning of December 14, 2012, after destroying the hard drive on his computer, Lanza loaded a Savage Mark II bolt-action .22-caliber rifle and went to his mother's bedroom, where he shot her four times in the head while she slept. He then took her car and drove toward Sandy Hook Elementary School, located in Fairfield County, Connecticut. There were 456 children in the school. Protocol was to lock the doors after 9:30 a.m. Adam Lanza arrived at 9:35 a.m., parked in the lot, and, wearing a black shirt and pants, sunglasses and yellow ear plugs from the range, along with an army-green vest stuffed with extra magazines for the Bushman XM15-E2S rifle, he blasted his way through the locked glass door. The shots could be heard over the intercom during the morning announcements.[5]

Principal Dawn Hochsprung and teachers Mary Sherlach and Natalie Hammond went into the hall when they heard the first shots. The principal screamed out, "Shooter, Stay put!" She then lunged toward the shooter, and it would later be determined the shots ripping across her chest showed she lunged to put her body in front of her students and died trying to save her children. Lanza fired a burst from his XM15, killing the principal and Mary Sherlach and wounding Natalie Hammond. Hammond was able to crawl into a conference room and hide after Lanza left the hallway. Lanza went into the main office and, seeing no one, left. Sally Cox, hiding under the desk, was close enough to see Lanza's boots.[6] A substitute teacher in the first grade looked up as Adam Lanza entered with his automatic weapon.

Lauren Rousseau had herded her students into the back of the room toward the bathroom. Behavioral therapist Rachel D'Avino was in the room when Lanza walked in and began firing. Fifteen children were murdered there, along with their teacher and the therapist. Many of the victims were shot multiple times.

Bullets from assault weapons travel twice as fast as regular bullets. They essentially destroy everything in their path and inside the human body they ricochet around, pulverizing bones and shredding organs. Later, a doctor in the documentary *Newtown* would attest that the bullets had exploded inside the small bodies; he would not describe the carnage further. Many of the dead students and teachers were found in the bathroom where they were hiding. A single six-year-old survived by playing dead in a cupboard and later told her mother that all her friends had died.[7]

After shooting everyone, Lanza left and headed to another first-grade classroom, reloading as he went. He entered Victoria Leigh Soto's classroom as she was moving to lock the door. First-grader Jesse Lewis yelled for his classmates to run, and Lanza shot and killed him. At that point, Lanza's gun momentarily jammed and several of the students were able to run to safety. Victoria Soto tried to shield her students with her body, but Lanza shot her dead and then continued firing at the children. Anne Marie Murphy, a teacher's aide, was killed as she covered a little boy's body with her own; the boy was also shot and killed.

The children would be left in place until late in the night during the subsequent investigation. All crime scene photos would be sealed. An officer on camera a year later would speak like a zombie when asked what it looked like when he entered the classroom.[8]

When he left Victoria Soto's classroom, Lanza went into the hallway and passed a classroom with black construction paper over the window on the door; inside, Kaitlin Roig was hiding with her students. School librarians hid children in a storage space and barricaded it with a filing cabinet. A music teacher hid her students in a small storage closet, staying silent when Lanza pounded on the door and demanded entrance. He moved on and his final shot rang out at 9:40 a.m. This was when Lanza shot himself in the head with his Glock.[9]

By the time the police entered it was all over. Eight boys and twelve girls were dead, all between the ages of six and seven. Six women lay dead as well. Lanza fired over one hundred rounds, not even emptying his clips before reloading. His car held more ammunition. An NRA certificate was found at his home, along with samurai swords, 1,400 rounds of ammunition, a .45 Henry rifle, .30 Enfield rifle, and a .22 Marlin rifle.[10]

Speaking at a press conference about the shooting, President Barack Obama became emotional and vowed to make gun control a central issue of his administration.[11] Immediately, the debate over universal background checks and banning assault weapons heated up. Limiting magazines to ten rounds was a major concern, since Adam Lanza had been able to fire 154 times in the space of only five minutes, killing twenty-six people with his XM 15 Bushmaster.[12] The NRA went into hiding immediately after Sandy Hook, and its president, Wayne La Pierre, was not to be seen until December 21, when he held a news conference and proposed armed guards for all schools. He said the shooting could have been avoided if Sandy Hook had not been a gun-free zone. He was surrounded by armed men as he spoke.[13]

The Sandy Hook School was razed in 2013, and Adam Lanza's home was demolished two years after that. A new school was constructed with the help of a fifty-million-dollar state grant. The shooting was so horrific to the community of Newtown that obliteration was preferable to any possible association of the tragedy with a building. Nine families who lost children sued the manufacturers of the Bushmaster AR-15.[14] The families also sued the estate of Nancy Lanza for not properly securing her firearms since she knew that her son had mental health problems. They were eventually awarded 1.5 million.[15]

Legislation to enact the assault weapons ban of 2013 and an amendment to expand background checks on guns were defeated in the US Senate on April 17, 2013. Not one law was passed to prevent a shooting like that which occurred at Sandy Hook from happening again. Families of the children who were murdered have been harassed by proponents of the Second Amendment ever since. They have received death threats, and one person was sent to jail for making such threats. A documentary on Sandy Hook aired in 2016 and included interviews with the parents of children who died, as well as police, teachers, doctors, and paramedics who had been at the scene. Most people cried on camera when talking about that day four years earlier. Some people couldn't talk at all.[16]

The most horrific scene of the documentary described the fire station. The parents waited in a fire station house for news of their children. They had been separated into two groups. While one group of parents was reunited with their children, the other group met with the governor, who told them that their children had been killed. People screamed. Some fell on the floor. People talking about the firehouse in the documentary said it was the worst moment of their lives.[17]

Many of the parents of the children who died were well-educated professionals. A number of them would later go to Washington to try to bring about change and outlaw AR-15s.[18]

Nothing happened.

CHAPTER 28

PORT EVERGLADES

11:00 p.m.

We have never been part of a large migration of people. We have never been in a flood, a hurricane, fire, war, famine, or any of the events necessary to get people fleeing from one area to another. We will find out later that the American Red Cross is there, providing food and water for the evacuating people. We do not see them. All we see are buses behind and in front and we don't care who else is there. We are leaving.

The buses start out of the airport following one another. People are standing in front of us and hanging onto the overhead railings. It is hard to see out the windows. We are leaving the Fort Lauderdale–Hollywood Airport twelve hours after we arrived. People look at each other like prisoners who have made it outside of the compound walls. No one says anything. We are simply leaving the airport behind, along with all the danger and carnage that exists there.

I look out the windows several times at the flashing strobes of police lights. It takes me a few minutes to realize that the buses are all being escorted by police cars. I lean over farther for a better view and see an endless line of swirling blue lights running along both sides of the bus, ahead of us and behind us. We are a great migration of ten thousand people, headed for an unknown destination. Our caravan of buses must be considered vulnerable to terrorists because why else would they escort all these buses? But the police are all around us and I realize that they are responsible for getting these people out of the airport and safely to another destination. We have just begun to think about what we will do and where we will stay. Getting out had consumed us and now that we are going somewhere we have to think about lodging and food and everything else associated with normal life. Normal life has been on hold while we struggle for survival. We had left the world for a while and now we are returning. Someone says that we are heading back to the cruise ships, and that would mean Port Everglades.

At the beginning of the twentieth century, Florida was in need of a deep water port, and in 1911 the Florida Board of Trade passed a resolution calling for just that.[1] The port was to be used for shipping produce north and west. Lake Mabel was a part of the Florida East Coast Canal System, and developers saw it as a good place to locate the new port. The problem with Lake Mabel was that it was too shallow and had to be dredged to make it possible for the big ships to enter. A cut was to be blasted out, connecting the lake to the Atlantic Ocean when President Calvin Coolidge pressed a button on February 28, 1928. The initial button push did nothing, but the engineers were able to try again and blast away the sand between Lake Mabel and the Atlantic, to the enthusiasm of the watching crowd. Two years later the name Bay Mabel Harbor was changed to Port Everglades.[2]

The port can handle fifteen cruise ships in a day, with thousands of passengers passing through in a single day.[3] This is the port we left this morning and are now returning to. I can already see one of the big cruise ships in the distance. We have heard that the ships have had to delay their departures because so many cruise passengers have been stranded at the airport. It is hard to believe that we had been on one of these monster ships not twelve hours ago. Time has collapsed in on itself and we have no sense of time passing; our vacation belongs to a different life, one that existed before Esteban Santiago opened fire.

Clay has already groused that people won't ask him about his vacation when he returns to work but about the shooting. My daughters will experience the same at their schools. We have all stumbled into a dim shadow of fame from landing near the media trucks, and in a sense the entire cruise has been erased. I remember a fight Kitty and I had gotten into the night before and now I can't remember what it was about; it just doesn't seem to matter now. We exist in the here and now moment and we still have to be concerned with survival. Right now that means a hotel.

We enter the port area, a football-field-sized expanse with the cruise ships humming and puffing smoke from their diesel-electric motors. The orange lighting of the ships cuts shapes out of the darkness, giving a bizarre scene an even more surreal quality. Are we rewinding time back to this morning when this whole experience began? Can we just ignore the last twelve hours and continue on with our lives?

"Quality Inn," Kitty says, getting off her phone as we pull into the giant open space of the port.

I nod. We have a destination. The buses are unloading and heading back to the airport to pick up more people. The crowd in front of the port and under the giant ships makes me think of people released from a stadium. Everyone is flowing toward the ships. We grab our suitcases as the bus groans to a halt and we disembark into the warm sea air. The ocean is beyond the ships, and lights dot the sea with buoys blinking their red eyes. We have forgotten for a time about the ocean, the beaches, the world. Life has gone on while we, along with ten thousand others, took a detour.

People move toward the ships. I don't know if they are all going on cruises or if people are just going toward the edge of the port. But then I realize that people are swarming toward the cars and taxis that are pulling in. There is a fleet of Uber cars, and I realize then that if we don't grab one now we will never get out. "I'm going ahead to get a car," I shout at Kitty, leaving her the suitcase.

She stares at me.

"How can you do that? We didn't call one!"

I look around at the sea of people under the orange klieg-light glare of the port and realize that while we have escaped the airport we have not escaped Florida. Essentially we are still in limbo, with no real way to get home. All flights have been canceled and the rumor is that they will not even start scheduling flights until Monday. It is still every man for himself.

"If we don't get a car now we will never get one with all these people," I shout back.

Kitty has already been trying to get an Uber but I know there was no way. Thousands of people are trying to do the same thing. I know I have to act quickly if we want to leave the port and get to a hotel. The port, while set up to handle lots of people, has never before had an entire airport evacuated to it at once. I run ahead of the crowd and see a single dark Lexus. The man is looking into the crowd and I know someone had called him.

"HEY!" I wave at him. The Indian driver looks through his window.

"Mr. Patton?"

I nod and wave my arms.

"Yes . . . Yes . . . I am Mr. Patton."

He puts his car in park and gets out. He is well-dressed in business casual and has a small mustache. He moves efficiently, popping open his trunk, smiling widely.

"It is good to see you Mr. Patton. I am your Uber driver."

"My family is coming," I tell him, breathlessly.

"Oh very good. I will keep the trunk open, Mr. Patton."

"Good. We have lots of luggage."

He smiles. "No problem."

And then the policewoman comes from nowhere. She is large, scowling, wearing the bright orange vest of traffic cops. Her face is red and shiny and, like everyone else, she is overwhelmed at the scope of the operation.

"You can't stop here," she shouts.

I look around. I am not sure where *here* is, but the policewoman is red-faced and pissed.

She points away from the ships and yells at the Uber driver. "You have got to move this car . . . NOW!"

"My family is coming," I shout back, not seeing my family.

I turn to the Uber driver. "Wait here."

"Very good, Mr. Patton," he says, looking nervously at the policewoman.

And then I take off back toward the buses, looking for Kitty and Clay and my daughters. I see more and more people running toward me as the endless line of buses and police cars keep pulling up. This is it. We either get this car or we will be stuck in Port Everglades for a very long time. I see Kitty and wave my arms frantically.

"Come on! . . . I have a car . . . LET'S GO!"

I grab two suitcases and we all begin to run. I can see the policewoman screaming at the Uber driver again, who is looking for Mr. Patton. Mr. Patton is running up with his wife and kids. The driver smiles and waves.

"Here Mr. Patton! Here!"

Kitty looks at me. "Mr. Patton?"

I wave her off as we put most of our luggage in the trunk and the rest in the backseat, and then we all cram into the Lexus. The Uber driver starts navigating our way out and I see cars lined up all the way out of the port, hopelessly snarled in a traffic jam. The soft hum of the air-conditioning and the light jazz inside the car seems absurd.

"So you going to the Holiday Inn, Mr. Patton?"

I turn.

"Ah. No . . . actually the Quality Inn," I explain.

The Uber driver frowns, "That is strange. It says Holiday Inn."

I am sitting up front with him and figure it is now or never.

"Look we were in that shooting in the airport. We need to get to a hotel and get some food and water and take a shower. Mr. Patton couldn't make it but I will pay you cash to take me to the Quality Inn."

The Uber driver stares at me.

"Are you saying, then, you are not Mr. Patton?"

I shake my head.

"No. I am not Mr. Patton. I am Mr. Hazelgrove, who will pay cash."

The Indian driver takes a deep breath as his phone buzzes. He looks at it and shakes his head.

"It is Mr. Patton," he says with great sorrow.

"Don't worry about Mr. Patton. I will pay you twice what the fare is."

He breathes heavily.

"Mr. Patton will not be very happy about this," he says.

I lean back into the leather seat. "Mr. Patton will find another ride," I murmur, as we leave the port and enter the world again.

CHAPTER 29

QUALITY INN

11:30 p.m.

The Quality Inn is by a Burger King about three miles from the airport, in an industrial area. The lobby is full of other refugees from FLL, and we are lucky to have gotten a room. Kitty had called from the airport and secured one of the last rooms. She also called United, who gave us the bad news that they will not be able to get us out until Monday morning. That has pushed us to call a series of rental car agencies, all of which tell us they have no cars left. Everyone is trying to find a way home and we resign ourselves to the fact we won't be leaving until Monday morning at the earliest.

Right now we just want to get to our room and get something to eat. The pool area is strangely bucolic under the moonlight, which casts shadows across the umbrellas and gleams in the water. The Quality Inn is an oasis in a sea of transportation companies that cluster around airports. The orange-lit landscape outside the gates of the hotel is the American otherworld of industry and squalor. But the Quality Inn is set up a like a series of bungalows surrounding the pool area and has a bar with chairs and umbrellas set up near the breakfast room just off the lobby. People are already sitting at tables in the shadowy darkness, their luggage piled up around them. Everyone is discussing their options, which center on how to get out of Florida. The focus has gone from trying to escape the airport to trying to escape Florida. The girls are eyeing the pool that seems so out of line with the hell we have left at the airport and the mob scene at Port Everglades.

We pass through the pool area and walk down a long portico facing the parking lot. Our room is at the end and has two double beds with a television between them. We will be cramped but we are happy to be in our own space again. After being in an airport for almost twelve hours and running from a shooter and then living with the knowledge a shooter might come back, this is paradise. The girls immediately turn on the television.

"Dad, it's you!" Careen shouts.

I looks at the television and see a slightly bloated, middle-aged man wearing a Fort Lauderdale hat and a black Brooklyn T-shirt and sporting a backpack. He is sweating and speaks with a slight lisp and looks like his mouth is always full. I have been told I mumble and this man is mumbling. The words under him read, "Witness to Shooting." He is talking about running from shots in Terminal 1 when the journalist stops him.

"But there were no shots in Terminal 1."

The man wipes his brow. He is sweating like a stuck pig.

"Yes, there were. Right by the United Terminal. We were there. We ran from those shots. Everybody ran from those shots."

Then the man is suddenly gone, and I'm not sure I would believe him either. Then there is Callie telling someone that she ran from the bullets. She is sitting on the ground by the cement pole and looks much better than I do. Television loves youth and I notice it doesn't make her look bloated and flushed and she is not shiny from perspiration.

"It's you, Callie," Careen squeals.

Callie stares at herself on national television. You do not think you will become part of a news cycle until you do. And I marvel at how television makes everything magical. There is none of the squalor, the diesel fumes, the dirty clothes, the sweat, the stress, the grime, the feeling of impending doom. There is just a beautiful news anchor interviewing people talking logically about what happened to them. In this way television tells a lie. The police say there was one shooter and this is what is broadcast to the world. No one asks why Terminal 1 was evacuated with people running for their lives. That is not the hook. The hook is really . . . death.

Death is what people watch for; someone else's death, of course. Someone else has gone to the great beyond unexpectedly and we find this fascinating. What did they find? What were their thoughts at the last second? Did they have thoughts? Did they bleed to death? Did they struggle, cry out, scream. The shooting is layered. The media doesn't tell about the man who cursed at Esteban Santiago while he murdered people. It doesn't tell about the man shot in the back with a laptop saving his life. It doesn't tell about Kitty hiding with an Asian woman who won't get off her phone until a man screams that she is going to get everyone killed. The woman with the baby pleading with the man to get in his car or the people hiding under seats while other people right by them get shot, or the people on the tarmac picked up by a pilot of a jetliner. It is all lost with some guy in a Brooklyn T-shirt giving his recitation of events. Some writer.

And it gets worse. Careen switches the channel, and I pop up two more times. The Fox News interview has gone national and everyone has picked it up. I would have killed for this kind of coverage for one of my books but I have become a messenger of death. I was there. I ran from shots. I could have been a statistic; that is behind every question. What was it like to be close to death, because those people can't tell us; they are gone so we are stuck with you and your family. So, tell us what was it like. I rattle on and on. And it's still not over. Not by a long shot.

We are now in a twilight between our old life and the life that began when Esteban Santiago pulled out his Walther 9mm. And it will not end until we walk in the door of our home and the roller coaster is put back on the track and we continue with our lives. Now we are in a Quality Inn for three days with nowhere to go and really nothing to do. We are with people who ran from bullets and with people who suffered unimaginable loss. We are with people whose lives will never be the same.

Watching the television coverage of the shooting, I realize all the people from the airport shooting have become part of history. We will be read about in books, searched online, referenced, and then, finally, forgotten. All shootings are eventually forgotten; they are too horrific and our brains quickly paper over the carnage. Victims of shootings are divided between the dead and the living; the dead don't care anymore, and the living can't get away from the experience fast enough. In this way mass shootings become our dirty secret. The permanently disabled become inconvenient truths from an event we would rather just not think about anymore. We don't realize how horrible the events were until we read about them again. We remember the big ones, Sandy Hook and Columbine, but the other ones start to blend until we see an old article or bump into someone who was there. The Fort Lauderdale–Hollywood Airport shooting will start to fade after the media cycle is finished. But I will never forget it, nor will my kids. And the people who were at Virginia Tech on April 16, 2007, will never forget that day either.

CHAPTER 30

VIRGINIA TECH

2007

Virginia Tech is the perfect example of a mental health system that failed. Seung-Hui Cho at three was frail, shy, and hated personal contact. By the time he was in junior high he was being treated for severe depression and suffered from selective mutism, a severe social anxiety disorder. Cho was so stressed he didn't even want to speak.[1] Family members said he had autism, but psychiatrists would later push back with the response that mutism and autism had no relation to each other. Cho was in therapy during high school. When he began attending Virginia Tech, however, privacy laws meant that the school remained unaware of his mental health history.[2]

By his junior year of college Cho had begun writing strange manifestos and acting oddly enough that a professor encouraged him to get help. He began stalking women on campus and after a university investigation a judge in Virginia in 2005 declared Cho mentally ill and ordered him to get outpatient help. He did not seek help, though, and became progressively worse.

A manifesto and videos that Cho sent to NBC News at the time of the shooting reveal his deteriorating mental state. Cho believed he would be remembered as a savior of the oppressed after he went on his shooting rampage.[3] Later studies would say he was riddled with anxiety about graduating and going into the real world.[4]

Cho bought a Glock 19 and a box of ammunition from Roanoke Firearms.[5] He also had .22 caliber Walther P22 semiautomatic he had purchased online from a website, the Gun Source.[6] Just before 7:15 a.m. on April 16, 2007, Cho entered West Ambler Johnson Hall, a coed dorm, and shot freshman Emily Hilscher. The dorm resident assistant Ryan Clark tried to help Hilscher and Cho shot and killed him as well. After this Cho went back to his room and changed out of his bloodstained clothes and removed his computer's hard drive. He then walked to a pond on campus where authorities believe he got rid of the hard drive, although it was never found. Cho then mailed his manifesto and videos to NBC, which explained why he was going to shoot people.

Cho was wearing a backpack when he entered Norris Hall around 9:40 a.m., a building filled with classrooms and offices. In his backpack were chains, ammunition, a hammer, and a knife. The backpack also held his two guns. In total he had over four hundred rounds of ammunition. Inside Norris Hall he chained the front doors and locked them, leaving a note saying a bomb would explode if the doors were opened.[7]

Cho began walking through the building and looking into classrooms. He opened the door to room 206, where G. V. Loganathan was teaching hydrology engineering, and unleashed a barrage of gunfire, killing the professor and nine students, and wounding three others. He entered room 207, where Professor Jamie Bishop was teaching German, and shot the professor. He then opened fire on the front row and killed four students, wounding another six. He reloaded and left, and students barricaded the door. He next went to room 211, where he killed French professor Jocelyne Couture-Nowak, and a student, Henry Lee, as they tried to barricade the door. He then walked down the aisle of the classroom shooting each person, many multiple times; eleven students died. He moved on down the hall and tried to enter room 204, but the professor, Liviu Librescu, had heard the gunfire and held the door shut with his body to give his students time to escape through the windows. Cho fired through the door multiple times, striking and eventually killing Librescu and one student, Minal Panchal.[8]

Then Cho reloaded his weapons again and went back to the other classrooms. He killed Waleed Shaalan, whom he had earlier shot, then walked to room 205. The professor and students had put a large table against the door, and Cho was unable to get it, despite shooting through the door several times. Cho then shot and killed Professor Kevin Granata, who had come downstairs after he locking his students in his office. By this time, the police were closing in. Cho turned his Glock 19 on himself and fired into his right temple. He had killed thirty people in this assault and wounded seventeen more, spewing out 174 rounds. Victims had many bullet wounds and all those who were killed were shot at least three times. Twenty-eight were shot in the head.

The police were later criticized for not issuing a campus-wide notification after the initial report of a double homicide in the dormitory. In response to the shooting, Virginia passed gun legislation closing the gaps between federal and state laws. And the first major federal gun-control law in over a decade was passed, strengthening background checks through the National Instant Crime Background Check System (NICS) to stop purchases by the mentally ill and criminals. President George Bush signed the bill into law on January 5, 2008. Privacy laws were also altered to make sure schools were able to transfer medical records for incoming students.[9]

Authorities discovered that Cho purchased ammunition on eBay, which led the site to prohibit the sale of firearms and ammunition.[10] Students at rival schools dressed up as victims for Halloween[11] and a video game V-Tech Rampage was created by Ryan Lamborun who also created one for Sandy Hook.[12] Virginia Tech was fined by the Department of Education for not notifying students quickly after the first two students were shot.[13] The school developed an early-warning system for students in which text messages would warn of danger.[14] Several books came out criticizing Virginia Tech for not helping Cho more when he contacted counseling staff three times for help.[15] Eleven million dollars was paid in a settlement to twenty-four of the thirty-two families by the State of Virginia.[16]

Cho became the poster child for the gun-control movement when it was discovered he purchased his Glock and Walther legally. His mental illness, which had been diagnosed as mutism and depression, did not trigger the NICS system. Gun advocates blamed the gun-free zone of the university and said that if someone else with a gun had been there they could have stopped Cho. It came to light that Virginia never transmitted Cho's mental health status to the NICS system, and did not report that in 2005 he had been declared a danger to himself by the courts.[17] He was by Federal Law ineligible to buy a gun because of the fact he had been declared a danger to himself and ordered to undergo outpatient treatment. On CNN, NRA board member Ted Nugent called for an end to gun-free zones at schools and universities.[18]

Thirty-three people died at Virginia Tech. The video diatribe Cho sent to NBC News, in which he ranted about "wealthy brats," was received two days after the shooting.[19] The tragedy is that Cho had severe mental illness and should have never been allowed to buy a gun. This is of no consolation to the twenty-eight students and five faculty members who lost their lives on April 16, 2007.

CHAPTER 31

SWIMMING UP FROM THE DEEP

Midnight

We go swimming in the pool and life seems to take on a flavor of normalcy. The girls squeal in the lighted pool and I swim from one side to the other, feeling the stress slithering away. Clay sits in a chair next to Kitty and watches. It is midnight and I think the pool is closed but rules seem to have been suspended. People are still sitting in the semi-darkness with their suitcases and talking. One man talks about running out of Terminal 1: "I was in Nam and I know what gunfire sounds like. I haven't run like that for years." Others sit quiet and exhausted among the palm trees and the Spanish façade plastered over a cheesy hotel. But it is isolated and bucolic and this is enough.

Everyone is hungry. There is a Burger King nearby and Clay and I take orders and then set out to walk there. A major expressway rumbles overhead as we leave the confines of the Quality Inn. The garish orange light of an American city close to midnight in an industrial area is unsettling. We are not in a bad neighborhood but, like most neighborhoods by expressways, airports, and factories, it has elements that make one question the wisdom of walking around in the middle of the night. We reach the Burger King and walk up to the counter.

"Dad," Clay says in a low voice, nudging me.

He gestures to the television mounted overhead and there I am again. There is no sound, mercifully; there is just this sunburned man with a backpack speaking on camera. I, like most people, do not like to see myself on television. We all have an image of how we look and television takes that image and shreds it in seconds and says, no, this is how you really look. Deal with it. Then I see Callie and Kitty and then the news cuts away to another story.

"Weird," I mutter, but this is local news and the shooting is sweeping the airwaves. I have become B-roll footage to be played over and over. Here is the witness, *the dad* from Chicago, as one station captioned me, or *the author*, as another said, or *witness to the shooting*. None of it is good and it adds to the surreal moment of standing in a Burger King in the middle of the night outside the airport. It hits me then that we would have been home by now. We would have been unpacking and greeting our dog and our cat and we would have had that feeling of being away replaced with the its-good-to-be-home feeling. Instead, I am waiting for several whoopers, a whopper junior, chicken nuggets, lots of fries, many drinks, and some apple pies in the middle of the night outside a Fort Lauderdale airport.

I look around and notice we are one of the few people in the restaurant. The people behind the counter are busily making our food. All seems to be normal, but then it comes, the strange thought that I would have never had in a million years before today. I think that we could all be shot at any minute. Someone could bust in through the door and swing up a 9mm and we would hear those four metallic sounding shots again. There is no safety here. A disgruntled employee, a jealous boyfriend, an estranged husband, someone with severe mental illness, a veteran with PTSD, a frustrated loner who decides in a haze of schizophrenic delusion that we people in the Burger King are the source of all his problems. Or just a psychopath wanting revenge on the world.

I look around and wonder if I will ever feel safe again. My basic confidence in the world has been shaken to the core. If I don't feel safe getting some fast food for my family in an area where there are only a few people, how will I feel back in the airport, or in a train station or a stadium or a classroom, or out on the street? Someone with a gun could be anywhere. I keep looking around, examining the few people eating their Burger King fare and then I look at the employees. Does one of them have an angry lover or someone they owe a debt? Or maybe a fired employee is even now walking toward us locked and loaded, about to scream out, "You think you're going to fucking fire me . . . think again motherfucker!"

"Here you are," the woman at the counter says, handing me three large bags and a stack of cups for the sodas.

I stare at her.

"You say thank you, Dad," Clay whispers.

"Thank you," I mutter.

I turn to Clay and murmur.

"Let's get the fuck out of here."

He frowns and gestures to the cups.

"Dad, what about the sodas?"

I head for the door. I am leaving, now. I want to get away from the danger I am sure is coming again out of the warm Florida night. There is a trigger there now, a tripwire that stretches across every public space where the unthinkable could occur. My heart is racing. I am sweating. I am that guy in the airport again, looking for his family, thinking he is about to get shot. Clay follows me out the door and into the parking lot.

"Dad, what about the drinks? We paid for them!"

I wipe my face, heart racing, blood pumping, the world around me swirling.

"Dad, the drinks—"

I turn on him, eyes blazing, a man clearly coming unhinged. "Fuck it. We can drink fucking water. Okay? Fucking water!" And then I turn and start walking again.

Clay must read my body language because he glances around and then nods. "Cool."

We walk quickly back to the Quality Inn with our fast food. I just want to get back to the hotel, where the environment is reasonably controlled. Kitty looks up from the table by the pool.

"Any problems?"

"No," I say, feeling like I am gritting my teeth.

I begin unloading the food. We are a family again, doing what families do best, eating fast food. I want to dive into the pool, float to the bottom, and stay there. I just want order in the universe, quiet. I want the world to remain at a moral level while I catch my breath.

"Something the matter?"

I shake my head. "No . . . No. All good," I mutter.

"Where are the drinks?" Careen demands.

"Drink water," Clay answers.

"I forgot to get them," I explain.

Kitty frowns. "But you have the cups."

"Yeah. I know. I just forgot," I mutter, slumping into a chair, closing my eyes, a headache coming on quickly.

"He forgot, Mom," Clay says, backing me up.

"But—"

"HE FORGOT, MOM."

Kitty stares at Clay, then nods. I stay in my chair, suddenly exhausted, jittery, my heart thumping crazily. I wonder if I am having some sort of delayed stress reaction. Maybe I am having a breakdown. I just want to go where all is still. I want to get as far away as possible from the airport and everything associated with it. I want to get back to the Midwest where it is three degrees and snowing. I want to get away from the sickening warmth and palm trees and the smell of jet engine fuel that is now linked in my mind with those four shots. I want to get away from Florida and go back to the icy tundra of frozen cornfields. I know nobody would dare shoot anyone when it is that cold out. But we are stuck like everyone else, and while we are out of the airport we are in a second limbo that cannot be escaped. If fear is losing control of one's fate then we still are not in control of ours. No car. No flight out. We are in a crappy Quality Inn around a small pool, sitting in the dark eating Burger King food after being in a shooting in a major airport. I look around at the other people at the tables, sitting in the shadows by their suitcases. We are all stuck for now, waiting in the dark for whatever comes next.

CHAPTER 32

THE DARK KNIGHT

2012

James Holmes might have seen himself as the Joker. No one is sure. He liked Batman, anyway. His father was a scientist educated at Stanford and UCLA. His mother was a nurse. When he was eleven, James Holmes complained about Nail Ghosts, and this was the first time anyone suspected he might have mental health problems. The ghosts hammered the walls at night, and he saw men fighting out of the corners of his eyes. He tried to commit suicide that same year. In high school, he played soccer and ran cross country. He graduated from Westview High School in San Diego and headed for the University of California, Riverside.[1]

Holmes was brilliant. He graduated with honors in the top one percent of his class with a degree in neuroscience. Letters of recommendation talked about his leadership skills. He worked at a summer school camp and then at a pill-capsule-coating factory. People he worked with said he was antisocial, however, and would often not talk at all. He left the factory in 2011 and enrolled at the University of Colorado in the neuroscience doctoral program. He received a 21,000 dollar grant and university stipends. Holmes was wooed by several universities with offers of free tuition and lucrative stipends but he chose to stay at the University of Colorado. While a student there, Holmes met with three mental health professionals. He expressed homicidal thoughts to them, and one, Dr. Lynne Fenton, told the campus police about Holmes's desire to kill. She considered putting an involuntary mental health hold on him but decided he was a borderline case and that he wasn't mentally ill enough to justify the restraining hold.[2] Holmes also told other students to stay away from him because he was bad news.

In 2012, Holmes chose a midnight screening of *The Dark Knight Rises* to kill as many people as possible. On May 22, he went to a Gander Mountain sporting goods store and picked up a Glock 22 and then a week later went to Bass Pro Shops and bought a Remington 870 Express Tactical shotgun. The week after that he failed his oral exams for his doctoral program and immediately purchased a Smith and Wesson M&P15 rifle. Holmes passed the background checks when purchasing all these weapons.[3] He went on to buy 3,000 rounds of ammunition for the pistol and rifle and 350 shells for the shotgun from the internet. He rounded out his arsenal with online purchases of body armor, an assault vest, gas mask, helmet, and a knife.[4]

On July 20, the day of the shooting and hours before he left for the theater, Holmes mailed his notebook to his psychiatrist at the university. In the notebook he had detailed his plans and thoughts leading up to the shooting. He also called a crisis hotline with the hope that someone might stop him from the shooting, but he was disconnected.[5] The notebook was never delivered and was found days later in a mail room.

That night, Holmes drove to the Century 16 multiplex theater in Aurora, Colorado. He had picked a midnight showing to avoid shooting children. He bought a ticket and sat in the front row for twenty minutes before slipping out of a side exit and propping it open with a plastic cup. He armed himself and put on his vest, helmet, gasmask, bullet-resistant leggings, bullet-resistant groin protector, and gloves. He returned dressed all in black, blending into the audience that had dressed up for the movie. Holmes also wore earbuds and blasted techno music, to block out the screams of the people he shot.[6]

Holmes began by throwing two tear gas canisters into the theater and then fired at the audience in the back of the theater with his shotgun. He used his semiautomatic rifle, equipped with a hundred-round drum, and started mowing down people in the aisles and in their seats. He whipped out the Glock and fired back and forth as well. In all, Holmes fired seventy-six bullets: six shotgun blasts, sixty-five from the rifle, and five from the Glock.[7]

People initially thought Holmes's appearance was part of the movie premier entertainment, and then, realizing what was happening, panicked, rushing the doors. Holmes left by the same emergency exit he had entered and went back to his car, where police arrested him. He was described by police as calm and disconnected.[8]

In total seventy people were shot, with twelve fatalities. Four men died protecting their girlfriends. Many were hit multiple times. Most were shot in the chest and head as they sat in their seats. The shotgun and the automatic rifle killed most of those who died. Ten died in the theater and two died at the hospital. One child, Veronica Moser-Sullivan, age six, died. Her mother was also shot and survived as a paraplegic.[9] Caleb Medley was the last to leave the hospital after three brain surgeries. He uses a wheelchair and has difficulty speaking.[10]

Holmes pleaded guilty by reason of insanity. He underwent several psychiatric evaluations and was found fit to stand trial. A psychiatrist said Holmes was legally sane during the shooting but that he suffered from schizoaffective disorder. The jury could not reach a unanimous decision on the death penalty and Holmes was sentenced to twelve life sentences, with an additional 3,318 years.[11]

Security guards began patrolling theaters nationwide. *The Dark Knight Rises*'s premiere in France, Mexico, and Japan were canceled. Colorado gun sales went through the roof, increasing by 43 percent in the week following the shooting.[12] The debate over the sale of automatic weapons flared up again, given Holmes's access to high-powered semi-automatic weapons designed to kill humans. The assault weapons ban of 1994 to 2004 was cited as a deterrent, but no changes were made to any law. Holmes's wide-eyed mug shot and flaming red hair became the new face of insanity on the internet.

CHAPTER 33

VICTIMS

January 7, 2017, 9:00 a.m.

Shootings are class conscious. It would seem the rich have not been caught in many mass shootings. If one were to follow the line through American shootings, it is usually a middle-class person shooting other middle-class people. Schools, colleges, restaurants, theaters, and concerts are all frequented by middle-class people. Not to say rich people are not there, but the images we see—the victims, the wounded—all belong to the middle class.

It is curious that mass shooters don't take it upon themselves to go after the one percent, but in truth the one percent is harder to find. Their tastes are more expensive, their homes more exclusive, their communities gated. Some don't frequent airports and instead fly on private jets. Some pass through airports and have others retrieve their baggage. Many of the rich have their children attend private schools. Many of the rich don't frequent concerts. They don't go to the latest Batman movie, and they send their kids to private, Ivy League colleges.

The middle class is simply more vulnerable and the shooters' ideas of revenge are not focused on the rich, whom they have little contact with, but other middle-class people just like themselves. It is the other rats in the cage they want to kill, not the cage owner. Their self-loathing extends to others they perceive to be like themselves. They turn their rage on their fellow students, fellow concert goers, movie watchers, fast food eaters, those who have no right to be happy when their lot is the same as that of the shooters, who will inflict death before taking their own lives. The upper class, the rich, are not recognizable, and in a shooter's death fantasy it is familiarity that breeds contempt and the penalty for commonality is death.

The breathless middle-class people are the ones being interviewed on television: the mom, the dad, the children, everyone in their Kohls and Target clothes with an iPhone in their hand. The consumer class is targeted by ease of their accessibility, their known habits, patterns, and shared frustrations, in addition to the shooter's inability to rise up out of this class. The shooter sees their friends and coworkers, the bystanders, students, and strivers, as competitors, and often the shooter feels that their final act will set them apart for all time. Anonymity is the enemy, and it is felt acutely at the end, and those who compete with the shooter shall die. Fame is only promised to the one willing to kill.

The only time the upper-class was breached was Sandy Hook, and in that case Adam Lanza was from the same community, he and his gun-loving mother seemed to have little in common with the upwardly mobile professionals living near them. The large woody lots in the area hid one neighbor from another. Did Adam Lanza, besides being severely mentally ill, go after the children of these more talented, driven people surrounding him? Did he go after the Achilles heel of all who would look down on him? Did he feel the rage of class consciousness, the club he and his mother could never belong to? He went after these upper-middle-class professionals in the one place where they were most vulnerable— their children.

Being a victim can be dehumanizing, no matter what class they are part of. Victims' families are not told right away. Hospitals have to be checked, dental records secured, and crime scenes need to be detailed. No one wants to make a mistake and so in Sandy Hook the children remained in the classroom for twelve hours. Without confirmation, the feeling of hope, that somehow the inevitable did not happen, is kept alive even when people know the worst.

After the 9/11 attack, people walked around for days with pictures of their loved ones. They held them up to cameras and posted them on boards. They had not heard from their family members since the attack, yet they hoped that somehow they would appear alive. Humans do not easily believe the worst. It is a coping mechanism. When men are lost at sea and never found, as in the *Andrea Gail* disaster in 1991, where a fishing boat was lost during a storm (as depicted in the book and movie *The Perfect Storm*), their wives and mothers sometimes still hold out hope that one day they will come back, even years later.[1]

Family members hope that there has been a colossal mistake and that the person was sent to the wrong hospital or that a body had been misidentified as their loved one. This is why the police have to be sure of a victim's identity before they notify the family or release names to the media. In some situations, dental records are required or identification by the family is needed. But in school shootings, where kids and parents are involved, it starts to come down to simple math. Four hundred and fifty kids attended the school that day and only 425 returned. Twenty-five kids are missing. In Columbine they bused the kids out to another location, where parents were waiting. As each bus came there were fewer parents waiting. Finally, the parents left were faced with the probability that their children had been victims. No more buses were coming.

No victims have been identified so far at the airport. But we hear immediately that some of the families of the victims are staying at the Quality Inn. We have become a small community of survivors and like every small community there are rumors that ripple through in waves. Someone says the airline will be picking up the hotel tab and paying for everyone. (This proves not to be true for us.) Another rumor says that there will be special shuttles taking us back to the airport. This turns out not to be true. Then it is rumored that our tickets will be reimbursed to us. This is not true either. The only rumor that sticks is the one about the victims' family also being at the Quality Inn. They are about to become victims too.

That first night has been chaotic, but in the morning we go back to the pool area for breakfast. It is mobbed, and people crowd around the hotel fare of plasticized eggs, Rice Krispies, and warm orange juice, swarming the waffle makers, the toast with sealed jellies, the pans of sausages, and the coffee that runs out instantly, as happy music plays in the background. Stressed out people eat a lot and we have to wait to get some coffee and some more eggs for the kids. The morning is strangely beautiful, with Florida giving up one of its seventy-degree days.

I have gotten up early and tried to jog around the parking lot, around the dumpsters and trucks making morning deliveries. This is something I do on vacations that I don't do at home. The let's-get-healthy bug kicks in and for a week I become a jogger. The night before has been an experiment. Could I sleep? Could any of us sleep in the hotel room with the air conditioner whirring through the night? Would I hear those four shots in my sleep and wake up sweating, disorientated, my peaceful slumbers destroyed forever by one Esteban Santiago?

I do wake up every few hours, wondering where I am. I wonder if I am suffering from PTSD; I look at my son and two daughters and hope the psychic scars will not be deep. Fortunately, they all seem peacefully asleep and I, too, fall asleep and wake in the early morning with the sun peeking around the curtains. That's when I decide to take control and go for a run. I put on my swimsuit, find my high-top tennis shoes, and quietly open the door. It is chilly out, but this feels good; it reminds me of Chicago, of going home. And then I start to jog and go around the hotel five times, breathing like an asthmatic, not thinking but just concentrating on dodging the cars, the people out walking dogs with plastic bags, the deliverymen, and the dumpsters, finally giving it up when I am sure one more lap will give me a heart attack.

After getting breakfast, Kitty and I sit at the table while the girls swim and Clay goes back to the room to sleep. He can sleep twelve hours straight and then go back to bed again. We sit with our lukewarm coffee, discussing how to get out of Florida, telling ourselves we won't have to wait until Monday morning, and swearing we will not return to Terminal 1. And then I look up and see a strange, lonely procession.

There are three young men with beards and two women. One woman looks to be in her late fifties and walks with her head down. They seem not to be of this earth and they pass through the pool area meeting no one's eyes. They look at the ground, pulling their suitcases behind them, dressed in shorts and colorful shirts. They look like they are headed for a cruise. Kitty and I watch them, not saying a word, and then Kitty looks at me.

"I wonder if they are family of one of the victims."

"I don't know," I murmur, watching them disappear toward the rooms.

I have seen human grief before. My uncle's funeral was something I have always remembered. His coffin was over the grave and about to be lowered when his wife threw her body on top of it and hugged the smooth lacquered wood. She cried in anguish and gasped out his name. But these people are mute, dour, moving through like ghost walkers from another world.

I watch the last person disappear and I can only imagine what they are feeling. Maybe their loved ones are missing but haven't been confirmed dead. Maybe we are mistaken and they are just a glum group of people.

"Maybe they missed their cruise," I suggest, knowing this is not the case.

Kitty looks at me. Neither of us speaks. What no one ever talks about is the survivors, the people who are wounded or the loved ones of someone who dies. the same muzzle flash that takes some lives leaves others who are never grazed by a bullet forever altered. The dead leave, but the living must go on and continue along on this new and unwanted path. The wounded heal, the dead are buried, and the survivors must cope.

CHAPTER 34

THE SURVIVOR

2011

Jared Loughner liked to smoke pot, and he dropped acid and did mushrooms. He was convicted for defacing a street sign and for possession of marijuana. His father, a local government employee and retired truck driver, didn't know what to do. His son had dropped out of high school in 2006 and it was all downhill from there. Jared's manager at Quiznos said Jared had changed drastically and he was soon fired from his job. He then got a job walking dogs but he would wander off into strange areas with the dogs and was asked not to return. He tried to join the Army in 2008 but was rejected after he told the recruiter that he regularly smoked marijuana.[1]

In 2010 Loughner was investigated by campus police five times at Pima Community College where he attended. Teachers complained of his bizarre behavior and campus police discovered a YouTube video that called the school a scam. He was suspended and asked to not return until he got a mental health clearance. Two months later, on November 30, he bought a Glock from Sportsman's Warehouse. On January 8, 2011, he tried to buy more ammo at a Walmart store but was turned away because of suspicious behavior.[2] He went to another Walmart and bought his ammo and headed for the Safeway where Congressman Gabrielle "Gabby" Giffords was giving a speech in the parking lot called "Congress on Your Corner."

Jared had told friends goodbye on his Myspace page that morning and asked them to "please not be mad at me."[3] On the way to the Safeway, an Arizona Game and Fish Department officer pulled Loughner over for running a red light but let him go when he saw that he had no out-standing warrants.[4]

Earlier that morning, his father had seen a black bag in the trunk of Loughner's car and tried to grab it. Loughner ran off and his father chased him on foot but lost him. Jared threw the bag away, but authorities would later determine that it held 9mm clips.[5]

Loughner arrived at the Safeway parking lot in a taxi and stepped out of the car. He approached Congresswoman Giffords, who was standing with a group of constituents and political aides, pulled out his Glock, and shot her in the head at close range. He then turned his gun on the crowd and began firing randomly; nineteen people were shot and six of them were killed. The dead included nine-year-old Christina-Taylor Green, who had been born on September 11, 2001; Dorothy Morris, a retired secretary; John Roll, a retired judge; Phyllis Schneck, a home-maker; Dorwan Stoddard, a retired construction worker; and Gabe Zimmerman, a congressional staffer who worked for Giffords.[6]

After Loughner emptied his Glock, he reached for another clip but it slipped and he dropped it on the ground. A woman kicked the clip away and another man hit Loughner in the back of the head with a folding chair. He was then tackled and restrained by several people who had come to meet Congresswoman Giffords. Giffords's intern, Daniel Hernandez, put pressure on the wound in her forehead to slow the bleeding until paramedics arrived. Giffords was rushed to University Medical Center, where doctors performed surgery to remove skull fragments and damaged brain tissue. The bullet had missed the center of her brain and exited the back of her skull.[7] A part of her skull was removed to alleviate swelling, and a neurologist gave her a more than fifty percent chance of recovery. She was placed in a medically induced coma and put on a ventilator. Eventually, a tracheotomy replaced the ventilator and Giffords was brought out of the coma. Doctors surgically repaired her eye socket, which had been damaged by the bullet, and began reconstructive surgery on her face. On May 18, 2011, a piece of molded plastic was attached to her skull with tiny screws to replace the bone removed after the shooting.[8] On June 15 she went home from the hospital, continuing therapy from there. Giffords's cognitive and physical abilities continued to improve. Three years later she was able to write and speak in short sentences and could walk with assistance.[9]

On August 1, 2011, Gabby Giffords returned to the House of Representatives to cast a vote. She walked without a cane as she entered the room. While she had been right handed before the shooting, she now wrote with her left hand, which was stronger. She resigned from Congress on January 22, 2012, to focus on her recovery. As of November 30, 2017, she still needed assistance walking, had no use of her right arm, and had difficulty finding the right word, due to her brain injury.[10] Gabby Giffords and her husband, Mark Kelly, formed Americans For Responsible Solutions to lobby for gun control. They support responsible gun ownership and increased gun laws, in order to keep guns out of the hands of criminals and the mentally ill.[11] Giffords appeared at a Senate hearing on gun violence in 2013 and spoke for gun control in a halting voice, saying, "Too many children are dying."[12]

Jared Loughner was sentenced to seven life terms in prison plus 140 years with no chance of parole.[13] His mugshot is similar to James Holmes's in the stare of insanity that dominates both photos. An eerie smirk is the final insult to the memory of the six people he murdered, including a nine-year-old girl.

CHAPTER 35
THE HORROR
January 8, 2017, 2:00 p.m.

I hear people talking around the pool. Everyone talks about leaving the Quality Inn and returning home. The airport reopened on Saturday but we can't get a flight out until Monday morning even though we have talked to United Airlines many times. They just can't find a flight for all of us until Monday. I go for my morning jog around the back parking lot and by the third time past the dumpster I have an idea and call my agent. She has left me several messages asking if I am alright.

I give her my idea for a book. She listens to me ramble for a while and thinks it sounds like a good idea. I really need something to occupy me and like a lot of writers I am not normal until I start writing. I want to try and make some sense out of what has happened. I have no idea what approach I will take or what I am even looking for, but we have gone through something horrific and I need to get a handle on it. So while Clay sleeps, the girls swim, and Kitty naps in a lounge chair, I tap away at my laptop.

I don't know where I am when I am writing. I could be in a desert or at the bottom of the ocean. I am just gone. I am working along when I hear some commotion. It is a scream, a cry for help, a throaty gasp, something that sounds like a wounded animal. Kitty opens her eyes and I look up and see the woman from the day before who had passed through. The woman is now falling down by the pool. Two people from the Quality Inn are assisting her. The woman is sobbing, screaming, lying on the wet cement. Two young men run up and help the hotel people. They get her to her feet but she continues to cry in agony. Her face is red and blotchy, her eyes are slits, and she continues her pained screaming, *Oh, Oh, Oh, Oh.* This is the horror we have all danced around. This is the grief of someone who has just been told their loved one has died. I know the authorities waited until they were sure, but I find out later this woman was called to the office of the Quality Inn where she was told that her mother was one of the victims of the shooting. And now she cannot walk, cannot talk; she simply cannot function.

This is the horror that lies beneath all shootings. There is a strange type of adrenaline that kicks in during a shooting, allowing people to function, to get to safety, to handle the unbelievable. It must be an evolutionary defense mechanism that keeps the brain from fully understanding what is too much to handle in the moment. This coping blocks the horror that a person has been murdered and what has happened can never be undone and the loved one taken away will never return.

Kitty is wiping her eyes as we watch the woman being escorted away from the pool area. "She must have just found out," she says, looking at me with red eyes.

"Yes," I mutter.

Suddenly I want to drink. I am not a big drinker but there are times when I don't want any more reality and this is one of those moments.

"You want a drink?" I ask, standing up.

"Yes!"

I head for the tiki hut with its folding sign advertising tropical drinks. It doesn't matter: gin, vodka, whiskey, anything to dull what we have just witnessed. I go in and see in the half-light the two men with beards who had been in the procession the day before. Their eyes are red and the bartender is speaking to them.

"Anything you want. You can have anything on the house."

His eyes are red, too. The men are about the same age as the woman who was so distraught One of the men, who has short blond hair, looks simply stunned, almost too much to speak. He wipes his eyes when the bartender speaks again.

"They were both there?"

The man nods. "Yes . . . we just got the news that my mother-in-law expired."

There are several other people there and no one speaks, no one moves. He smiles strangely, his eyes welling. I feel compelled to ask. I have not talked to anyone who had been in the lower baggage area of Terminal 2. Here is the tragedy we have all been running from for two days.

"You were there?" I ask.

He looks at me and then wipes his eyes again.

"Yes. They were together and then they weren't. My father-in-law was shot through the eye and it went out the back of his head." He pauses. "My mother-in-law just expired."

And then he says something I will think about for a long time afterward. "It was all in the blink of a kiss."

He looks at me as if looking for an answer. All I can do is shake my head. No one moves.

"It's just fucking surreal," he mutters.

And here in this silly bar in a Quality Inn by the pool lives are being altered for all time. *All time.* There will be pictures on mantles that will take on different meaning. There will be albums that would be dated before the tragedy. There will be photos of the days before. There will be videos of lives that will be shown at funeral homes. Pictures will be rounded up for display to explain a life lived fully as people pay their respects. Then the pictures will quietly be put away forever. And then it will all just stop. Time will stop on this day for those families. The history of families detours and veers away from the darkness and there will be whispers by grandkids about what happened. This family will remember this day for the rest of their lives. Funerals will be held. Wills read. Houses and belongings sold. Anniversaries altered. Cars sold or given to family members. No part of these families' lives will stay the same. January 6, 2017, will be quietly remembered with loss, grief, and horror. Eventually, the day will be ignored and pushed back as lives are rebuilt. Some people will simply move away and not be heard from again. Nothing will resemble what came before the shooting.

I say something about being in the other terminal and offer my condolences, then order a couple of gin and tonics. Words have lost all meaning. For a writer this is a strange moment but the magnitude of what has happened has stripped away meaning. This man's mother-in-law has been murdered by Esteban Santiago and his father-in-law is fighting for his life. *I'm sorry for your loss. I'm sorry this happened to you. I'm sorry your mother-in-law was shot down and your father-in-law critically wounded.* Still I say it. You have to, and he thanks me, but it feels so much like a Band-Aid for a terminal wound. There is nothing to say and for the first time I understand the tragedy of a mass shooting. There we were in our bathing suits and sandals and T-shirts, ready to enjoy whatever life could offer, and now we are all in some dark night of the abyss. I take the drinks and go back to the pool.

"The son-in-law was in there . . . pretty ripped up," I say, handing the drink to Kitty.

We both turn to the tiki bar. A small group of people are at one end of the bar now. *All in the blink of a kiss*: that phrase haunts me. Did he mean they were kissing at the moment Esteban let loose with his Walther 9mm, or was it just that life was altered in that moment forever? That their love affair ended in that moment and all love ended? I don't know. Life is evanescent and more so in unspeakable tragedy.

"It's all so sad," Kitty says, shaking her head and wiping her eyes.

I nod and drink the gin. Then I drink some more, not wanting to think any more about anything. It is a sunny day, but the darkness has moved in. We are back there at the airport again and those four shots are exploding and we are running for our lives. Like a horror movie you want to turn away from, the dark night has returned.

CHAPTER 36

THE BUMP STOCK KILLER

Las Vegas

2017

To this day no one can say for sure why Stephen Paddock murdered fifty-eight people during an outdoor concert on the Las Vegas Strip on October 1, 2017. As of the spring of 2018, this is the deadliest mass shooting in United States history. Paddock, a sixty-four-year-old retired accountant and real-estate investor who saw himself as a high-stakes gambler, had lost a lot of money.[1] His doctor had diagnosed him as bipolar and given him anxiety medication, but he refused to take it. He said he was in pain most of the time. He had no children, was twice divorced, drank heavily, played primarily video poker, and had a girlfriend whom he had quit being "intimate" with. He left no suicide note and seemed to take pains to cover his tracks by destroying hard drives. His father was Benjamin Paddock, a bank robber who was on the FBI's most wanted list in the sixties and seventies. But Stephen Paddock had no known interaction with law enforcement until the shooting.[2]

On September 25, 2017, Stephen Paddock began to amass an arsenal in his hotel room at the Mandalay Bay Hotel in Las Vegas. He took Room 32135 and then booked Room 32134 four days later. Both rooms peered down on Las Vegas Village, a fifteen-acre site and the venue for the Route 91 Harvest Country Music Festival. The festival would host 22,000 people on its final day, October 1, 2017, when country music star

Jason Aldean was scheduled to give a performance. It would be a day no one would forget.

Paddock began to stockpile weapons in his hotel rooms. He had two AR-10s and ten AR-15 rifles, with hundred-round magazines and bump stocks, as well as multiple pistols. He had telescopic sights, and the AR-10s were mounted on bipods.[3]

Colt started selling the AR-15, a gas-operated semiautomatic weapon, as a civilian version of the military M16 in 1964. The Colt version took a twenty or thirty-round staggered column detachable magazine and supported a flash suppressor, sound suppressor, or muzzle brake, which kept the barrel from rising up when fired. In 1977 Colt's patent expired, and other gun manufacturers began to make their own versions under different names, but all were known as "AR-15 rifles." Adding a bump stock made an AR-15 capable of firing ninety rounds in ten seconds.

> The Bump Fire stock . . . provides an effective means of engaging a gun's trigger extremely quickly. Instead of pulling back the trigger to fire, the user places his or her finger slightly in front of the trigger and pushes the whole gun forward with steady pressure. The trigger hits the finger and the round goes off. Recoil pushes the gun back, but the shooter's forward pressure immediately returns the trigger back to the finger, and so the gun fires off another round faster than the blink of an eye.[4]

Paddock was readying himself for killing on a massive scale.

Just before 10:00 p.m. a security guard, Jesus Campos, noticed a door accessing the thirty-second floor wouldn't open. An L-shaped bracket had been screwed into the door and the floor of the hallway to block access from the stairs. Campos went back down to the floor below and took the elevator up to see what was going on. When he heard what sounded like drilling he walked down the hallway toward the door of Paddock's room. As he approached, Paddock opened fire through the wood of the door, spraying two hundred bullets into the hallway. Campos collapsed, shot in the right thigh, and dragged himself into an alcove between two rooms, where he radioed for help. A maintenance worker, Stephen Schuck, had also arrived on the floor, and Campos screamed at him to take cover. Schuck too radioed for help.[5]

Paddock knew time was growing short. He smashed two of the room's windows with a hammer, and at 10:05 p.m. he began murdering people five hundred yards away. There was a sea of people below him. He did not have to aim but sprayed bullets over the festival crowd. When he did use the telescopic sites, he fired bullets with deadly accuracy. The bump stock allowed him to fire continuously for ten minutes. Many people at first thought the shots were fireworks, but then panic took over and people ran toward the security fence that surrounded the grounds. Jason Aldean ran off the stage without a word and would later be criticized for not warning people as to what was happening.[6] All the concertgoers could do is run for their lives as they were cut down.[7]

Fifty-eight people were shot dead and over five hundred wounded. Seventy-five minutes after the attack began the police would reach Paddock's room with explosives to find him dead from a self-inflicted gunshot wound through the mouth.[8] Jesus Campos had radioed in the location of the shooter and that along with the muzzle flash allowed police to determine where the shots were coming from.[9]

Upon investigation, authorities determined that Paddock had considered other venues for his rampage, such as the Lollapalooza music festival in Chicago.[10] He had no known associations or links to any hate groups. He was found to have ammonium nitrate in his truck, along with Tannerite, a binary explosive that explodes upon impact from a high-velocity bullet. A large tank of aviation fuel near the concert was found to have bullet holes and authorities determined that Paddock had fired into it to try and ignite the fuel.[11] It did not explode, however, since aviation fuel does not ignite easily.

Those killed in Paddock's massacre ranged in age from twenty to sixty-seven; thirty-six were women and twenty-two were men Thirty-one of them were pronounced dead at the scene. Nearby McCarren International Airport was closed for four hours for fear of shots being fired at the planes. Three hundred people ran onto the airport grounds to escape. President Trump called Paddock "a demented man with a lot of problems." Paddock's girlfriend returned from the Philippines and said Paddock had sent her 100,000 dollars days before the attack and told her to buy a house for her family there. In conversations with the FBI she said her fingerprints would be on the bullets because she had helped him load the high-volume magazines.[12]

No motivations could be subscribed to Stephen Paddock except maybe the rage of his gambling losses, though he was solvent at the time of the shooting. One can only surmise that Stephen Paddock had slowly changed over the years into a psychopath who felt nothing, a human animal bent on self-destruction and wishing for final revenge against a world he perceived had destroyed him.[13] Fully armed like a battle-hardened solider, he exacted his revenge using altered weapons and a sniper's lair.

After the Las Vegas shooting President Trump vowed to ban the manufacture and use of bump stocks. As of this writing in 2018, however, no federal law has been passed prohibiting bump stocks, although several states have banned them.[14]

CHAPTER 37

HOME

January 9, 2017

Monday finally comes and we return to the airport. I would like to say it is eerie being back in Terminal 1. I would like to say that being dropped off in the same terminal and talking to the skycap men is weird. I would like to say that I see death all around, but the truth is that all that is gone. The airport is a busy place of human activity once again. People are there to board planes and fly away from Florida. And so are we. The truth is that humans are very present-minded.

The cab drops us off as before and this time we check our bags through at the curb and head for security. I stare at the bench where Callie's glasses had been left along with all our luggage. There is nothing at all to mark those moments of terror just three days ago. I do not look toward Terminal 2 when we walk into the building. I look at the area where I had spoken with the SWAT officer and then I look down the terminal where the stampede of humans had come running. I listen for those four shots again and then push them from my mind. The mission is to get through security as fast as possible.

Kitty and I exchange glances several times in the security line. You can't help but think someone might come in any minute and start shooting. We take off our shoes, belts, and watches and place our cellphones, laptops, and keys into bins. We are scanned, x-rayed, and photographed, while Careen triggers an extra alarm. She has used talcum powder and the chemical composition ignites one of the sensors looking for the residue of bomb-making material. They wipe her hand and she goes through and then, for the first time, we are on the secure side of the Fort Lauderdale–Hollywood Airport.

We put our shoes back on, pick up our belongings, and grab some coffee and donuts while we wait for the plane. Even on this side I look around at people as possible shooters. I see happy families with children and marvel at the how the door to horror is so thin. I see the family at the poolside again and the woman crumpling in grief and the son-in-law with the red eyes. I want that plane to pull up to the terminal as quickly as possible. And when it does pull up and we are aboard I feel like this might be one of those movies where people are yanked off a plane at the last minute. I look out the window at the tarmac where three days before people ran for their lives while planes taxied around with nowhere to go. We have heard that the airlines are slowly catching up and in a day all the flights will be back to normal.

And then we lift off. Kitty and I are across from each other and we exchange glances as Florida recedes and becomes a flat checkerboard of sand, golf courses, hotels, and street grids. I see the ocean in the early morning light and I realize then that I have stopped thinking of Florida as a seaside state that offers the ocean and sunshine, an idea I'd had that went all the way back to when I was in college on spring break. There have been no other association up until now, but in these last few days Florida has suddenly become the place to get the hell away from as fast as possible.

The captain signals that we are at cruising altitude and I lean back and shut my eyes. Going home has seemed like a fantasy for days. There were moments when I hadn't thought we would ever get home. It just seemed that the dark place we had stumbled into had taken over the world. But we do go home, and Chicago is snowy and freezing when we land. The Uber driver hoists our bags and we drive home talking about weather, the Bears, the Cubs, the economy, and Donald Trump. The driver had another job that he has either left, retired from, or been fired from. We are not really sure, but he keeps up a steady stream of conversation.

"So you were on vacation?"

"Yes."

"Florida?"

"Yes."

"They had that shooting in Lauderdale."

I feel something shift in me. "Yes."

The driver shakes his head. "Crazy."

And then we are home, at our house in the suburbs with the dog, the cat, and the snow in the drive and covering the sidewalk. The fireplace smells like creosote and the house has the musty, slightly woody scent I always associate with when we first moved in. The dog and the cat are happy to see us and the girls run upstairs to their rooms, already connecting with friends. Clay goes to his room and falls asleep but not before he turns to me.

"Dad, you were so right to move out here." He pauses. "The world is fucking crazy."

I nod. I know what he is saying. We were 9/11 refugees when we moved away from Chicago, escaping the possible danger of a dirty radioactive bomb. We had taped up our doors and stockpiled water. In Oak Park we were only about three miles west of downtown Chicago and we felt that a second wave of al-Qaeda bombers was sure to come. So we had moved thirty miles west to one of the far suburbs. Clay and I have never talked once about our reasons for the move, but he knows now. He sees a great danger out in the world, an uncontrollable element that living in a house in a suburban setting might save him from.

"Thank God we are home," Kitty says, after I bring in the last piece of luggage.

I stand up and look at our house, with the paintings, my books, the pictures of the kids, of all of us on previous vacations. This life has been quietly waiting here for us under the snow and ice. This Midwestern life of cornfields under low skies and five-degree temperatures and months when the sun barely shines. We have returned and it goes without saying that five other people will never return to their homes.

But it is January again. The warmth of Florida no longer exists. We will build a fire tonight and watch television or read and probably order pizza. We will get the kids ready for school and I will have to finish my proposal for a book and send it to my agent. Kitty will go back to marketing, and life will continue. The dog and the cat will have to be fed and the garbage cans will go down by the curb and we will revel in the luxurious drudgery of our middle-class life. We have passed through another door and we are simply back in the land of the living.

CHAPTER 38

A PROFESSIONAL SCHOOL SHOOTER

Marjory Stoneman Douglas High School

2018

President Trump called out as a coward the school resource officer who stayed outside Marjory Stoneman Douglas High School, in Parkland, Florida, while Nikolas Cruz went on a six-minute rampage inside, firing rounds from his semiautomatic AR-15.[1] The policeman was put on leave immediately and then he retired.[2] He was the man who was charged with protecting the students, yet he took cover outside the school behind a car while seventeen people were murdered. It gets worse. When other Broward County police arrived they, too, stayed outside and did not enter.[3] When the Coral Springs police arrived, they were astounded that the other officers had not entered. By the time the Coral Springs Police entered the school it was too late: seventeen people were dead of massive gunshot wounds.[4]

So what happened at Stoneman Douglas High School? Let's start with Nikolas Cruz. He has become the poster child for missed red flags. The nineteen-year-old was a former student at Stoneman Douglas. Nikolas Cruz was adopted. His parents had died. He had been in trouble since middle school. He suffered from depression, autism, and ADHD. He had been transferred six times between schools for behavior issues. He talked incessantly about guns. He posted racist, homophobic, and xenophobic views on Instagram: "I wanna die Fighting killing shit ton of people."[5] He wanted to emulate the Texas Tower shooter. The police received twenty-three calls about Cruz over ten years' time. He was not allowed to carry a backpack to school. He posted on YouTube, "I'm going to be professional school shooter." An anonymous tip to the FBI weeks before the shooting detailed Cruz's "desire to kill people, erratic behavior, and disturbing social media posts as well as potential of him conducting a school shooting."[6]

If Nikolas Cruz had stood in front of the police station with a megaphone and said he intended to kill people in schools, he could not have been clearer. But no action was taken by the police or FBI or school officials except to shuffle him off to one school after another. Even though he was severely mentally ill, had posted his intention to kill, and told friends he wanted to shoot up a school, he had no problem buying an AR-15 and ammunition a year before the shooting.

On February 14, 2018, Cruz took an Uber to the high school, arriving at 2:19 p.m. He then followed some students and entered the east stairwell of Building 12, which held mostly freshman classes, with his AR-15 in a black case.[7] He stopped in the stairwell, opened the case, and began shoving the magazine into the weapon. Freshman Chris McKenna saw Cruz loading his weapon. "You better get out of here," Cruz told him. "Things are gonna start getting messy." McKenna ran, and Cruz began walking down the first-floor hallway with his assault rifle, hunting people.[8]

When Chris McKenna fled, he ran into Aaron Feis, a thirty-seven-year-old assistant football coach and father, and told him about Cruz. "Let me check it out," Feis said, and then they heard the first shots. Feis ran down the hallway and when he saw the gunman he began pushing students out of the way and shielding them with his body. Cruz shot and killed him, and witnesses later said that Feis was a hero who had saved lives. As Cruz continued down the hallway he fired indiscriminately into classrooms.[9]

Ivy Schamis was just finishing a lesson on the Holocaust when Cruz shot through the window of the door, hitting six students. Two of them, Helena Ramsay and Nick Dworet, both seventeen years old, were killed by the high-velocity rounds. Cruz continued down the hallway, firing in all directions. The AR-15 does not have be precisely aimed but simply pointed in a general direction as bursts of gunfire spray the victims. English teacher Dara Hass in room 1216 dropped to the floor as bullets blasted through the door, hitting eight of her students; three of them died on the floor in front of their classmates. Hass texted her husband and hugged the students around her. Cruz was still moving, still firing.

The smoke from the gunfire set off the smoke alarms, and students on the third floor, not hearing the shots, assumed it was yet another fire drill. On the second floor, math teacher Shanti Viswanathan heard the gunshots and screams. She told her students to get on the floor in the corner and she placed computer paper over the door's window to block the view from the hallway.[10] When Cruz climbed to that floor, he passed her classroom without shooting.

On the third floor, Cruz saw geography teacher Scott Beigel unlocking a door to let students in and shot and killed him with a quick burst of gunfire. Chris Hixon, the school's athletic director, was running toward the sound of shots, trying to pull students out of harm's way, when Cruz killed him.

The fire alarm was still buzzing. Cruz went into the third-floor teachers' lounge and tried to fire from the windows at students escaping the building. The hurricane-resistant glass fragmented the bullets, however, and he was unable to hit any targets. Six minutes after he entered the building, he stopped shooting.[11] He dropped his rifle and went back into the hall, joining the students who were rushing down the stairs and out of the building to get away from the shooter. Cruz ran outside with them, right past the police still crouching behind their cars.

In the parking lot, school resource officer Scot Peterson and other officers from the Broward County Police Department were behind cars. They had heard the shots and yet they violated the protocol that had been in place ever since Columbine, which was to immediately confront the shooter.[12] The AR-15 shots clattered through the school, they heard the multiple bursts, and they were not going to confront a killer armed with a military weapon while they were armed with handguns. Peterson's attorney later argued that Peterson thought the shots were coming from the outside of the building.[13]

Our society expects police officers to sacrifice their lives for others. But when the moment of a mass shooting comes and an officer hears the rapid *booms* of a semiautomatic weapon, the cold fear of death becomes very real. The shooter is not a man armed with a pistol. This is a killer armed with a killing machine that sprays out high-velocity bullets, leaving wounds like those seen on battlefields in Iraq and Afghanistan.[14]

By the time the officers entered the school, Cruz had already walked to a nearby Walmart, where he got a soda at Subway and then went on to McDonald's. He eventually left the restaurant and was arrested at 3:40 p.m. A surveillance camera in the school confirmed his identity as the school shooter. Cruz was charged with seventeen counts of murder. The prosecutors have stated they will seek the death penalty but, as of May 2018, no firm decisions had been made.[15]

Fourteen students and three teachers died in Parkland.[16] In the days after the shooting, the president declared his desire to arm teachers and spoke of turning schools into fortresses.[17] High school students around the country protested with walkouts and a march on Washington. A CNN town hall meeting was held the week after the shooting, with discussions between the students, Senator Marco Rubio, and a representative of the NRA. Once again lawmakers debated gun legislation, arguing about bump stocks, background checks, and more mental health restrictions. Students from Marjory Stoneman Douglas High School have been vocal at rallies and on national television, declaring that they will no longer tolerate the status quo on guns. Many began to view this shooting as a tipping point for gun control.

On March 7, 2018, Florida passed a 400 million dollar gun-control bill, with the NRA in opposition. The legislation "would raise the minimum age to purchase any firearm to 21 from 18; impose a three-day waiting period on gun purchases; fund school police officers and mental health counselors; and allow local school districts and sheriffs to arm certain school personnel. It would also ban so-called bump stocks, which make guns fire faster, and give law enforcement more power to commit people deemed a threat."[18]

Student activists wanted a more sweeping bill, but this is the first significant gun-control legislation to emerge in the last ten years. Governor Rick Scott signed the bill into law March 9, 2018.[19]

CHAPTER 39

MALES WHO FAIL

I f an alien came down from another planet and examined the shootings that have occurred in the United States beginning with Howard Unruh in 1949 and ending with Dimitrios Pagourtizs, who killed ten people at Santa Fe High School on May 18, 2018, he or she or it would make several observations. The shooters were all suburban males. They were all young men, with the oldest being Stephen Paddock at sixty-four (an unusual rarity). They were all white, with the exception of Seung-Hui Cho. They had little or no ideological motivation. They were all mentally ill, with the Santa Fe High School shooter still a question mark as of this writing. And they all were failing.

The alien then might study the Second Amendment of the United States and find that it is intertwined into the foundation of our society. The right to bear arms is as much a right as free speech. The right to bear arms ensures that no government will run amuck and trample the other rights. The alien would understand how taking away guns in any form will not work. People fail and there is nothing to be done about that. A ban on young white males having guns will not work. The assault weapons ban has already been tried and appealed. So the alien might throw up his hands and walk back to his ship in disgust. He might then turn and shout, "At least keep guns out of the hands of the mentally ill." Then he would fly away and leave earthlings to their strange problem of people shooting people.

What the alien doesn't know is that there is such a rule on the books. There is a federal law that keeps the mentally ill from buying guns, but states are not required to report people to the FBI's NICS system. So people like Esteban Santiago, who was clearly mentally ill and told the FBI he heard voices telling him to kill, was still able to buy a gun.[1] The alien would be amazed to know that Congress repealed a law that kept guns from mentally ill people on Social Security.[2]

When you begin a book you do not know where you will end up. Fiction, nonfiction, it is all a journey and you are after the discoveries. In a book like this the journey is even more important. I did not want to begin this with preconceived notions or have an axe to grind for or against guns. I did not want to hit people over the head with statistics. I have purposely stayed away from writing a "gun book." A lot of the books I consulted were brimming with stats that became meaningless because there was always another statistic that countered it. So I wanted to blend my journey with shootings in the United States that were not ideologically motivated.

I wanted to know about the shootings where there was no reason. There was no overwhelming motive. And as I went through the shootings beginning with Howard Unruh in 1949 and ending with Nikolas Cruz in 2018, there were discoveries. American shooters are mostly young men. All the shooters were in some stage of mental illness and all the shooters were males who had failed in life. And all the victims of the shootings had their lives changed forever.

The people who died in shootings were not even given the honors of someone dying in a war. At least those killed in war get a twenty-one gun salute and a flag and a letter from the president. No, people who are killed in shootings just die and the media moves on and they are forgotten. They are put in the category of freak accidents, tornados, lightning strikes, rare incurable diseases. They are just gone and the survivors who are wounded physically or psychically are left to pick up the pieces of their lives and do the best they can.

There is no Veterans Administration for victims. There is nothing beyond the lawyers who can try and sue for compensation. You could say there is a war between vested interests in the gun debate in America but that would not get you very far. Basically, victims have had the bad luck to be in the wrong place at the wrong time. In this life, in America, we live with the ever-present danger of being shot. Statistically, the odds are increasing that we or someone we know will be involved in a firearm-related incident, if not a mass shooting. There are mothers who have had children in two separate school shootings.[3] The odds of that happening are incalculable and this is the very reason that in the end the numbers are meaningless.

Veterans suffering from PTSD, young men who are failing, young men who are schizophrenic, paranoid, delusional, psychotic, insane, bipolar, psychopathic, depressed, and are armed with automatic weapons are a hazard to our health. There is no doubt. If the alien stopped at a different world they might have a psychological test for all gun owners to complete, with a waiting period, and only the sane could own a gun. And there would be no automatic weapons. On earth, this will never happen.

This is no great epiphany. Everyone knows that crazy people should not own guns and civilians should not have military weapons. So what? I grew up playing with guns my whole life and drawing pictures of men with guns and playing war games and fantasizing about being a western gunslinger. Guns are in our DNA in America. They are intertwined with who we are. So how can we survive in this gun-rich environment?

What we really have is a national health crisis, much like cancer or heart disease. The difference between this disease and the others is that we have chosen not to study this one. Where is the Presidential Commission on Mass Shootings in America? Where are the congressional committees mandating studies? With any other health crisis, from AIDS to Ebola, we throw millions and millions at the problem. We are strangely silent on guns. There are a few strangled gasps after each shooting, and then we go back to sleep. If we did have a national study we would probably find that the crisis stems from a confluence of trends in America. A plethora of guns in an increasingly urbanized society. A culture that promotes violence. A media that inadvertently promotes the shootings they cover with their glorification of the shooters. A lack of recognition that the old model of open schools should be replaced with metal detectors and single entrances, closer to a TSA approach. The problem is that we don't know because we have chosen to not even study this spreading cancer, which is multiplying every month and every year.

Personally, I won't ever do a layover in an airport again. I won't hang around public areas unless I must. I will always look for a nearby exit or a door to escape through. After that, it is the luck of the draw. Most people in shootings never see it coming. They are here one moment and gone the next. Some see their executioner and have that last thought that is terror, amazement, finality. *So this is how it ends. A fucking shooting. This is how I am leaving.* Many who survive have survivor's guilt and wonder—why not me?

I don't own a gun. I won't buy a gun to protect myself. That is not in my personality. But others think having a weapon might change the outcome and guns give them a sense of safety in their home. I get it. That is their right. I used to have a friend in Baltimore and whenever I would do something really stupid he would say, "Duuuuuumb." He would almost sing it and later in life when I do something stupid I will often murmur to myself, *duuuuuuuuuumb.*

And if that alien returned in his spaceship years later and ran through our news cycles and saw the same kinds of shootings with the same talking heads, the same SWAT teams, the same memorials and funerals and the same quadriplegics, the same school massacres, people in wheelchairs and families destroyed, people scarred for life with PTSD, the same fights in Congress going nowhere, and the same arguments trotted out, the same accessible automatic weapons, and the same mentally ill young men shooting people down, you can see that alien putting his spacecraft into gear and taking off, shaking his head, and singing out just like my old friend . . .

"Duuuuuuuuuuuumb."

CHAPTER 40

TWELVE HOURS OF CHAOS

I am buying a ticket for the train to go to Chicago. The lady behind the ticket window stares at me. "I saw someone on television in that shooting in Florida. Was that you?"

I nod.

"Oh my gosh. I thought that was you. That is amazing!"

I smile and take my ticket and have some time to kill. I have been holed up working on the proposal for this book for a few weeks and this is my first time out in public since I got back. I walk next door to get a cup of coffee. The same guy I see every time I take the train and who wears shorts all winter takes my order then looks at me.

"Were you on television?"

I nod.

"I thought that was you."

And that's it. He doesn't want to know any more beyond the confirmation that I have been on television. I take my coffee and go outside to wait for the train. Friends and family wanted to hear the story and Kitty and I have told them obligingly. It has become an adventure story, something we lived through and now we could relate our perilous journey.

Some people don't want to hear it. One couple at dinner after telling us all about their vacation in Europe only nod when I mention that we were in the shooting in the Fort Lauderdale airport.

"That's weird," the woman says, looking at her menu. It is already in the realm of the fantastic and weird and as more time passes it will become more so. Normal people are not in shootings in airports and we are normal people. And so we just quit talking about it. It requires too much energy from the listener and we become fatigued with trying to relate the story in a way that makes people understand.

A week after we came back the house phone rang. It rarely ever rang and I rarely answered it but that time I did.

"You don't know me but I am the photographer who let your kids stay in my car."

"Oh. Yes. Thank you for doing that. We really appreciate it."

"Yes . . . well. I don't know how to say this but one of your kids urinated in my backseat and I cannot get the smell out."

And then it all came back: the long day and the girls sitting in the car. There was nowhere to go to the bathroom except to be escorted into Terminal 2 by a policeman. Kitty and the girls eventually went but they were in that car a long time before that. Probably six hours.

"I am really sorry about that. We can pay for any damage."

"Yeah, I've been trying to scrub it out but I can't get rid of the smell."

"I am so sorry. We can pay you for the damages."

"Well, that's cool . . . Your girls alright?"

"Yes. They seem to be."

"And your son. I never did use that picture of him being searched by the police."

"Yes . . . he seems fine also."

There was a pause on the line.

"Well, the only thing I want to know is did they use my car to go to the bathroom . . . you know, figure they could do it there."

I hesitated and shook my head. It was a logical question, I suppose. Some people might use a car to urinate in if they weren't so terrified that urinating was the last thing they were worried about.

"No. No. Absolutely not. This is the first I heard of it. We appreciate what you did and, like I said, we can send you something for the damage . . . ah, why don't you give me your address."

I wrote down her address and hung up the phone. It was as if a hand had reached out and pulled me all the way back to that hot sticky day of terror. It was another world and this woman had done a humane thing and she wanted to make sure we had not played her for her kindness. I understood. It is a cynical world and you do something nice and you end up with urine in your backseat. What it said beyond this I didn't want to think about. Two girls too scared to get out of a car to go the bathroom so they urinate quietly in the back seat. There are things we cannot control and one of the most frustrating is losing control of what affects our children. Esteban Santiago and whoever shot off the rounds in Terminal 1 was still in our lives and might be for a long time.

Kitty ends up sending the photographer a nice card and a check. We never hear from her again, but she did a very human thing on a very bad day.

The kids never skip a beat. No bad dreams or nightmares. They are celebrities at their schools for a few days from being on television and then it is forgotten. Kids seem to compartmentalize, and I go with the police story that there was only one shooter and that we probably just heard some loud noises. Clay isn't buying it, of course, but the girls seem to accept this and so our time in the airport becomes the weird time we ran like crazy from the loud noises.

A second shooter has never been identified. I could list all the people who ran from those shots but to what end? This is not a conspiracy book. I am not trying to prove there was a second shooter. There was. I heard the shots. I ran for my life from the shots. So did everyone else. They shut down the airport because of that second shooter. They had to evacuate ten thousand people because of that second shooter. I have no idea why the police cling to the lone gunman scenario when Terminal 1 was evacuated and searched and person after person said they heard the shots.

Another book could take this on and make a very strong case. The shots could have come from the police, maybe a SWAT team member. Maybe it was an individual whose gun went off. Or it could have been a coordinated attack. I have no idea. All I know is what I heard and what my family heard and how we ran with a thousand other people to get away from those shots. The rest is left to history to decide what happened.

I did not run from a folding chair falling or someone yelling fire, and neither did anyone else.

If you surf the internet, you can find the interviews I gave at the airport. I found the CNN interview where the man said I didn't know what I was talking about. It is on a right-wing website that cites it as fake news put up by gun-control activists. There is another clip of Callie being interviewed and the site claims she is an actress. I can only imagine what the Sandy Hook parents went through when people accused them of staging the deaths of their children for an agenda. But this is the world we live in.

I didn't include the Pulse Nightclub shooting in this book as it was deemed the act of a terrorist, although it was horrific. Sadly, there have been many shootings since I began this book and there will be many more. There was a domestic shooting in our very sleepy town recently. A father killed his two daughters. I happened to be at a Starbucks working when I heard the police cars. Later, Kitty and I went to a restaurant down the street and we saw all those police cars and ambulances. It looked like Fort Lauderdale all over again. We both had trouble sleeping that night. I would say we both have a touch of PTSD because the strange uneasiness returned and I felt the same emotions of that day in the Florida airport. But it passed eventually.

Esteban Santiago took a plea deal where he will be sentenced to life in prison and the state will not pursue the death penalty.[1] He is on medication for schizophrenia. The wounded have all been released from the hospital. Fort Lauderdale hired a consultant to examine the police response to the shooting. The ninety-page report said the Broward Country Police mishandled the response to the shooting at the airport.

"The words 'shots fired' spread throughout the airport and triggered pandemonium as thousands of travelers, airline and airport employees began to escape from the concourses, gates, baggage claim areas, curbside loading areas and parking garages of all four terminals," the report states.[2]

Another report, by an outside consultant, concluded that the police and the airport did little to control the situation: "The shooting was followed by panic in other terminals, as rumors of additional shooters led to stampedes onto the tarmac. Some of those rumors were caused by law enforcement officers yelling unconfirmed reports of shots fired. The panic was worsened by TSA officials running from their posts to the exits as they are trained to do. Approximately 12,000 passengers were displaced, the review found, and many were stuck for hours without food, water or shelter and without timely information about what was happening to them."[3]

We lived the twelve hours of chaos and survived. The dead have been buried and the living endure. And now it is months later and spring is here. Chicago is finally warming up. I work a lot in Starbucks, and there is not a day that goes by when I don't think that someone could come in with a gun and start shooting. I think this in passing but it is there like a rock in my shoe, something I forget about until I suddenly feel it again.

We recently went to the Museum of Science and Industry in Chicago and had a great time over spring break. But a little dark bat would flap out of the corner of my mind at odd times in those crowds and I would look around for that young man with a Glock, a Walther 9mm, an AR-15, or a shotgun, and I would know what many others know at that moment . . . that it all can end, in the blink of a kiss.

ACKNOWLEDGMENTS

Many thanks to Steven L. Mitchell and the great folks at Prometheus Books for taking on a very tough book on a very tough subject and pushing me to make the book even better.

NOTES

PROLOGUE

1. Mark Follman, Gavin Aronsen, and Deanna Pan, "US Mass Shootings, 1982–2018: Data from Mother Jones' Investigation," *Mother Jones*, March 10, 2018, https://www.motherjones.com/politics/2012/12/mass-shootings-mother-jones-full-data/ (accessed March 23, 2018).

2. Joe Palazzolo and Alexis Flynn, "US Leads World in Mass Shootings," *Wall Street Journal*, October 3, 2015.

CHAPTER 1: REENTRY

1. Brett Clarkson, Brooke Baitinger, et al., "Timeline: How the Fort Lauderdale Airport Shooting Unfolded," *Sun Sentinel*, January 14, 2017, http://projects.sun-sentinel.com/projects/fll-airport-shooting-timeline/ (accessed April 2, 2018).

2. Ibid.

CHAPTER 2: THE AMERICAN PAYOFF

1. Andrea Torres, "Father Celebrating Birthday Dies in Fort Lauderdale Airport Shooting," Local 10 ABC News, January 7, 2017, https://www.local10.com/news/crime/father-celebrating-birthday-dies-in-fort-lauderdale-airport-shooting (accessed April 2, 2018).

2. Paul Scicchitano, "All 5 Fort Lauderdale Airport Victims Had Planned Cruises," *Miami Patch*, January 12, 2017, https://patch.com/florida/miami/all-5-fort-lauderdale-airport-victims-had-planned-cruises (accessed March 23, 2018).

3. Ibid.

4. Siobhan Morrissey and Steve Helling, "Friends and Family Mourn Shirley Timmons, Killed in the Fort Lauderdale Airport Shooting," *People*, January 12, 2017, http://people.com/crime/friends-and-family-mourn-shirley-timmons-killed-in-the-fort-lauderdale-airport-shooting/ (accessed April 12, 2018).

5. Juan Ortega, "Shirley Timmons: Airport-Shooting Victim Was 'Amazing Daughter,

Wife, Mother and Grandmother,'" *Sun Sentinel* (Broward County, FL), January 9, 2017, http://www.sun-sentinel.com/news/fort-lauderdale-hollywood-airport-shooting/fl-shirley-timmons-airport-shooting-20170107-story.html (accessed April 12, 2018).

6. Johnny Diaz, "Michael Oehme: Airport-Shooting Victim Was Known For His Love of Cruises," *Sun Sentinel* (Broward County, FL), January 7, 1017, http://www.sun-sentinel.com/news/fort-lauderdale-hollywood-airport-shooting/fl-michael-oehme-20170107-story.html (accessed April 12, 2018).

7. Rebeca Piccardo, "Mary Louise Amzibel Identified as Fifth Victim of Fort Lauderdale Airport Attack," *Orlando Sentinel*, January 11, 2017, http://www.orlandosentinel.com/news/sfl-fifth-victim-of-airport-massacre-identified-20170111-story.html (accessed April 12, 2018).

CHAPTER 3: FORT LAUDERDALE–HOLLYWOOD INTERNATIONAL AIRPORT

1. "Fort Lauderdale, FL: Fort Lauderdale-Hollywood International (FLL)," Bureau of Transportation Statistics, May 2011, https://www.transtats.bts.gov/airports.asp?pn=1&Airport=FLL&Airport_Name=Fort%20Lauderdale,%20FL:%20Fort%20Lauderdale-Hollywood%20International&carrier=FACTS (accessed March 23, 2018).

2. Ibid.

3. Lisa J. Huriash, "A Look at History of Fort Lauderdale–Hollywood International Airport," *Sun Sentinel*, March 23, 2017, http://www.sun-sentinel.com/news/sfl-fort-lauderdale-hollywood-international-airport-photo-gallery-20170323-photogallery.html (accessed April 13, 2018).

4. Hillary Mayell, "Bermuda Triangle: Behind the Intrigue," *National Geographic News*, December 15, 2003, https://news.nationalgeographic.com/news/2002/12/1205_021205_bermudatriangle.html (accessed April 13, 2018).

5. "About Us: Timeline," Fort Lauderdale–Hollywood International Airport, http://www.broward.org/Airport/About/Pages/Timeline.aspx (accessed April 13, 2018).

6. Joseph B. Treaster, "Hurricane Drenches Florida, Leaves 7 Dead," *New York Times*, August 27, 2005, https://www.nytimes.com/2005/08/27/us/hurricane-drenches-florida-leaves-7-dead.html (accessed April 13, 2018).

7. "Wilma's Wrath: Ft. Lauderdale–Hollywood Airport Still Closed," Aero News Network, October 27, 2005, http://www.aero-news.net/index.cfm?do=main.textpost&id=5fc02238-e8b7-43b6-9156-04c7bd2ea725 (accessed April 13, 2018).

8. "Accident Description: McDonnell Douglas DC-9-31, N8961E, Fort Lauderdale International Airport, FL," Aviation Safety Network, May 18, 1972, https://aviation-safety.net/database/record.php?id=19720518-1 (accessed March 23, 2018).

9. Amy Stromberg, "Cuba Frees Skyjacker," *Sun Sentinel*, June 18, 1988, http://articles

.sun-sentinel.com/1988-06-18/news/8802050382_1_air-piracy-air-florida-cuba (accessed April 13, 2018).

10. Richard N. Aarons, "Multiple Failures Put Learjet 35A into the Atlantic," Aviation Week Network, April 27, 2016, http://aviationweek.com/business-aviation/multiple-failures-put-learjet-35a-atlantic (accessed April 13, 2018).

11. Eliott C. McLaughlin, "Plane Catches Fire on Runway at Fort Lauderdale Airport," CNN, October 30, 2015, https://www.cnn.com/2015/10/29/us/fort-lauderdale-plane-catches-fire-runway/index.html (accessed March 23, 2018).

12. Jon Ostrower and Ralph Ellis, "FedEx Cargo Plane Burns at Fort Lauderdale Airport," CNN, October 28, 2016, https://www.cnn.com/2016/10/28/us/fedex-cargo-plane-fire/index.html (accessed April 13, 2018).

13. *Wikipedia*, s.v. "Airport Security," last edited April 1, 2018, https://en.wikipedia.org/wiki/Airport_security (accessed April 2, 2018).

CHAPTER 4: WEAPONIZED HUMANS

1. Paula McMahon, "Airport Shooting Suspect Is Being Treated for Schizophrenia, Defense Team Says," *Sun Sentinel*, March 13, 2017, http://www.sun-sentinel.com/news/fort-lauderdale-hollywood-airport-shooting/fl-reg-esteban-santiago-diagnosis-airport-shooting-20170313-story.html (accessed March 23, 2018).

2. Charles Rabin, "Airport Shooter's Life in Alaska Was Falling Apart, Though Few Seemed to Notice," *Miami Herald*, January 11, 2017, http://www.miamiherald.com/news/nation-world/article126025249.html (accessed April 13, 2018).

3. Mike Clary, Megan O'Matz, Lisa Arthur, and Carl Prine, "How Accused Airport Killer Esteban Santiago Spun Out of Control—With No One to Stop Him," *Sun Sentinel*, January 14, 2017, http://www.sun-sentinel.com/news/fort-lauderdale-hollywood-airport-shooting/fl-airport-shooting-santiago-profile-20170113-story.html (accessed April 13, 2018).

4. Megan O'Matz, Deborah Ramirez, and Stephen Hobbs, "Airport Shooter Esteban Santiago Had Florida Driver's License," *Sun Sentinel*, January 19, 2017, http://www.sun-sentinel.com/news/fort-lauderdale-hollywood-airport-shooting/fl-santiago-gun-license-pr-20170119-story.html (accessed April 13, 2018).

5. Nathaniel Herz, Chris Klint, Suzanna Caldwell, and Jerzy Shedlock, "Esteban Santiago, the Suspect in Florida Airport Shooting, Was an Anchorage Resident," *Anchorage Daily News*, January 6, 2017, https://www.adn.com/alaska-news/crime-courts/2017/01/06/suspect-in-florida-airport-shooting-has-same-name-age-as-anchorage-man/ (accessed April 17, 2018); Carol Currie, "Alaska Authorities: He Broke No Laws Here," *Florida Today*, January 7, 2017, https://www.floridatoday.com/story/news/local/2017/01/07/alaska-authorities-broke-laws/96299070/ (accessed April 17, 2018).

6. Ray Sanchez, "What We Know about the Fort Lauderdale Airport Shooting Suspect,"

CNN, January 7, 2017, https://www.cnn.com/2017/01/06/us/fort-lauderdale-airport
-shooting-suspect/index.html (accessed April 17, 2018).

7. Jason Dearen and Rachel D'Oro, "Suspected Florida Airport Gunman's Life Unraveled Over the Past Year," *Valley News*, January 12, 2017, http://www.vnews.com/Suspected-airport -gunman-s-life-unraveled-over-past-year-7442631 (accessed April 17, 2018).

8. Brandy Zadrozny, "Ft. Lauderdale Gunman Esteban Santiago Was Being Prosecuted for Strangling His Girlfriend," *Daily Beast*, January 7, 2017, https://www.thedailybeast.com/ ft-lauderdale-gunman-esteban-santiago-was-being-prosecuted-for-strangling-his-girlfriend (accessed April 17, 2018).

9. Kyle Clayton, Nicol Jenkins, and Leonard Greene, "Esteban Santiago's Brother Blames FBI for Killings as Fort Lauderdale Shooting Suspect May Face Death Penalty," *Daily News*, January 7, 2017, http://www.nydailynews.com/news/national/terrorism-probed-motive-fort -lauderdale-airport-shooting-article-1.2939003 (accessed March 23, 2018).

10. Currie, "Alaska Authorities."

CHAPTER 5: BAGGAGE CLAIM TERMINAL 2

1. Brett Clarkson, Brooke Baitinger, Linda Trischitta, Catie Peterson, Irfan Uraizee, and Yiran Zhu, "Timeline: How the Fort Lauderdale Airport Shooting Unfolded," *Sun Sentinel*, January 14, 2017, http://projects.sun-sentinel.com/projects/fll-airport-shooting-timeline/ (accessed April 18, 2018).

2. Joey Aguirre and Lihn Ta, "Iowa Man Killed in Fort Lauderdale Shooting 'a Good Husband, Father,'" *Des Moines Register*, January 7, 2017, https://www.desmoinesregister.com/ story/news/2017/01/07/iowa-man-killed-fort-lauderdale-shooting-good-husband-father/ 96292046/ (accessed April 18, 2018).

3. David Ng, "Answer: Do Most Soldiers Intentionally Shoot to Kill in Combat? . . ." Quora, November 19, 2015, https://www.quora.com/Do-most-soldiers-intentionally-shoot -to-kill-in-combat-Does-the-modern-soldier-differ-from-those-of-past-wars-Does-training -effectively-desensitize-killing-When-your-life-is-threatened-does-that-remove-all-inhibitions (accessed April 20, 2018).

4. Aguirre and Ta, "Iowa Man Killed."

5. Clarkson et al., "Timeline."

6. Ibid.

CHAPTER 7: THE RIGHT TO BEAR ARMS: A LIBERAL IDEA

1. James Thomas Flexner, *The Face of Liberty: Founders of the United States* (New York: Random House, 1977), p. 128.

2. Ibid.

3. English Bill of Rights 1689: An Act Declaring the Rights and Liberties of the Subject and Settling the Succession of the Crown, Avalon Project, http://avalon.law.yale.edu/17th _century/england.asp (accessed May 17, 2018).

4. Richard Burn, *The Justice of the Peace, and Parish Officer*, vol. 5 (London: A. Strahan, 1810), p. 757.

5. Charles A. Weisman, "Origin of the Right to Bear Arms in America," *Chalcedon*, February 28, 2000, https://chalcedon.edu/magazine/origin-of-the-right-to-bear-arms-in -america (accessed May 17, 2018).

6. An Act Concerning Crossbows and Handguns, 1541, 33 Hen. 8, c. 6.

7. US Const. amend. II (Bill of Rights), https://www.archives.gov/founding-docs/bill-of -rights-transcript (accessed May 17, 2018).

8. David Bodenhamer and James Ely Jr., *The Bill of Rights in Modern America* (Blooming-ton: Indiana University Press, 2008), p. 91.

9. Jeff Garzik, *The Founding Papers*, vol. 2, *The Federalist Papers* (Morrisville, NC: Lulu, 2004), p. 157.

10. Robert J. Cottrol, ed., *Gun Control and the Constitution: Sources and Explorations on the Second Amendment* (New York: Garland, 1994), p. xvi.

11. Gerard N. Magliocca, *The Heart of the Constitution: How the Bill of Rights Became the Bill of Rights* (Oxford, UK: Oxford University Press), p. 13.

12. A. John Simmons, *The Lockean Theory of Rights* (Princeton, NJ: Princeton University Press, 1994), p. 225.

CHAPTER 8: GRACE UNDER PRESSURE

1. Aviation Security Improvement Act of 1990, Pub. L. No. 101-604, 104 Stat. 3066.

2. Thomas H. Kean et al., *9/11 Commission Report* (Washington, DC: National Commission on Terrorist Attacks upon the United States, July 22, 2004), p. 270, http://avalon .law.yale.edu/sept11/911Report.pdf (accessed April 20, 2018).

3. R. William Johnstone, *9/11 and the Future of Transportation Security* (Westport, CT: Praeger Security International, 2006), p. 37.

4. Kean et al., *9/11 Commission Report*, p. 2.

5. Johnstone, *9/11 and the Future of Transportation Security*, p. 50.

6. Clark Kent Ervin, *Major Management Challenges Facing the Department of Homeland Security*, Department of Homeland Security, Office of Inspector General, December 2004, OIG-05-06, https://www.oig.dhs.gov/assets/Mgmt/OIG_05-06_Dec04.pdf (accessed April 20, 2018).

CHAPTER 9: ONE IN THREE HUNDRED

1. Dave Mosher and Skye Gould, "The Odds that a Gun Will Kill the Average American May Surprise You," *Business Insider*, March 25, 2018, http://www.businessinsider.com/us-gun-death-murder-risk-statistics-2018-3 (accessed Msy 25, 2018).

2. Dave Mosher and Skye Gould, "How Likely Is Gun Violence to Kill the Average American? The Odds May Surprise You," *Business Insider*, February 15, 2018, http://www.businessinsider.com/mass-shooting-gun-statistics-2018-2 (accessed March 23, 2018).

CHAPTER 10: THE FIRST MASS MURDER

1. Patrick Sauer, "The Story of the First Mass Murder in US History," *Smithsonian*, October 14, 2015, https://www.smithsonianmag.com/history/story-first-mass-murder-us-history-180956927/ (accessed March 23, 2018).

2. Ibid.

3. Charles Rabin, "Airport Shooter's Life in Alaska Was Falling Apart, Though Few Seemed to Notice," *Miami Herald*, January 11, 2017, http://www.miamiherald.com/news/nation-world/article126025249.html (accessed April 23, 2018).

4. Sauer, "Story of the First Mass Murder."

5. Ibid.

6. Ibid.

7. Ibid.

8. Mark Follman, Gavin Aronsen, and Deanna Pan, "A Guide to Mass Shootings in America," *Mother Jones*, March 10, 2018, https://www.motherjones.com/politics/2012/07/mass-shootings-map/ (accessed April 23, 2018).

CHAPTER 11: THE FEEDING FRENZY

1. Douglas Gentile, *Media Violence and Children: A Complete Guide for Parents and Professionals* (Westport, CT: Praeger, 2003), p. 2–3.

2. National Television Violence Study, 1998, cited in ibid., p. 3.

3. Gentile, *Media Violence and Children*, p. 11.

4. Ibid., p. 58 [italics added],

CHAPTER 13: THE TEXAS TOWER SNIPER

1. Gary M. Lavergne, *A Sniper in the Tower: The Charles Whitman Murders* (Austin: University of Texas Press 1997), pp. 18–19.

2. Ibid., p. 5.

3. Ibid., pp. 22–23.

4. Ibid., pp. 93–94.

5. Sarah Brash et al., eds., *Mass Murderers* (Alexandria, VA: Time-Life Books, 1993), p. 34.

6. Saul Pett and Jules Loh, "Whitman's Losing Battle Against Hate, Cruelty," *Ottawa Citizen*, August 15, 1966, p. 7.

7. Pamela Colloff, "96 Minutes," *Texas Monthly*, August 2006, https://www.texasmonthly.com/articles/96-minutes/ (accessed April 23, 2018).

8. Garth Jones, "Beginning of an Era: The 1966 University of Texas Clock Tower Shooting," NBC News, July 31, 2016, https://www.nbcnews.com/news/us-news/beginning-era-1966-university-texas-clock-tower-shooting-n620556 (accessed April 23, 2018).

9. "Charles Whitman Sniper Coverage," YouTube video, 1:54, posted by senortecolote, June 3, 2010, https://www.youtube.com/watch?v=1oK72g7mfvA (accessed April 26, 2018).

10. "KTBC UT Tower Shooting story during The Huntley-Brinkley Report | 8/1/1966," YouTube video, 5:06, posted by KTBC FOX 7 Austin, August 8, 2016, https://www.youtube.com/watch?v=-1Tty29I9m0 (accessed April 26, 2018), at 2:58–3:35.

11. David Wolcott, *Crime and Punishment in America* (New York: Infobase, 2010), p. 218.

12. Eva Frederick, "Experts Still Disagree on Role of Tower Shooter's Brain Tumor," *Daily Texan*, July 30, 2016, http://www.dailytexanonline.com/2016/07/30/experts-still-disagree-on-role-of-tower-shooters-brain-tumor (accessed March 23, 2018).

CHAPTER 15: CHICKEN NUGGETS: THE McDONALD'S SHOOTING

1. Arthur S. Brisbane, "To Father of Mass Murderer, Son's Violence Is Inexplicable," *Washington Post*, July 21, 1984, https://www.washingtonpost.com/archive/politics/1984/07/21/to-father-of-mass-murderer-sons-violence-is-inexplicable/377d77bd-97ff-4f22-b2a3-15c747f70ea3/?utm_term=.642238b630ad (accessed April 27, 2018).

2. Sarah Brash et al., eds., *Mass Murderers* (Alexandria, VA: Time-Life Books, 1993), pp. 114–15.

3. Ronald D. Brown, *Dying on the Job: Murder and Mayhem in the American Workplace* (Lanham, MD: Rowman and Littlefield, 2013), p. 194.

4. Brash et al., *Mass Murderers*, pp. 118–23.

5. Ibid., pp. 126–27.

6. Ibid.

7. Jim Kavanagh, "Slaughter at McDonald's Changed How Police Operate," CNN, July 24, 2009, http://edition.cnn.com/2009/CRIME/07/23/california.mcdonalds.massacre/index.html (accessed April 30, 2018).

8. John E. Douglas and Mark Olshaker, *The Anatomy of Motive* (New York: Pocket Books, 2000), p. 296.

CHAPTER 16: SHELL SHOCK

1. Ernest Hemingway, *A Farewell To Arms* (New York: Scribner's, 1929), p. 32.

2. Ryan Jaslow, "Soldiers' Brain Damage Similar to Football Players', Study of Chronic Traumatic Encephalopathy Shows," CBS News, May 16, 2012, https://www.cbsnews.com/news/soldiers-brain-damage-similar-to-football-players-study-of-chronic-traumatic-encephalopathy-shows/ (accessed May 3, 2018).

3. Peter Leese, *Shell Shock: Traumatic Neurosis and the British Soldiers of the First World War* (Basingstoke, UK: Palgrave Macmillan, 2014), p. 10.

4. "Shell Shock," *Inside Out*, BBC, March 3, 2004, http://www.bbc.co.uk/insideout/extra/series-1/shell_shocked.shtml (accessed May 3, 2018).

5. Taylor Downing, "How Shell-Shock Shaped the Battle of the Somme," *Telegraph*, April 16, 2016, https://www.telegraph.co.uk/books/authors/how-shell-shock-shaped-the-battle-of-the-somme/ (accessed May 3, 2018).

6. "Shell Shock," *Inside Out*.

CHAPTER 17: A SHORT HISTORY OF THE GUN

1. Jeff Schogol, "Are New Recruits Secretly Given Saltpeter?" *Stars and Stripes* (blog), June 15, 2010, https://www.stripes.com/blogs-archive/the-rumor-doctor/the-rumor-doctor-1.104348/are-new-recruits-secretly-given-saltpeter-1.107251#.Wvn9uqSUtpg (accessed May 14, 2018).

2. The Conestoga Company's Big-Bang Cannons, https://www.bigbangcannons.com/Home (accessed April 30, 2018).

3. "Firearms," History.com, 2018, https://www.history.com/topics/firearms (accessed May 5, 2018).

4. Carl P. Russell, Guns on the Early Frontiers: A History of Firearms from Colonial Times through the Years of the Early Fur Trade (Lincoln: University of Nebraska Press, 1980), p. 93.

5. Matthew Moss, "How the Colt Single Action Army Revolver Won the West," *Popular Mechanics*, November 3, 2016, https://www.popularmechanics.com/military/weapons/a23685/colt-single-action/ (accessed May 5, 2018).

6. Bill O'Neal, *Encyclopedia of Western Gunfighters* (Norman: University of Oklahoma Press, 1991), p. 4.

7. Dan Haar, "Gun That Won the West: Two Claim Bragging Rights," *Hartford Courant*, January 22, 2006, http://articles.courant.com/2006-01-22/business/0601210317_1_oliver-winchester-winchester-model-winchester-family (accessed May 5, 2018).

8. William Hazelgrove, *Al Capone and the 1933 World's Fair* (Lanham, MD: Rowman and Littlefield, 2017), p. 7.

9. Osha Gray Davidson, *Under Fire: The NRA and the Battle for Gun Control*, rev. ed. (Iowa City: University of Iowa Press, 1998), p. 4.

10. "Slaughter in a School Yard," *Time*, January 24, 2001, http://content.time.com/time/magazine/article/0,9171,151105,00.html (accessed April 30, 2018).

11. Wayne King, "Weapon Used by Deranged Man Is Easy to Buy," *New York Times*, January 19, 1989, https://www.nytimes.com/1989/01/19/us/weapon-used-by-deranged-man-is-easy-to-buy.html (accessed April 30, 2018).

12. "Slaughter in a School Yard."

13. Jay Mathews, "Schoolyard Massacre Refuels Drive for Stricter Gun Control," *Washington Post*, January 20, 1989, https://www.washingtonpost.com/archive/politics/1989/01/20/schoolyard-massacre-refuels-drive-for-stricter-gun-control/a309140e-7666-44d0-b684-30e5e43c5e21/?utm_term=.b8a65debc2e6 (accessed April 30, 2018).

14. Ron Irwin, *Mass Murders in America* (Lulu, 2016), p. 81.

15. William Booth, "Texas Killer Said to Have 'Problem with Women,'" *Washington Post*, October 18, 1991, https://www.washingtonpost.com/archive/politics/1991/10/18/texas-killer-said-to-have-problem-with-women/0af79d27-5ed2-4a1a-afb2-f6a38e9c32c2/?utm_term=.ae9b72b8b2f5 (May 1, 2018).

16. Don Terry, "Portrait of Texas Killer: Impatient and Troubled," *New York Times*, October, 18, 1991, https://www.nytimes.com/1991/10/18/us/portrait-of-texas-killer-impatient-and-troubled.html (accessed May 1, 2018).

17. Booth, "Texas Killer Said to Have 'Problem with Women.'"

18. Kyle Blankenship, "25 Years Later: Memories of Luby's Shooting Fade but Don't Die," *Killeen Daily Herald*, October 15, 2016, http://kdhnews.com/news/local/years-later-memories-of-luby-s-shooting-fade-but-don/article_c9b9b2b0-9357-11e6-ad69-abfb3fb48883.html (May 1, 2018).

19. Jon Stokes, "The Assault Weapons Ban Didn't Work. A New One Won't, Either," *Los Angeles Times*, March 1, 2018, http://www.latimes.com/opinion/op-ed/la-oe-stokes-assault-weapon-ban-20180301-story.html (accessed May 5, 2018).

20. Jason Ryan, "Obama to Seek New Assault Weapons Ban," ABC News, February 25, 2009, http://abcnews.go.com/Politics/story?id=6960824&page=1 (accessed April 3, 2018).

21. Meghan Keneally, "How 15 Democrats Helped Tank the 2013 Assault Weapons Ban," ABC News, October 5, 2017, https://abcnews.go.com/Politics/15-democrats-helped-tank-2013-assault-weapons-ban/story?id=50275295 (accessed May 5, 2018).

CHAPTER 18: RETURN TO TERMINAL 1

1. Radley Balko, *Overkill: The Rise of Paramilitary Raids in America* (whitepaper; Washington, DC: Cato Institute, July 17, 2006), https://object.cato.org/sites/cato.org/files/pubs/pdf/balko_whitepaper_2006.pdf (accessed April 3, 2018), pp. 12.

2. Sukanya Menon, "Mother Shot Dead by Police as They Raided Home to Arrest Her Son for Marijuana," *Meaww*, January 20, 2018, https://meaww.com/read/news/mother-shot-dead-by-police-as-they-raided-home-to-arrest-her-son-for-marijuana (accessed May 3, 2018).

3. Radley Balko, Rise of the Warrior Cop: The Militarization of America's Police Forces (New York: PublicAffairs, 2013), p. 258.

4. Matt Apuzzo, "War Gear Flows to Police Departments," *New York Times*, June 8, 2014, https://www.nytimes.com/2014/06/09/us/war-gear-flows-to-police-departments.html (accessed May 14, 2018).

5. Christopher Ingraham, "American Gun Ownership Drops to Lowest in Nearly Forty Years," *Washington Post*, June 29, 2016, https://www.washingtonpost.com/news/wonk/wp/2016/06/29/american-gun-ownership-is-now-at-a-30-year-low/?noredirect=on&utm_term=.e56e0aea111b (accessed May 14, 2018).

6. Kim Parker, Juliana Menasce Horowitz, et al., "America's Complex Relationship with Guns: 1. The Demographics of Gun Ownership," Pew Research Group, Washington, DC, June 22, 2017, http://www.pewsocialtrends.org/2017/06/22/the-demographics-of-gun-ownership/ (accessed April 3, 2018).

7. Dave Mosher and Skye Gould, "How Likely Is Gun Violence to Kill the Average American? The Odds May Surprise You," *Business Insider*, February 15, 2018, http://www.businessinsider.com/mass-shooting-gun-statistics-2018-2 (accessed March 23, 2018).

CHAPTER 19: COWBOYS AND INDIANS

1. Charles Dickens, *Martin Chuzzlewit*, in *The Works of Charles Dickens* (repr., 1842; Oxford: Oxford University Press, 2003), p. 458.

2. Garry Wills, "Spiking the Gun Myth: Review of *Arming America: The Origins of a National Gun Culture*, by Michael A. Bellesiles," *New York Times*, September 10, 2000, https://www.nytimes.com/2000/09/10/books/spiking-the-gun-myth.html (accessed May 14, 2018).

3. "Frederick Jackson Turner's 'Frontier Thesis,'" Gilder Lehrman Institute of American History, http://oa.gilderlehrman.org/history-by-era/development-west/timeline-terms/ frederick-jackson-turners-frontier-thesis-0 (accessed May 3, 2018).

4. Jervis Anderson, *Guns in American Life* (New York: Random House, 1984), p. 23.

5. William Hazelgrove, *Forging a President: How the Wild West Created Teddy Roosevelt* (Washington, DC: Regnery, 2017), p. 20.

6. Anderson, *Guns in American Life*, p. 49.

7. Ibid., p. 50.

8. "Frederick Jackson Turner's 'Frontier Thesis.'"

9. Ibid.

10. Michael R. Federspiel, *Picturing Hemingway's Michigan* (Detroit: Painted Turtle, 2010), p. 70.

11. "Hemingway's Suicide Gun," *Garden and Gun*, October 20, 2010, http://gardenand gun.com/articles/hemingways-suicide-gun/ (accessed May 14, 2018).

12. Marc Fisher, "Bang: The Troubled Legacy of Toy Guns," *Washington Post*, December 22, 2014, https://www.washingtonpost.com/lifestyle/style/bang-the-troubled-legacy-of -toy-guns/2014/12/22/96494ea8-86f8-11e4-9534-f79a23c40e6c_story.html?utm_term =.ea524ad31bd9 (accessed May 14, 2018).

13. *A Christmas Story*, directed by Bob Clark (Los Angeles, CA: Warner Bros., 1983).

CHAPTER 21: A SHORT HISTORY OF THE NRA

1. "A Brief History of the NRA," National Rifle Association, https://home.nra.org/about -the-nra/ (accessed May 5, 2018).

2. Lily Rothman, "The Original Reason the NRA Was Founded," *Time*, November 17, 2015, http://time.com/4106381/nra-1871-history/ (accessed May 14, 2018).

3. Nicholas J. Johnson, David B. Kopel, George A. Mocsary, and Michael P. O'Shea, *Firearms Law and the Second Amendment: Regulation, Rights, and Policy* (New York: Wolters Kluwer Law & Business, 2012), p. 531.

4. Robert Singh, "Gun Control," *Governing America: The Politics of a Divided Democracy*, ed. Robert Singh (Oxford, UK: Oxford University Press, 2003), p. 370.

5. Richard M. Skinner, More Than Money: Interest Group Action in Congressional Elections (Lanham, MD: Rowman & Littlefield, 2007), p. 144.

6. Cydney Hargis, "No, the NRA Is Not Actually the United States' 'Oldest Civil Rights Organization,'" *Media Matters for America*, April 28, 2017, https://www.mediamatters.org/ blog/2017/04/28/no-nra-not-actually-united-states-oldest-civil-rights-organization/216186 (accessed May 14, 2018).

7. David Knowles, "NRA Spent $15 Million to Oust President Obama from Office in 2012, and Donated Overwhelmingly to Republican Candidates," *New York Daily News*, February 4, 2013, http://www.nydailynews.com/news/politics/nra-spent-15-million-defeat -obama-2012-article-1.1254996 (accessed May 14, 2018).

8. Joel Roberts, "Assault Weapons Ban Expires," CBS News, September 13, 2004, https://www.cbsnews.com/news/assault-weapon-ban-expires/ (accessed May 14, 2018).

9. Eric Lichtblau and Motoko Rich, "NRA Envisions 'a Good Guy With a Gun' in Every School," *New York Times*, December 21, 2012, https://www.nytimes.com/2012/12/22/us/nra-calls-for-armed-guards-at-schools.html (accessed May 14, 2018).

10. Jay Nordlinger, "Chuck and Clint and Guns, &c.," National Review, September 13, 2017, https://www.nationalreview.com/2017/09/charlton-heston-clint-eastwood-guns-and-more-jay-nordlingers-impromptus-september-13/ (accessed May 14, 2018).

11. "NRA to File Suit Against San Francisco Gun Ban," Fox News, November 13, 2005, http://www.foxnews.com/story/2005/11/13/nra-to-file-suit-against-san-francisco-gun-ban.html (accessed May 14, 2018).

12. "NRA to Settle Suit Over Katrina Gun Seizures," NBC News, October 8, 2008, http://www.nbcnews.com/id/27087738/ns/us_news-life/t/nra-settle-suit-over-katrina-gun-seizures/#.WvpMEaSUvDc (accessed May 14, 2018).

13. Azam Ahmed, "NRA Sues Chicago, 3 Suburbs to Repeal Their Firearms Bans," *Chicago Tribune*, June 28, 2008, http://articles.chicagotribune.com/2008-06-28/news/0806270541_1_gun-ban-gun-control-activists-second-amendment-foundation (accessed May 14, 2018).

14. Tom Precious, "Appeals Court Upholds SAFE Act but Rules Against Seven-Bullet Limit," *Buffalo News*, October 19, 2015, http://buffalonews.com/2015/10/19/appeals-court-upholds-safe-act-but-rules-against-seven-bullet-limit/ (accessed May 14, 2018).

15. Dan Nephin, "NRA Sues Lancaster over Gun Law," *Lancaster Online*, December 15, 2015, https://lancasteronline.com/news/local/nra-sues-lancaster-over-gun-law/article_8b9ef60c-b780-11e4-90a5-b7ac691de4fc.html (accessed May 14, 2018).

16. Jay Weaver, "Man Accused of Fort Lauderdale Mass Shooting has Mental Illness but Can Stand Trial," *Miami Herald*, March 15, 2017, http://www.miamiherald.com/news/local/article138704713.html (accessed May 14, 2018).

CHAPTER 23: COLUMBINE

1. Dave Cullen, *Columbine* (New York: Grand Central, 2009), p. 357.
2. Ibid., p. 310.
3. Ibid., p. 158.
4. Ibid., p. 335.
5. Ibid., p. 141.
6. Ibid., p. 52.
7. Ibid., p. 53.
8. Ibid., p. 163.
9. Ibid., p. 59.
10. Ibid., p. 60.

11. Ibid., p. 66.

12. Ibid., p. 112.

13. Ibid., p. 195.

14. Michael W. Chapman, "Flashback—Charlton Heston: 'From My Cold, Dead Hands!'" CNS News, January 14, 2013, https://www.cnsnews.com/news/article/flashback-charlton -heston-my-cold-dead-hands (accessed May 15, 2018).

15. Cullen, *Columbine*, p. 342.

16. Ibid., p. 165.

17. Ibid., p. 167.

18. Ibid., p. 204.

19. Ibid., p. 261.

20. John D. Sutter, "Columbine Massacre Changed School Security," CNN, April 20, 2009, http://www.cnn.com/2009/LIVING/04/20/columbine.school.safety/ (accessed May 15, 2018).

21. "Columbine Student Jailed for Alleged Threat Not a Danger, Lawyer Says," CNN, October 22, 1999, http://www.cnn.com/US/9910/22/columbine.threat.02/ (accessed May 15, 2018).

22. Caroline Mimbs Nyce, "Dress Codes After Columbine," *Atlantic*, April 7, 2016, https://www .theatlantic.com/notes/2016/04/dress-codes-after-columbine/477375/ (accessed May 15, 2018).

23. "Cleaned-Up Columbine Reopens Monday; Decision on Fate of Library Remains," Fox News, January 26, 2001, http://www.foxnews.com/story/2001/01/26/cleaned-up-columbine -reopens-monday-decision-on-fate-library-remains.html (accessed May 15, 2018).

24. Ryan Parker, "Colorado Gun Background Check System Tops Out as Checks Still Pour In," *Denver Post*, December 26, 2012, https://www.denverpost.com/2012/12/26/colorado-gun -background-check-system-tops-out-as-checks-still-pour-in/ (accessed May 15, 2018).

25. Cullen, *Columbine*, p. 321.

26. Jeremy Rogalski and Tina Macias, "Suspected Santa Fe HS Shooter Violated District Trench Coat Policy," KHOU, May 24, 2018, https://www.khou.com/article/news/ investigations/suspected-santa-fe-hs-shooter-violated-district-trnch-coat-policy/285-557195480 (accessed May 29, 2018).

CHAPTER 24: ESCAPE FROM FLL

1. Kyra Gurney, "Hero Shields Mother of Two from Fort Lauderdale Airport Shooter," *Miami Herald*, January 8, 2017, http://www.miamiherald.com/news/nation-world/national/ article125275384.html (accessed May 15, 2018).

CHAPTER 25: TAXI DRIVER

1. Del Quentin Wilber, *Rawhide Down: The Near Assassination of Ronald Reagan* (New York: Henry Holt, 2011), p. 50.

2. Ibid., p. 60.

3. Jennifer Rosenberg, "Reagan Assassination Attempt," ThoughtCo, April 11, 2018, https://www.thoughtco.com/reagan-assassination-attempt-1779413 (accessed May 15, 2018).

4. Wilber, *Rawhide Down*, p. 90.

5. Ibid., p. 154.

6. Amanda Douville, "The Attempted Assassination of Ronald Reagan," *Daily News*, March 30, 2018, http://www.nydailynews.com/news/attempted-assassination-ronald-reagan-gallery-1.2728503 (accessed May 15, 2018).

7. Michelle Hackman, "Ex-Reagan Press Secretary James Brady Dies at 73," Wall Street Journal, August 4, 2014, https://www.wsj.com/articles/ex-reagan-press-secretary-james-brady-dies-1407176076 (accessed May 15, 2018).

8. Adam Howard, "John Lennon's Death 35 Years Ago Also Sparked a Gun Control Debate," MSNBC, December 8, 2015, http://www.msnbc.com/msnbc/john-lennons-death-35-years-ago-also-sparked-gun-control-debate (accessed May 15, 2018).

9. Brady Handgun Violence Prevention Act, H.R. 1025, 103rd Cong. (1993–1994), https://www.gpo.gov/fdsys/pkg/BILLS-103hr1025rh/pdf/BILLS-103hr1025rh.pdf (accessed May 4, 2018).

10. Jose Pagliery and Aaron Smith, "How Gun Background Checks Work," CNN, February 15, 2018, https://www.cnn.com/2018/02/15/us/gun-background-checks-florida-school-shooting/index.html (accessed May 15, 2018).

11. Brady Handgun Violence Prevention Act, p. 8.

12. "Meaning of Terms," 27 CFR 478.11, https://www.law.cornell.edu/cfr/text/27/478.11 (accessed May 4, 2018).

13. Jaime Fuller, "It's Been 20 Years Since the Brady Bill Passed. Here Are 11 Ways Gun Politics Have Changed," *Washington Post*, February 28, 2014, https://www.washingtonpost.com/news/the-fix/wp/2014/02/28/its-been-20-years-since-the-brady-law-passed-how-have-gun-politics-changed/?utm_term=.b7357c9f3586 (accessed May 4, 2018); Ronald Reagan, "Why I'm for the Brady Bill," *New York Times*, March 29, 1991, https://www.nytimes.com/1991/03/29/opinion/why-i-m-for-the-brady-bill.html (accessed March 25, 2018).

14. Trevor Hughes, "John Hinckley Jr. Released from Mental Hospital after More than 30 Years," *USA Today*, September 10, 2016, https://www.usatoday.com/story/news/2016/09/10/would--reagan-assassin-john-hinckley-jr-released-mental-hospital/90191312/ (accessed May 15, 2018).

CHAPTER 27: THE WORST: SANDY HOOK

1. "5 Years after Sandy Hook, the Victims Have Not Been Forgotten," CNN, December 14, 2017, https://www.cnn.com/2017/12/14/us/sandy-hook-newtown-shooting-victims -profiles/index.html (accessed May 15, 2018).

2. Daniel Bates and Helen Pow, "Lanza's Descent to Madness and Murder: Sandy Hook Shooter Notched Up 83,000 Online Kills Including 22,000 'Head Shots' Using Violent Games to Train Himself for His Massacre," *Daily Mail*, December 1, 2013, http://www.dailymail.co .uk/news/article-2516427/Sandy-Hook-shooter-Adam-Lanza-83k-online-kills-massacre.html (accessed May 15, 2018).

3. Andrew Solomon, "The Reckoning: The Father of the Sandy Hook Killer Searches for Answers," *New Yorker*, March 17, 2014, https://www.newyorker.com/magazine/2014/03/17/ the-reckoning (accessed May 15, 2018).

4. Liz Goodwin, "Sandy Hook Report: Shooter's Mom Wanted to Buy Him Gun for Christmas," Yahoo News, November 25, 2013, https://www.yahoo.com/news/sandy-hook -report--shooter-s-mom-wanted-to-buy-him-gun-for-christmas-210859068.html (accessed May 15, 2018).

5. Joshua Gardner, "Newtown Students Heard Principal's Murder Over Intercom," ABC News, December 15, 2012, https://abcnews.go.com/US/newtown-elementary-students-heard -principals-screams-intercom/story?id=17983828 (accessed May 15, 2018).

6. John Clarke, "'Petrified' Sandy Hook Nurse Hid in Closet for Four Hours Listening to Screams and Gunshots," *Daily Mail*, December 18, 2012, http://www.dailymail.co.uk/news/ article-2249768/Sandy-Hook-nurse-Sally-Cox-hid-closet-hours-listening-screams-gunshots .html (accessed May 15, 2018).

7. Alexander Abad-Santos, "This 6-Year-Old Survivor's Story May Be the Most Intense from Newtown Yet," *Atlantic*, December 17, 2012, https://www.theatlantic.com/politics/ archive/2012/12/6-year-old-survivor-newtown/320428/ (accessed May 15, 2018).

8. Pamela Engel, "Police Officer Describes the Grisly Scene at Sandy Hook Elementary after the Mass Murder," *Business Insider*, December 27, 2013, http://www.businessinsider.com/ police-officer-describes-scene-in-sandy-hook-2013-12 (accessed May 15, 2018).

9. "Gunman Adam Lanza Killed Himself as Police Closed In, Shot All Victims Multiple Times," *National Post*, December 16, 2012, http://nationalpost.com/news/gunman-adam -lanza-killed-himself-as-police-closed-in-shot-all-victims-multiple-times (accessed May 15, 2018).

10. Sarah Childress, "What Police Found in Adam Lanza's Home," *Frontline*, PBS, March 28, 2013, https://www.pbs.org/wgbh/frontline/article/what-police-found-in-adam-lanzas -home/ (accessed May 15, 2018).

11. Igor Bobic, "Conservatives Mock Obama for Crying about Newtown School Shooting," *Huffington Post*, January 5, 2016, https://www.huffingtonpost.com/entry/conservatives-mock -obama-crying_us_568c091be4b014efe0dbdf2c (accessed May 15, 2018).

12. Matt Friedman, "Sandy Hook Families Say Ammo Magazine Limit Would Save Lives," NJ.com, February 24, 2014, http://www.nj.com/politics/index.ssf/2014/02/sandy_hook_families_say_ammo_magazine_limit_would_save_lives.html (accessed May 15, 2018).

13. "Remarks from the NRA Press Conference on Sandy Hook School Shooting, Delivered on Dec. 21, 2012 (Transcript)," *Washington Post*, December 21, 2012, https://www.washingtonpost.com/politics/remarks-from-the-nra-press-conference-on-sandy-hook-school-shooting-delivered-on-dec-21-2012-transcript/2012/12/21/bd1841fe-4b88-11e2-a6a6-aabac85e8036_story.html?utm_term=.2212a378d343 (accessed May 15, 2018).

14. Rick Rojas and Kristin Hussey, "Appeal Offers Hope for Newtown Families in Suit Against Gun Companies," *New York Times*, November 12, 2017, https://www.nytimes.com/2017/11/12/nyregion/appeal-offers-hope-for-newtown-families-in-suit-against-gun-companies.html (accessed May 15, 2018).

15. Dave Altimari, "Sandy Hook Families Settle Lawsuits Against Lanza Estate for $1.5M," *Hartford Courant*, August 6, 2015, http://www.courant.com/news/connecticut/hc-sandy-hook-lawsuit-settled-20150803-story.html (accessed May 15, 2018).

16. Bilge Ebiri, "The Documentary *Newtown* Grapples With the Memories of Sandy Hook Without Exploiting Them," *Vulture*, January 27, 2016, http://www.vulture.com/2016/01/sundance-review-the-heart-wrenching-newtown.html (accessed May 15, 2018).

17. Peter Applebome and Michael Wilson, "'Who Would Do This to Our Poor Little Babies,'" *New York Times*, December 14, 2012, https://www.nytimes.com/2012/12/15/nyregion/witnesses-recall-deadly-shooting-sandy-hook-newtown-connecticut.html (accessed May 15, 2018).

18. Ana Radelat, "Sandy Hook Parents Watch as Gun Bill Dies in Congress," *CT Mirror*, April 18, 2013, https://ctmirror.org/2013/04/18/sandy-hook-parents-watch-gun-bill-dies-congress/ (accessed May 15, 2018).

CHAPTER 28: PORT EVERGLADES

1. Kristen Andersen, *Port Everglades: A Century of Opportunity* (Fort Lauderdale, FL: Port Everglades Department of Broward County, 2000), p. 15, https://res.cloudinary.com/simpleview/image/upload/v1/clients/porteverglades/Port_Everglades_A_Century_of_Opportunity_for_Web_ADA_6820a847-a20c-4350-90e0-258bd2d33ce8.pdf (accessed May 7, 2018).

2. Ibid., pp. 26, 32.

3. Susan Piperato, "Top 10 Busiest US Ports," National Real Estate Investor, January 27, 2014, http://www.nreionline.com/public-infrastructure/top-10-busiest-us-ports (accessed March 25, 2018).

CHAPTER 30: VIRGINIA TECH

1. N. R. Kleinfield, "Before Deadly Rage, a Life Consumed by a Troubling Silence," *New York Times*, April 22, 2007, https://www.nytimes.com/2007/04/22/us/22vatech.html (accessed May 16, 2018).

2. Brigid Schulte and Tim Craig, "Unknown to Va. Tech, Cho Had a Disorder," *Washington Post*, August 27, 2007, http://www.washingtonpost.com/wp-dyn/content/article/2007/08/26/AR2007082601410.html (accessed March 25, 2018).

3. M. Alex Johnson, "Gunman Sent Package to NBC News," NBC News, April 19, 2007, http://www.nbcnews.com/id/18195423/ns/us_news-crime_and_courts/t/gunman-sent-package-nbc-news/#.WvxHMKSUtpg (accessed May 16, 2018).

4. Emma Ketteley, "Killer's History of Social Disorders," *This World*, BBC, April 8, 2008, http://news.bbc.co.uk/2/hi/programmes/this_world/7336053.stm (accessed May 16, 2018).

5. "The 'Unremarkable Sale' of Gun to Student Killer," NBC News, April 18, 2007, http://www.nbcnews.com/id/18170761/ns/us_news-crime_and_courts/t/unremarkable-sale-gun-student-killer/#.WvxJkaSUtpg (accessed May 16, 2018).

6. Sean Alfano, "Va. Tech Killer Bought 2nd Gun Online," CBS News, April 19, 2007, https://www.cbsnews.com/news/va-tech-killer-bought-2nd-gun-online/ (accessed May 16, 2018).

7. Fred Burton, "The Virginia Tech Shootings: A Case for Redundant Communications," Stratfor, April 17, 2007, https://www.stratfor.biz/weekly/virginia-tech-shootings-case-redundant-communications (accessed May 16, 2018).

8. Virginia Tech Review Panel, *Mass Shootings at Virginia Tech, April 16, 2007: Report of the Review Panel*, August 2007, p. 27, https://governor.virginia.gov/media/3772/fullreport.pdf (accessed May 16, 2018).

9. Rick Jervis, "10 years after Va. Tech Shooting: How Gun Laws Have Changed," *USA Today*, April 14, 2017, https://www.usatoday.com/story/news/nation/2017/04/14/va-tech-shooting-gun-laws-debate/100458024/ (accessed May 16, 2018).

10. Matt Halprin, "Message from Matt Halprin—New Listing Restrictions on Gun Parts," eBay, July 30, 2007, http://www2.ebay.com/aw/core/200707301000452.html (accessed May 16, 2018).

11. Theresa Vargas and Michael Laris, "Costumes of Cho Victims Rile Va. Tech Community," *Washington Post*, December 9, 2007, http://www.washingtonpost.com/wp-dyn/content/article/2007/12/08/AR2007120801537.html (accessed May 16, 2018).

12. James Nye, "Video Game Designer behind Sick Sand Hook Shoot-Em-Up Was Also behind Banned Virginia Tech Game Which He Said He Made Because He's a 'Heartless B*****d,'" *Daily Mail*, November 20, 2013, http://www.dailymail.co.uk/news/article-2510991/Ryan-Jake-Lambourn-Sandy-Hook-video-game-Virginia-Tech-Rampage.html (accessed May 16, 2018).

13. Kyle McDonald, "Va. Tech Fined $55K for Clery Act Violations," Student Press Law Center, March 30, 2011, http://www.splc.org/article/2011/03/va-tech-fined-55k-for-clery-act-violations?id=2206 (accessed May 16, 2018).

14. Ned Potter, "Shooting at Virginia Tech: Did Campus Alerts Work?" ABC News, December 8, 2011, https://abcnews.go.com/Technology/virginia-tech-alerts-shooting-message-boards-text-messages/story?id=15116102 (accessed May 16, 2018).

15. See, for example, Lucinda Roy, *No Right to Remain Silent: The Tragedy at Virginia Tech* (New York: Crown, 2009).

16. "Settlement Reached in Virginia Tech Shootings," NBC News, April 10, 2008, http://www.nbcnews.com/id/24050712/ns/us_news-crime_and_courts/t/settlement-reached-virginia-tech-shootings/#.WvxmZqSUtpg (accessed May 16, 2018).

17. Richard Brusca and Colin Ram, "A Failure to Communicate: Did Privacy Laws Contribute to the Virginia Tech Tragedy?" *Washington and Lee Journal of Civil Rights and Social Justice* 17, no. 1 (2010), https://scholarlycommons.law.wlu.edu/cgi/viewcontent.cgi?article=1274&context=crsj (accessed May 16, 2018).

18. Ted Nugent, "Nugent: Gun-Free Zones Are Recipe for Disaster," CNN, April 20, 2007, http://www.cnn.com/2007/US/04/19/commentary.nugent/index.html (accessed May 16, 2018).

19. Sean Alfano, "Va. Tech Killer Picked On, Classmates Say," CBS News, April 19, 2007, https://www.cbsnews.com/news/va-tech-killer-picked-on-classmates-say/ (accessed May 16, 2018).

CHAPTER 32: THE DARK KNIGHT

1. Nick Allen, "James Holmes, the 'Brainiac' Who Grew Up to Be a Mass Murderer," *Telegraph*, July 15, 2015, https://www.telegraph.co.uk/news/worldnews/northamerica/usa/11564962/James-Holmes-the-brainiac-who-grew-up-to-be-a-mass-killer.html (accessed May 16, 2018).

2. Allison Sylte and Brandon Rittiman, "Theater Shooter's Psychiatrist Found His Behavior Bizarre," *USA Today*, June 16, 2015, https://www.usatoday.com/story/news/nation/2015/06/16/aurora-theater-shooting-psychiatrist/28812505/ (accessed May 16, 2018).

3. Michelle Castillo, "Colo. Shooter Purchased Guns Legally from 3 Different Stores," CBS News, July 20, 2012, https://www.cbsnews.com/news/colo-shooter-purchased-guns-legally-from-3-different-stores/ (accessed May 16, 2018).

4. Jack Healy, "Suspect Bought Large Stockpile of Rounds Online," *New York Times*, July 22, 2012, https://www.nytimes.com/2012/07/23/us/online-ammunition-sales-highlighted-by-aurora-shootings.html (accessed May 16, 2018).

5. "Colorado Theater Gunman Says He Called Crisis Line Before Shootings," *Chicago Tribune*, June 2, 2015, http://www.chicagotribune.com/news/nationworld/ct-james-holmes-murder-trial-20150602-story.html (accessed May 16, 2018).

6. Jack Healy, "Video Shows James Holmes Recalling Colorado Theater Shooting," *New York Times*, June 2, 2015, https://www.nytimes.com/2015/06/03/us/video-shows-james-holmes-recalling-colorado-theater-shooting.html (accessed May 16, 2018).

7. Phil Tenser, "240 Ballistic Impacts Found after Theater Shooting, Aurora Police CSI Testifies in Holmes' Trial," Denver7, May 14, 2015, https://www.thedenverchannel.com/news/movie-theater-shooting/240-ballistic-impacts-found-after-theater-shooting-aurora-police-csi-testifies-in-holmes-trial-051415 (accessed May 16, 2018).

8. Keith Coffman, "Colorado Police Officer Says Movie Theater Gunman Was 'Very Calm,'" Yahoo News, April 30, 2015, https://www.yahoo.com/news/colorado-police-officer-says-movie-theater-gunman-very-165639024.html (accessed May 16, 2018).

9. "Woman Who Lost Everything Caps Prosecution in Holmes Trial," CBS News, June 19, 2015, https://www.cbsnews.com/news/james-holmes-trial-prosecutors-wrap-up-case/ (accessed May 16, 2018).

10. Stephanie Wolf, "The Aurora Theater Shooting Recasts 'In Sickness and in Health' for One Family," Colorado Public Radio, July 19, 2017, http://www.cpr.org/news/story/in-sickness-and-in-health-takes-on-new-meaning-for-couple-that-survived-aurora-theater (accessed May 16, 2018).

11. Sadie Gurman, "WATCH LIVE: Day 2 in the Sentencing of Aurora Theater Shooting Gunman," Gazette, August 25, 2015, http://gazette.com/watch-live-day-2-in-the-sentencing-of-aurora-theater-shooting-gunman/article/1558038 (accessed May 16, 2018).

12. Mike Baker and Kristen Wyatt, "Fear Prompts Gun Sales after Colorado Theater Massacre," Salt Lake Tribune, http://archive.sltrib.com/article.php?id=54556710&itype=CMSID (accessed May 16, 2018).

CHAPTER 33: VICTIMS

1. Gail McCarthy and Terry Weber, "Lost Crew Still Remembered in Gloucester," Eagle Tribune, October 29, 2011, http://www.eagletribune.com/news/local_news/lost-crew-still-remembered-in-gloucester/article_fa158634-fedf-5463-a3c0-0abfaa0aa4ba.html (accessed May 16, 2018).

CHAPTER 34: THE SURVIVOR

1. Mark Thompson, "How Marijuana Use Aborted Jared Loughner's Military Career," Time, January 10, 2011, http://content.time.com/time/nation/article/0,8599,2041634,00.html (accessed May 17, 2018).

2. Philip Bump, "Walmart, Guns, and Money: What's Inside Gabby Giffords Files for the Gun Debate," Atlantic, March 27, 2013, https://www.theatlantic.com/national/archive/2013/03/gabby-giffords-files-gun-debate/316906/ (accessed May 17, 2018).

3. Eric Lipton, Charlie Savage, and Scott Shane, "Arizona Suspect's Recent Acts Offer

Hints of Alienation," *New York Times*, January 8, 2011, https://www.nytimes.com/2011/01/09/us/politics/09shooter.html?pagewanted=all (accessed May 17, 2018).

4. Ashleigh Banfield, Jessica Hopper, Josey Crews, and Emily Cohen, "Tucson Shooting: Jared Loughner Stopped for Traffic Violation Hours Before Shooting," ABC News, January 12, 2011, https://abcnews.go.com/US/tucson-shooting-jared-loughner-stopped-authorities-hours-shooting/story?id=12597092 (accessed May 17, 2018).

5. David Nakamura and Sari Horwitz, "Police Recover Black Bag, Ammunition Believed to Belong to Tucson Suspect," *Washington Post*, January 13, 2011, http://www.washingtonpost.com/wp-dyn/content/article/2011/01/13/AR2011011303515.html (accessed May 17, 2018).

6. "Arizona Safeway Shootings Fast Facts," CNN, December 25, 2017, https://www.cnn.com/2013/06/10/us/arizona-safeway-shootings-fast-facts/index.html (accessed May 17, 2018).

7. Marc Lacey and David M. Herszenhorn, "In Attack's Wake, Political Repercussions," *Gainesville Sun*, January 9, 2011, http://www.gainesville.com/article/LK/20110109/news/604129277/GS/ (May 17, 2018).

8. Dan Childs, "Giffords' Brain Surgery Safe, but Not Risk-Free, Surgeons Say," ABC News, May 18, 2011, https://abcnews.go.com/Health/rep-gabrielle-giffords-brain-surgery/story?id=13631297 (accessed May 17, 2018).

9. Susan Page, "Gabby Giffords' Comeback: Word by Word, Step by Step," *USA Today*, September 28, 2014, https://www.usatoday.com/story/news/politics/2014/09/28/day-in-the-life-of-gabby-giffords/16281013/ (accessed May 17, 2018).

10. Gabby Giffords and Mark Kelly, "Gabby Giffords and Mark Kelly: The New Year Is a Time for Hope, Even After Tragedy," *Time*, November 30, 2017, http://time.com/5041049/gabby-giffords-husband-after-shooting/ (accessed May 17, 2018).

11. Tom Watson, "Gabby Giffords' New Firearms Reform PAC Goes Viral," *Forbes*, January 11, 2013, https://www.forbes.com/sites/tomwatson/2013/01/11/gabby-giffords-new-firearms-reform-pac-goes-viral/#4e5c2302c7d5 (accessed May 17, 2018).

12. Jennifer Steinhauer "Senate Hearing on Guns Suggests an Uphill Fight on New Limits," *New York Times*, January 30, 2013, https://www.nytimes.com/2013/01/31/us/politics/senate-hearing-to-focus-on-gun-violence.html (accessed May 17, 2018).

13. Alan Duke, "Loughner Sentenced to Life for Arizona Shootings," CNN, November 8, 2012, https://www.cnn.com/2012/11/08/justice/arizona-loughner-sentencing/index.html (accessed May 17, 2018).

CHAPTER 36: THE BUMP STOCK KILLER: LAS VEGAS

1. "Las Vegas Shooter Stephen Paddock Had Lost Money, Been Depressed, Sheriff Says," CBS News, November 4, 2017, https://www.cbsnews.com/news/las-vegas-shooter-stephen-paddock-had-lost-money-been-depressed-sheriff-says/ (accessed May 17, 2018).

2. Sabrina Tavernise, Serge F. Kovaleski, and Julie Turkewitz, "Who Was Stephen Paddock?

The Mystery of a Nondescript 'Numbers Guy,'" *New York Times*, October 7, 2017, https://www
.nytimes.com/2017/10/07/us/stephen-paddock-vegas.html (accessed May 17, 2018).

3. Larry Buchanan et al. "Inside the Las Vegas Gunman's Mandalay Bay Hotel Suite," *New York Times*, October 4, 2017, https://www.nytimes.com/interactive/2017/10/04/us/vegas -shooting-hotel-room.html (accessed March 25, 2018).

4. Alex Yablon, "AR-15 Lovers Are Getting Fully Automatic Thrills with Barely Legal Gadgets," *Trace*, November 16, 2015, https://www.thetrace.org/2015/11/ar-15-bump-fire -legal/ (accessed May 17, 2018).

5. Matt Pearce, David Montero, and Richard Winton, "Las Vegas Gunman Shot Security Guard a Full Six Minutes Before Opening Fire on Concertgoers, Police Reveal," *Los Angeles Times*, October 9, 2017, http://www.latimes.com/nation/la-na-vegas-shooting-20171009-story .html (accessed May 17, 2018).

6. "Las Vegas Shooting: Jason Aldean Fans Jump to His Defense after Trolls Call Him a 'Coward,'" Fox News, October 2, 2017, http://www.foxnews.com/entertainment/2017/10/02/ las-vegas-shooting-jason-aldean-fans-jump-to-his-defense-after-trolls-call-him-coward.html (accessed May 17, 2018).

7. Maria Puente, "Las Vegas Mass Shooting Raises New Doubts about Safety of Live Entertainment," *USA Today*, October 2, 2017, https://www.usatoday.com/story/life/ 2017/10/02/las-vegas-mass-shooting-raises-new-doubts-safety-live-entertainment/723197001/ (accessed May 17, 2018).

8. "Why Did It Take Police So Long to Breach Las Vegas Gunman's Room? Here's a New Timeline," *Los Angeles Times*, October 4, 2017, http://www.latimes.com/nation/la-las-vegas -shooting-live-updates-why-did-it-take-police-so-long-to-1507174474-htmlstory.html (accessed May 17, 2018).

9. Nick Visser, "Unarmed Hotel Security Guard Who Found Las Vegas Shooter Hailed as Hero," *Huffington Post*, October 10, 2017, https://www.huffingtonpost.com/entry/jesus -campos-las-vegas-shooter_us_59d5c607e4b0cde45872e30e (accessed May 17, 2018).

10. Jeremy Gorner, "Las Vegas Gunman Booked Chicago Hotel Rooms Overlooking Lollapalooza: Sources," *Chicago Tribune*, October 6, 2017, http://www.chicagotribune.com/news/ local/breaking/ct-las-vegas-gunman-lollapalooza-20171005-story.html (accessed May 17, 2018).

11. Michael Y. Park, "Why the Las Vegas Shooter Couldn't Blow Up Jet Fuel Tanks at LAS," *The Points Guy*, October 5, 2017, https://thepointsguy.com/2017/10/why-stephen -paddock-couldnt-blow-up-jet-fuel-tanks-in-las-vegas/ (accessed May 17, 2018).

12. Jason Silverstein, "Las Vegas Gunman Stephen Paddock's Girlfriend Had Fingerprints on His Ammunition, Documents Show," *Newsweek*, January 14, 2018, http://www.newsweek .com/las-vegas-gunman-stephen-paddock-girlfriend-fingerprints-ammunition-781028 (accessed May 17, 2018).

13. "Las Vegas Shooting: Gunman Was on Losing Streak and 'Germophobic,' Police Say," *Guardian*, January 20, 2018, https://www.theguardian.com/us-news/2018/jan/20/las-vegas -shooting-police-report-gunman-motive-mystery-stephen-paddock (accessed May 17, 2018).

14. Lydia Wheeler, "Trump Sets Up Legal Fight Over Bump Stocks," *Hill*, March 27, 2018, http://thehill.com/homenews/administration/380369-trump-sets-up-legal-fight-over-bump-stocks (accessed May 17, 2018).

CHAPTER 38: A PROFESSIONAL SCHOOL SHOOTER: MARJORY STONEMAN DOUGLAS HIGH SCHOOL

1. Todd J. Gillman, "Trump Calls Florida School Guard a Coward, Compares Immigrants to Poisonous Snakes," *Dallas News*, February 23, 2018, https://www.dallasnews.com/news/politics/2018/02/23/after-calling-florida-school-guard-coward-trump-cpac-keeps-push-arm-teachers (accessed May 17, 2018).

2. Sarah Gray, "'Coward' Cop Defends His Actions During Parkland School Shooting," *Time*, February 26, 2018, http://time.com/5176090/scot-peterson-not-coward-parkland-cop/ (accessed May 17, 2018).

3. Max Greenwood, "Additional Deputies Did Not Enter Florida High School During Shooting: Report," *Hill*, February 23, 2018, http://thehill.com/homenews/news/375392-officers-from-second-fla-police-department-found-four-deputies-hadnt-entered (accessed May 17, 2018).

4. Emily Stewart, "Multiple Armed Officers Hung Back During Florida School Shooting, Reports Say," *Vox*, February 25, 2018, https://www.vox.com/policy-and-politics/2018/2/24/17048720/florida-shooting-law-enforcement-gun (accessed May 17, 2018).

5. Sara Dorn, "Cruz Spewed Vile Hatred in Online Rants," *New York Post*, February 17, 2018, https://nypost.com/2018/02/17/cruz-threatened-violence-in-disturbing-online-rants/ (accessed May 17, 2018).

6. Mark Berman and Matt Zapotosky, "The FBI Said It Failed to Act on a Tip about the Suspected Florida School Shooter's Potential for Violence," *Washington Post*, February 16, 2018, https://www.washingtonpost.com/news/post-nation/wp/2018/02/16/as-florida-town-mourns-authorities-revisit-possible-warning-signs-before-school-massacre/?utm_term=.8214d65f014a (accessed May 17, 2018).

7. Jake Newby, "Pace Mom Petitions Santa Rosa, Escambia District to Lock All School Doors," *Pensacola News Journal*, February 16, 2018, https://www.pnj.com/story/news/local/2018/02/16/pace-mother-petition-santa-rosa-florida-schools-lock-doors-school/344433002/ (accessed May 17, 2018).

8. Wayne T. Price and John McCarthy, "Step by Step: How the Parkland Shooting Unfolded," *Florida Today*, February 17, 2018, https://www.floridatoday.com/story/news/2018/02/17/minute-minute-how-parkland-school-shooting-unfolded/345817002/ (accessed May 17, 2018).

9. Elizabeth Chuck, "Parkland School Shooting: Football Coach Aaron Feis Died Shielding Students," NBC News, February 15, 2018, https://www.nbcnews.com/news/us-news/parkland-school-shooting-hero-football-coach-aaron-feis-died-shielding-n848311 (accessed May 17, 2018).

10. Amanda Woods, "Second Alarm Spurred Hero Teacher into Action During Florida Shooting," *New York Post*, February 16, 2018, https://nypost.com/2018/02/16/second-alarm-spurred-hero-teacher-into-action-during-florida-shooting/ (accessed May 17, 2018).

11. Patricia Mazzei, "Parkland Gunman Carried Out Rampage Without Entering a Single Classroom," *New York Times*, April 24, 2018, https://www.nytimes.com/2018/04/24/us/parkland-shooting-reconstruction.html (accessed May 17, 2018).

12. Ruth Brown, "Four Sheriffs' Deputies Hid During Florida School Shooting," *New York Post*, February 23, 2018, https://nypost.com/2018/02/23/four-sheriffs-deputies-hid-during-florida-school-shooting/ (accessed May 17, 2018).

13. Luis Sanchez, "Florida Deputy Thought Shooting Was Outside School: Lawyer," *Hill*, February 26, 2018, http://thehill.com/homenews/news/375640-florida-deputy-thought-shooting-was-outside-school-lawyer (accessed May 17, 2018).

14. Heather Sher, "What I Saw Treating the Victims from Parkland Should Change the Debate on Guns," *Atlantic*, February 22, 2018, https://www.theatlantic.com/politics/archive/2018/02/what-i-saw-treating-the-victims-from-parkland-should-change-the-debate-on-guns/553937/ (accessed May 17, 2018).

15. Alan Binder, "Florida Will Seek Execution of Nikolas Cruz in Parkland Shooting Trial," *New York Times*, March 13, 2018, https://www.nytimes.com/2018/03/13/us/nikolas-cruz-death-penalty.html (accessed May 17, 2018); David Ovalle, "'I Don't Want This Case Treading Water.' Judge Nudges Lawyers in Parkland Massacre Case," *Miami Herald*, April 27, 2018, http://www.miamiherald.com/news/local/crime/article209983584.html (accessed May 17, 2018).

16. Rene Rodriguez, Monique O. Madan, Alex Harris, and Martin Vassolo, "The Victims of the Parkland School Shooting," *Tampa Bay Times*, February 16, 2018, http://www.tampabay.com/news/publicsafety/The-victims-of-the-Parkland-school-shooting_165511796 (accessed May 17, 2018).

17. David Smith, "Trump's Solution to School Shootings: Arm the Teachers with Guns," *Guardian*, February 21, 2018, https://www.theguardian.com/us-news/2018/feb/21/donald-trump-solution-to-school-shootings-arm-teachers-with-guns (accessed May 17, 2018).

18. Patricia Mazzei, "Florida Gun Control Bill Passed by House, Defying N.R.A.," *New York Times*, March 7, 2018, https://www.nytimes.com/2018/03/07/us/florida-shooting-gunman-indicted.html (accessed May 17, 2018).

19. Ray Sanchez and Holly Yan, "Florida Gov. Rick Scott Signs Gun Bill," CNN, March 9, 2018, https://www.cnn.com/2018/03/09/us/florida-gov-scott-gun-bill/index.html (accessed May 17, 2018).

CHAPTER 39: MALES WHO FAIL

1. Benjamin Mueller, "Limiting Access to Guns for Mentally Ill Is Complicated," *New York Times*, February 15, 2018, https://www.nytimes.com/2018/02/15/us/gun-access-mentally-ill.html (accessed March 25, 2018).

2. Kristen Korosec, "Trump Undid Obama Rule That Added Mentally Ill People to Gun Check Register," *Fortune*, February 15, 2018, http://fortune.com/2018/02/15/trump-shooting-mental-illness/ (accessed May 17, 2018).

3. Georgina Rannard, "Florida School Shooting: One Mother, Two Gun Attacks," BBC News, March 4, 2018, http://www.bbc.com/news/world-us-canada-43156477 (accessed May 17, 2018).

CHAPTER 40: TWELVE HOURS OF CHAOS

1. Paula McMahon, "Airport Shooter Esteban Santiago to Plead Guilty, Spend Life in Prison," *Sun Sentinel*, May 1, 2018, http://www.sun-sentinel.com/news/fort-lauderdale-hollywood-airport-shooting/fl-reg-esteban-santiago-death-penalty-decision-20180430-story.html (accessed May 17, 2018).

2. "New Report Details Florida Airport Shooting That Killed 5," *US News and World Report*, October 7, 2017, https://www.usnews.com/news/us/articles/2017-10-07/new-report-details-florida-airport-shooting-that-killed-5 (accessed May 17, 2018).

3. Stephen Hobbs and Megan O'Matz, "Fort Lauderdale Airport Unprepared for Shooting, Outside Review Finds," *Sun Sentinel*, August 16, 2017, http://www.sun-sentinel.com/news/fort-lauderdale-hollywood-airport-shooting/fl-airport-shooting-after-action-release-20170815-story.html (accessed May 17, 2018).